Emerging Global Scarcities and Power Shifts

Bernard Berendsen (ed.)

Emerging Global Scarcities and Power Shifts

Bernard Berendsen (ed.)

KIT Publishers – Amsterdam

Emerging Global Scarcities and Power Shifts
Bernard Berendsen (ed.)

KIT Publishers
Mauritskade 63
P.O.Box 95001
1090 HA Amsterdam
The Netherlands
E-mail: publishers@kit.nl
www.kit.nl/publishers

© 2009 KIT Publishers, Amsterdam, the Netherlands

This publication was supported by the Society for International Development (SID) and World Wildlife Fund (WWF).
Emerging Global Scarcities and Power Shifts is also the title of the lecture series organised by SID in partnerschip with The Ministry of Foreign Affairs, Clingendael/IEP, Socires and the Dutch National Committee for International Cooperation and Sustainable Development (NCDO).

Editing: Sarah Ream, Amsterdam, the Netherlands
Design: DéTéPé, Meppel, the Netherlands
Production: Bariet, Ruinen, the Netherlands

ISBN 978 90 6832 689 5
NUR 754

Contents

Preface

No 'Limits to Growth' as the Club of Rome warned and predicted in 1972, rather 'a vacuum cleaner without a stop button' as Prof. Ben Knapen, former editor-in-chief of a leading Dutch newspaper puts it: the approach that has been applied for the last thirty-five years to the seemingly inexhaustive sources of raw materials, energy, timber, agricultural products, water, and clean air has been careless. For years, confirmation of their abundance was to be found in the paradoxical combination of growing demand and declining prices, or – as is the case for water – no price at all.

The first to experience the unsustainability of this myth of abundance and inexhaustiveness were the poorest in the world. Their firewood became scarce, their water wells drier and drier, and their food supplies more and more expensive. The poor of this world, and especially women, who were the first to be confronted with increasing journeys – sometimes of many hours per day – to obtain clean water or to collect fire wood, were paying the higher prices, which indicated and demonstrated that something was essentially false with the dominant presupposition of easy and affordable lifestyles. In truth, the situation was increasingly the inverse of this. Scarcities of resources, which have been the determining reality for the poor of this world for several decades and generations, have become even more pressing.

In the richer countries too, the finiteness of natural resources, and especially of energy sources, became apparent. Prices of food, energy and basic materials started to rise to unprecedented levels. Nonetheless, it did not lead to new poverty, because until last year one abundance remained: financial resources! But

the pattern of new increasing scarcities became even more difficult to reverse because of another unforeseen consequence: a
redrafting of the world map of economic and politic power, including factors such as the role of China in Africa and Latin America;
the curse of the possession of natural resources for the economy –
known worldwide as 'the Dutch disease'; the political systems and
even the human-rights situations in the nations which are the
beati possidentes; holding 'hostage' those countries that are fully
dependent on the import of energy and natural resources, such as
those in Central and Eastern Europe today; and the advent of new
important economic players and their subsequent eligibility as
partners and allies, regardless of their autocratic governance or
even of their human-rights records.

With this background in mind the Netherlands Chapter of
the Society for International Development – a global network of
individuals and institutions concerned with development which is
participative, pluralistic and sustainable and one of the few global
networks with a stronger constituency in the South than in the
North – decided that it was high time to flag up all these aspects
of the new scarcities dilemma.

Throughout the series the other side of the coin became
apparent. For the South the new scarcities can also imply new challenges, chances and opportunities. Our scarcity could be matched
by their capacities: solar energy; biomass under strict, very strict
conditions; their indispensability in the preserve of bio-diversity
and the lungs of the world with their tropical forestry; and above
all, the rediscovery of the role of agriculture: the role of food and
broader agricultural production and its potential for national and
regional development.

The role of SID in this debate about 'Emerging Global
Scarcities and Power Shifts' did not become superfluous; rather than
falling into the trap, strongly prevalent in the North, of relating the
new scarcities to the preservation of progress and growth of the
richer nations and emerging economies, SID Netherlands has made
a conscious effort to factor the role of the South into the overall
global debate about this new phenomenon, which will determine

the lives and economies of individuals, their societies, the globe as a whole and, above all, the future of the earth.

We are very grateful that in our exploration of this vast subject we were supported by strong collaborators. The World Wildlife Fund was a notably strong partner in our dialogues and reflections. The National Commission on Sustainability and Development (NCDO) created the financial conditions for the implementation of this series. The institutional relationship with the Round Table of Worldconnectors for People and the Planet has been highly relevant in the whole process. The Senate Conference was a joint venture of SID Netherlands and the Worldconnectors under the stimulating leadership of Ruud Lubbers. In the months leading up to the conference a special working group of committed Worldconnectors with interest and expertise in this subject was assigned the task of exploring the subject further and preparing a statement to be shared with the conference participants. The group stated that 'increasing food prices may slow down the process of achieving the Millennium Development Goals, in particular the commitment to eradicate extreme poverty and hunger (MDG 1). Energy scarcity may jeopardize the international community's commitments towards environmental sustainability and reducing the loss of biodiversity (MDG 7). Clean drinking water and fertile land are other growing scarcities that endanger the livelihoods of increasing numbers of people in the South.' In so doing, the Worldconnectors recognized the importance of the interdependence of the scarcities, a phenomenon which will ensure new scarcities are an omnipresent part of the global picture in the years to come.

We hope and believe that these partnerships and this cooperation will last longer than the series mentioned above, especially with the Worldconnectors. During this series it became apparent that there are so many dimensions to the issue of new scarcities. Our series of lectures and their concluding conference in the Dutch Senate could therefore only be seen as a voyage of discovery, which has to be continued beyond this series. This publication is therefore much more than simply a record of the lectures, conference and working papers. The extremely valuable contributions to this book provide a much-needed starting-point for further and deeper exploration. In the course of the last three years it has become evident that the trinity of a lecture series, a Senate Conference and a subsequent high-level publication brings the SID initiatives to an outstanding and international level. We are once again grateful to the KIT (Royal Tropical Institute) publishers for their engagement. But above all, we are thankful to Ambassador Berendsen, who volunteered anew for the difficult, cumbersome and time-consuming task of editing this publication.

To return to the statement in the first sentence of this preface, the vacuum cleaner should not be without a stop button and the button should definitely be used more often. In the dramatic changes of behaviour and policies that we have to undergo in the face of the new realities, it is the poorest and the most vulnerable who deserve our special attention and care. But let this publication also contribute to that other dimension. In his comments on this discussion, Dr Herman Wijffels, who succeeded Ruud Lubbers as co-chair of the Worldconnectors, pinpointed the real change that is needed in view of the overarching reality of the new scarcities. Over the generations, he said, mankind has learned to grasp its energy sources, generally by exploring and exploiting the soil, digging in the ground, bending down; but the new realities and perspectives demand another attitude from mankind: looking forward and upwards, to the sea, the sun, the air. There lies the future of mankind and of the earth.

Let us hope that this publication also contributes to that goal.

Jos J. van Gennip
President SID Netherlands

Introduction

Bernard Berendsen

This book contains the lectures that were organised by the Netherlands Chapter of the Society for International Development (SID) in the 2007 to 2008 season. The lecture series was rounded off with a closing conference in the Dutch Senate in September 2008, organised together with the World Connectors, a Netherlands-based NGO chaired by the former Dutch prime minister, Ruud Lubbers. The lecture series focussed on the emerging global scarcities of food, energy and water, on how these scarcities are inter-related and affected by considerations and policies dealing with climate change, on how these developments influence the relative position of individual countries and groups of countries, and on the development prospects of developing countries.

After all, shifts in the economic domain do not fail to have an impact on global political power relations. With rising energy prices, political leaders in energy-rich countries such as Russia and Venezuela, but also Angola and Bolivia, are exhibiting a renewed self-confidence, both internally and on the international scene. Inversely, governments of the countries that depend on others for their energy supply or food are increasingly aware of their vulnerability and set energy and food security high on the political agenda. Subsequently their policy intentions, for example in the area of renewable energy and bio-fuels, are reflected on the different markets. For example, bio-fuels compete for scarce resources like land and water with food and feed (for meat production).

In addition, public concerns about climate change and consumption patterns are increasingly making themselves felt in the economic and geopolitical landscape.

The organizers of the lecture series considered that energy, water and food are obviously not just commodities. They are more than that: they are strategic commodities, i.e. the object of direct monitoring and intervention by the state that perceives them as crucial to national interests, security and sovereignty. At the international level, they are assets in negotiations, power relations and conflicts. The conduct of states and political leaders is increasingly influenced by the access to and control over those commodities and by the ongoing and fundamental shifts in the structures of prices and incomes. Inversely and consequently the markets for those commodities are increasingly influenced by geopolitical conditions at the international level, as well as by regional and individual state interventions and their underlying policies and perceptions.

As the Society for International Development has as its main objective the stimulation of debate on current development issues, the main issues addressed were what all this means for the position of developing countries, what their options are, and what this means for international cooperation. Like the economic and geopolitical world map, the one for international cooperation might be in need of serious revision.

This has become even more so the case since the arrival of the financial crisis in 2008 and the global economic downturn that followed upon it and became evident during the course of the lecture series. At the closing conference in September 2008, the downward trend of energy and raw material prices was already becoming apparent and the geopolitical consequences were beginning to be seen. These events demonstrated that the issues that were the subject of the lecture series, even more than could be expected at its inception, were at the centre of the debate on international cooperation and development.

The lectures presented in this book are arranged in the following way: the first part of the book deals with *food, energy and water;* the second part looks at the way these commodities interact with *climate change* and are affected by climate-change policies; and the third part looks at *the geopolitical consequences* of these developments in the area of commodities and climate change.

In the opening lecture, Gerda Verburg did not only deal with *food*, but also drew attention to the issue of biodiversity and the importance of preserving our ecosystem in order to enable it to meet the needs of future generations. Rudy Rabbinge discussed the relationship between food and bio-fuels and doubted the wisdom to go along with the trend to introduce agricultural production for bio-energy. Kornelis Blok and Andre Faaij, on the other hand, basing themselves among others on scenario analyses by the International Panel on Climate Change (IPCC), were expecting a huge contribution from biomass to our future energy supply. Both pointed out that land availability might not pose a problem, provided further increases in productivity as a consequence of new technological developments. Both acknowledged the importance of increased water efficiency and the introduction of sustainability criteria related to soil conservation, water and air pollution, biodiversity, the conservation and preservation of forests, and the effects on climate change.

In the area of *energy*, Michael Klare looked at the geopolitical consequences of the emerging global scarcity of energy as a result of a likely further expansion of global demand for energy. He saw an increasing risk of the military presence of superpowers in parts of the globe where the remaining energy resources are concentrated: the Middle East, the Caspian Sea area, a few countries in Africa and Latin America. He also considered the risk of the increasing likelihood of violence in those countries, and raised the prospect off another world war resulting from increased competition for energy and the tendency of oil to exacerbate the internal divisions in energy-producing countries.

Jonathan Stern focussed on the European position with regard to Russia and Europe's perceived (over)dependence in oil and gas from external resources. He also pointed to problems such as the lack of new investments and the consequences of the break-up of the former Soviet Union into newly independent CIS countries, in particular Ukraine, Belarus and Poland; and to Russia trying to solve its transport dependence by building new corridors in the North and in the South. But the main problem for Europe remains that not only oil, but also gas, will eventually run out and alternative sources of energy will be required.

Catrinus Jepma drew attention to growing domestic energy demand in Russia and the CIS countries, which is not likely to be slowed down by rising prices. So he believes that in the longer term there will simply not be sufficient gas left to be delivered to Western Europe.

This is exactly what Coby van der Linde is most worried about: how to organise a transition from the present situation to a more sustainable energy situation envisaged in long-term strategies after 2030. Those transition problems follow on from the fact that the demand for energy will for the time being continue to increase and that reserves are concentrated in only a few countries that are hesitant to invest. With market prices going down, she concluded, new investments will become even more problematic.

Turning to *water*, Jan Lundqvist argued that we should be looking more closely at what is happening in the food chain if we want to better understand the relationship between the amount of food produced, and wasted, and the amount of water required for food production. He also drew attention to the relationship between rising income levels and the diet people consume, and drew attention to the amount of water required to produce bio-fuels for energy. All in all, he concluded, we could expect a substantial increase in additional water requirements to produce additional food and bio-fuels and to sustain the existing aqua systems. Ways to deal with this are (1) reducing losses in the food chain, (2) dealing with post-harvest losses, (3) changing our diet and (4) reducing losses in the household sector.

Water was also the subject of the lecture of Michel Camdessus, who connected water to sanitation and pointed out that there is a widening gap between sub-Saharan Africa and the rest of the world as regards the satisfaction of this basic human need in a global context.

In the second part, focussing on *climate change*, both Gurmit Singh and Pier Vellinga gave a brief exposé of the causes and mechanisms of the greenhouse effect and made clear that global warming as a result of growing greenhouse gas emissions is undeniable and that humankind will have to deal with it. Singh went on to look at the way we have been trying to deal with the problem in the past: by agreeing on ways to reduce CO_2 emissions, introducing mechanisms to share the costs and in particular making sure that those costs are equitably distributed, taking into account the principle of common but differentiated responsibilities. He also made it clear that climate change is not only a global threat but is also totally submerged in politics and centres around the question of who will dominate and who will lose out. Developed countries have, on an annual basis, been emitting vastly more than developing countries, but emissions from the latter will overtake those of the developed world from 2020 onwards. So he sees global warming as an emergency, but submitted that we cannot talk about climate change alone: we should tackle the problem of global poverty at the same time.

Here Pier Vellinga agreed. After summarising the theory of global warming, he went on to explain how feedback mechanisms exacerbate the climate-change problems with possible dramatic effects on the rise in sea level. So he concluded that we have to deal with this issue urgently. Technically and economically, we are able to avoid most of the projected climate change, but we will have to pay a price and the measures required will have an effect on the distribution of wealth and income. Therefore strong political leadership is required at the local as well as at the international level.

In conclusion, Vellinga presented four dilemmas. The first is that we will have to accept that the present level of climate change is already endangering continuous economic prosperity and social stability. The second is that, even if it is difficult to make a distinction between climate change and climate variability, we will inevitably have to solve the issue of compensation for the costs of mitigation and adaptation of developing countries who are most vulnerable to the consequences of climate change. Thirdly, we will have to solve the issue of what we mean by common but differentiated responsibilities. But we will also have to solve the problem of the limited capabilities of governments that have to deal with the consequences of climate change, in particular in developing countries. Finally, we will have to deal with the question of whether to prioritise poverty and climate change. Vellinga concludes that we cannot afford to postpone reducing greenhouse gas emissions until all national and international redistribution issues have been resolved.

Jan Pronk reflected on his high-level engagement with climate change in the past, underlining the principles which should inform policy today but which were not adequately addressed at the recent UN Conference on Climate Change in Bali. He takes us through the policy responses required to counter the dire consequences of climate change that we, as he says, ignore at our peril.

After climate change, the final part of the book deals with *the geopolitical consequences* of the recent developments in the area of food, energy and water that are connected to climate change. Special attention is given to the increasing economic role on the world scene played by India and China, on the consequences thereof for Africa and Latin America, and the way energy relations have redefined politics in Latin America.

Ronaldo Figueredo looked at the consequences of the first oil crisis in the beginning of the 1970s and the way the OECD countries dealt with it. He concluded that the way chosen was not conducive to dispel deeper misunderstandings between producing and consuming countries. In the meantime, the world has changed, globalisation has become the dominant theme and new issues have come to the fore, including clean water, climate change and alternative energy resources such as bio-fuels. He believes that in the area of global warming and other environmental concerns convergence among producers and consumers would yield more positive outcomes than in the past, including a comprehensive regional or sub-regional approach that complements specific national or bilateral action.

Cor van Beuningen agreed and looked at possible implications for European policy-making then moved on to the prospects of an EU-Latin American partnership and alliance. In view of what he considers as a likely transition of the world order from a unipolar to a multipolar system, he proposes that all efforts be directed to facilitating a peaceful transition to a viable and more sustainable new world system in which the different actors feel recognised in their existence and their legitimate interests. He also envisaged that Europe and Latin America could cooperate in this enterprise as natural partners, both sharing a preference for multilateralism and rule-based international order and institutions. This new partnership could also be instrumental in addressing a number of current problems in Latin America, including a rational and fruitful use of the rich natural resources of the continent for growth and development.

Javier Santiso looked at the changing trade relationship between Latin America and China and India as a consequence of the latter countries regaining the dominant position in the world economy that they had had 150 years earlier. China, as an economy that is far more open than it was 150 years ago, now attracts much more foreign trade, including from Latin America with its abundance of natural resources. In the short term, this is good news for Latin American countries but in the longer term it raises the challenge of how to diversify their foreign trade beyond commodities.

The increasing demand from China explains why for the first time in its history Latin American foreign trade is shifting towards Asia. For Latin America to retain its competitiveness, new investments will be required, because it will not come from lower wages. Other commodity-exporting countries like Canada, Australia and New Zealand have demonstrated that it is possible to overcome the 'commodities malediction'. Santiso submits that Latin America will only be resilient in the face of the financial crisis if China is resilient.

Yang Guang acknowledged that with rapid economic growth over the past thirty years China's demand of energy has significantly increased and as a consequence Africa has gradually become a more important supplier. Since 2000 the value of trade and investments has increased, but China has also increased its assistance to African countries. Typically, Guang adds, China has always observed principles of equality and mutual respect and is reluctant to impose any political conditions. Chinese companies also invested in oil production, but Yang Guang believes that

China-Africa oil relations have contributed to the development of the countries where it has invested. They have helped African countries to improve their production structure and promote the industrialisation process. Chinese companies are also increasingly aware of their corporate social responsibility and pay attention to environmental concerns. Finally, China heeds the political situation in Africa and contributes substantially to peace-keeping operations.

Frank Heemskerk insists that open markets in a globalising environment are the best answer if we want to care for people that are in danger of exclusion. On the other hand, he is aware that social justice is not something to be left to markets and that governments and regulators have a very important role to play. On the question of climate change, he doubts whether trade is part of the problem or part of the solution. Taking carbon leakage as an example, he argues that trade measures are not very effective in solving the problem of carbon leakage. The best and most efficient solution most likely lies in mechanisms to control the cost of doing business, in stimulating innovation and in allocating emission rights more freely.

In the final conference representatives of the private sector and the scientific community, NGOs and political parties contributed to the debate. Contributions were partly made in the context of a panel discussion under the chairmanship of Hans Opschoor, a former Rector of the Institute of Social Studies, and partly in the form of two statements by the World Connectors[1] on Climate Change and Sustainable Bio Energy.

Their message on climate change is that we should consider it as both a responsibility and an opportunity. It contends that saving energy and making use of renewable energy sources are key to combating climate change and suggests a number of measures and initiatives for governments, private companies, NGO's and international organisations:

- mandatory reporting by companies of their carbon footprint;
- introducing payments for the Reduction of Emissions from Deforestation and Degradation (REDD);
- developing and introducing carbon capture and storage (CCS);
- offering assistance for adaptation to climate change in the South;
- making institutions deal more effectively with sustainable development;
- ensuring mature economies take the lead in preparing for successful negotiations on climate change in Copenhagen.

In their statement on new scarcities the World Connectors drew particular attention to the issue of bio-energy as one of the prime cross-cutting issues in the ongoing debate on scarcities, basing their views on the Earth Charter and the UN Millennium Declaration. They referred to the discussion on the relationship between bio-energy and food security, making a distinction between first- and second-generation bio-energy. They also drew attention to the fact that, taking the full lifecycle of bio-energy production, only certain types of bio-energy have a favourable greenhouse-gas balance. They thirdly pointed out that increased demand for agricultural land is an incentive for deforestation and that tropical forests and wetlands must at all times be protected against exploitation for bio-energy.

They recommend implementing the Cramer criteria on sustainability both in legal and in practical terms: they should be translated into binding national and EU legislation on the sustainable production and use of bio-energy. Private business and companies in the food and energy sector as well as governmental agencies should already adhere to the principle in practical terms as of today. An international certification scheme for bio-energy, including a monitoring system, should be developed and implemented. Finally, opportunities for small farmers to participate in the profitable and sustainable production of bio-energy should be maximised.

The panel discussion brought together representatives of government, NGOs, the private sector and political parties. They agreed on the importance of investments in research and argued that the

Dutch government should set parameters for an effective market in bio-fuels in cooperation with all other EU member states.

The NGO representative, Danielle Hirsch of Both ENDS, argued that developing countries should be trusted to solve their own problems. 'They have many bright ideas but we have to make sure that they get included in our international adaptation strategies.' She admits that NGOs like Both ENDS should themselves be more active in exploring the potential of public-private partnerships. And she wants businesses to think not only in terms of doing less harm but also in terms of how they can do good.

World Connector Herman Mulder, as a representative of the private sector and former ABN-AMRO risk manager, speaks of the need to develop a price for water and ecosystems in general. 'Pricing water,' he says, 'can be an incentive for investing in this sector in developing countries.'

Antony Burgmans, former CEO of Unilever, added a number of practical suggestions at the closing of the conference: enhance global cooperation; invest in research in the areas of food, energy and water; initiate unprecedented measures for the conservation of food, energy and water; abolish agricultural subsidies in Europe and the US; refrain from using food crops for bio-fuel; invest in bio-mass; engage in CO_2 Capture and Storage and develop nuclear energy, initiate a broad transfer of technology to the developing world and initiate a wide public debate on those often painful measures: the public will need to understand and support those measures.

This is exactly what the purpose has been of this lecture series: to encourage debate and contribute to a better understanding of the complex relationships between food, energy and water, climate change and the shifting power relations in the world. The Society for International Development Netherlands Chapter deserves credit for this initiative that was undertaken together with its traditional partner organisations, in particular the Vrije Universiteit in Amsterdam, the Radboud University in Nijmegen and Maastricht University. They were closely involved in scheduling, choosing subjects and speakers and hosting meetings at their institutions.

From the start of this series SID Netherlands worked together closely with the Clingendael International Energy Program (CIEP), sharing speakers and contributing to the programme in the form of a lecture by its head, Coby van der Linde. Likewise, the Netherlands Ministry of Foreign Affairs contributed in many different ways and participated in meetings on the subjects to be selected and speakers to be invited. Also the Netherlands Centre for Sustainable Development (NCDO) and the World Wildlife Fund (WNF) Netherlands gave their support in various ways.

On a personal basis this series has benefitted from the input of individuals and staff members of the institutions mentioned: Ruerd Ruben of Nijmegen University, Kees Kouwenaar of the Vrije Universiteit in Amsterdam and Chris Leonards and Huud Mudde of Maastricht University; Coby van der Linde and Lucia van Geuns of the CIEP; Gerben de Jong, Simon Smits, Timothy Boon von Ochssée and Paul Hassing of the Ministry of Foreign Affairs; Frank van den Heuvel of Delta NV who generously offered his views in the inception phase of the lecture series; Ellen Lammers who reported on the final conference; Louk de la Rive Box and Hans Opschoor of the Institute of Social Studies; Hennie Helmich and Alide Roerink of NCDO; Rein Willems, member of the Dutch Senate; and World Connectors Ruud Lubbers, Tineke Lambooy, Johan van de Gronden and Herman Mulder.

As before, the staff of SID Netherlands has been very supportive in the preparation of this publication, namely Annette de Raadt and Veronica Rivera Santander who were responsible for the organisation of the lecture series; Iem Roos, its director; Gordana Stancovics, coordinator of its European Programme and ever-present support-staff member Wilma Bakker. I am also indebted to Cor van Beuningen, who made a substantial contribution to the conceptualisation of the subject of the lecture series and its realisation and to the board members of SID Netherlands, in particular its chairman Jos van Gennip. Jan Donner, as chairman of the board of the Royal Tropical Institute (KIT), has been encouraging this publication from the start.

A special thanks to Lianne Damen who, after last year's publication on *Democracy and Development*, once again offered the services of KIT publishers to realize this publication and managed to keep up her, and my, good spirits in the process.

As was the case with the earlier publication on *Democracy and Development*, the lecturers were invited to provide a written version of their lectures so that editing could remain limited to fitting them into the structure chosen for the book. In most instances, however, the lecturers were provided with a transcript of the lectures and invited to prepare a final text for publication. In many instances as editor I was given liberty to finalise the text. As before, I aimed for a certain conformity in format while at the same time preserving some of the flavour of the spoken word. To enhance their comprehensibility I also included some illustrations that were used in their PowerPoint presentations.

The result will hopefully contribute to a better understanding of the complex issues involved and stimulate the debate on them. The ongoing financial crisis and the economic downturn that we have been experiencing in the course of 2009 only demonstrates that we will have to continue to think about the implications for the preservation of the environment; the provision of food, energy and water requirements of the world economy; and the continuation of global social and political stability.

NOTE

1   Worldconnectors The Roundtable for People and the Planet, '(Draft) Statement on New Scarcities: bio-energy and food security in developing countries', 18 September 2008, http://www.worldconnectors.nl/upload/cms/ 147_ Draft_Statement_on_New_Scarcities.pdf

PART I

Emerging Global Scarcities

Food, Bio-Fuels and Biodiversity

Gerda Verburg

S ociety today is constantly faced with different forms of scarcity – not just economic, but also social and ecological scarcity. In economics, scarcity is linked to the nature of the commodity. For example, biodiversity and climate are regarded as public goods, and land and water resources as semi-public. On the other hand, food and fuels may be regarded as private resources, which are subject to market forces.

In a perfect market, supply and demand are balanced. However, markets are not always perfect, and governments sometimes have to intervene and regulate.

As we are faced with these scarcities it becomes more evident that economic, social and ecological scarcities are interconnected, and interact with each other. The concept of 'competing claims' refers to the claims that different, competing uses make on both private and public resources.

We are well aware of this interaction at the Ministry of Agriculture, Nature and Food Quality (LNV). Since the creation of the Ministry in its current form, our dilemma has been to find a balance between agriculture and nature, as well as between different types of non-agricultural land use, such as urbanisation and infrastructure on the one hand and green functions including landscape and recreation on the other. As Minister of Agriculture, Nature and Food Quality, I am continually faced with this kind of dilemma, on both a national and an international level.

In this chapter I want to focus on three LNV policy areas where various developments, particularly in the international context, are challenging agriculture and society to find a new balance between social, economic and ecological interests. I will consider these issues with regard to food, bio-fuels and biodiversity.

Food production

Over 800 million people in the world face structural food insecurity. Of these, 60 percent live in Southeast Asia and sub-Saharan Africa. And things are not really improving. Indeed, despite huge investments, we have been unable to counteract the problem. In fact things have got worse. The number of people in sub-Saharan Africa classed as 'food insecure' rose from 125 million in 1980 to 200 million in 2005.

If the inputs for food production were distributed more evenly throughout the world, food insecurity would be less severe. Farmers would be able to grow enough food, and deliver it to where it was needed. In terms of grain, this would require just a 2 to 5 percent increase in current world production. So it would certainly be possible to achieve the UN's first millennium goal, to eradicate extreme hunger in the world by 2015.

But this is not a perfect world. It is a stubborn problem and there are no simple solutions. Hunger is often found where people are marginalized, as a result of poverty and war, disasters and poor governance. Only structural developments of sufficient impact can offer any relief. However, there are some rays of hope. In recent years there have been great improvements in the food security situation in Asia and Latin America, thanks to all-round economic growth in these regions. Agriculture has also contributed to this social and economic development and shows that investing substantially (10 to 15 percent) in the primary sector pays off. Unfortunately, Africa is lagging behind in this respect. Despite the fact that 65 percent of the working population is engaged in agriculture and related activities, only 4 percent of the national budget is spent in the sector.

As the world population has increased from 2.5 billion in 1950 to over 6.5 billion today, the area of irrigated agricultural land has doubled and water withdrawals have tripled. World food production has outstripped the enormous growth in population. In just forty years the average grain yield has doubled from 1.4 to 2.8 tonnes per hectare. New crop varieties, fertilizers and other quality inputs have boosted agricultural productivity: it has been a 'green revolution'.

The green revolution therefore seems to have had the desired effect in its time. However, the cost of inputs, such as seed and fertilizer, is rising, and there is little scope to increase the area of land or the amount of fresh water available for agriculture. As a result, we still cannot be sure whether we will be able to feed the projected world population of 9 billion in 2050. Looking to the future, there is once again a real need to invest in agriculture.

When I talk about investment, I don't mean investment in machinery or new irrigation systems only. If we want to find effective solutions to the problem of food scarcity, we need to find many more innovative solutions in relation to production. We need to be intelligent here. In order to make agricultural production sustainable we have to invest in management, knowledge and human capacity. Such solutions do not just appear out of thin air. They require significant investments. Local agriculture and local conditions will determine the best mix of investments, policy and research. It is a matter of improving productivity, facilitating chain development (from growing to processing to sale), stimulating local and regional markets and improving access to the international markets. We have to design a global policy and create an economic environment to allow this new strategy to be brought into practice.

Agricultural development is key

In its recent World Development Report, the World Bank supported this view and called for joint action by the public and private sectors. This report, entitled 'Agriculture for Development', clearly indicates that agriculture is vital for development and that we need to achieve a smallholder-based productivity revolution for Africa, in order to trigger growth.

The report also calls for greater investment in agriculture in developing countries, and warns that, if the goals of halving extreme poverty and hunger by 2015 are to be realised, the agricultural sector must be placed at the centre of the development agenda.

The re-discovery of agriculture as a main driver of economic development is very important, especially for developing countries. Allocating development funds and other resources to agriculture, even at a local level, can have a huge impact on relieving poverty and hunger.

The Netherlands Minister for Development Cooperation, Minister Koenders, and I recognize this necessity and this challenge. Innovative agriculture is regarded as an important driving force for rural development. The Dutch government will therefore reinforce its investment in applied agricultural research and in education programmes in developing countries. For example, in providing assistance for the establishment of innovation centres and advisory services. Or contributing to research into smart solutions, green (gene) technology, better use of the plant properties that enable them to grow under difficult conditions. And encouraging more careful use of phosphates – essential building blocks for plants – to counter the impending phosphate shortage.

We can also engage in non-technological cooperation, for example in WSSD (World Summit on Sustainable Development) partnerships, where we work with companies, NGOs and the governments of partner countries on market access, by introducing sustainable forms of agricultural chain management.

Finally, we also need investments by business in both local producer holdings *and* the processing industries (SMEs). Foreign Direct Investments and micro-credits could play an important role. There may be a role for Dutch companies in joint ventures but there is also a role for the governments of the countries concerned, particularly when it comes to commitment to good governance and infrastructure.

Food and fuel crops compete

However, what will happen if the cultivation of fuel crops has to compete with food production in developing countries?

The impact of the potential competition between food and fuels is still unresolved. There is concern that unbridled, worldwide demand for biomass to generate energy could threaten the process of sustainable development.

It will take a great concerted effort from all the players involved to amalgamate production for food and production for energy. In any case it can only be done on the basis of sustainable and chain-based agriculture. Rudy Rabbinge and Kornelis Blok will deal more extensively with the technological aspects of this issue in their contributions to the lecture series.

In this context, let me take a closer look at the policy side of the issue of bio-fuels. Part of the world is dependent on oil, or as Al Gore says, addicted to it. It is the same part that is largely responsible for CO_2 emissions and that contributes to climate change. Certain regions in the world are already experiencing the many negative effects of climate change. Rising sea levels endanger alluvial areas around the world. These deltas are often densely populated and the fertility of the soil makes them indispensable for food production.

The increasing scarcity of fossil fuels also affects our economic prospects. Furthermore, we are confronted with the impact of CO_2 emissions on our planet. In the Netherlands we have recognized this problem. The Dutch government is committed to making the Netherlands less dependent on fossil fuels and to reducing the emissions. Amongst other initiatives it is our vision is to encourage the intelligent use of biomass. Intelligent use of biomass means a co-production of foods and non-foods. Non-food production is not only for bio-fuels. As a government we are also in favour of the use of biomass for chemicals and materials currently based on fossil feedstock. Further scientific research is required and industry will be encouraged to convert from fossil-based to bio-based production. The Dutch government is also looking at wind and solar power and other forms of renewable energy. We need to use them all to counter climate change. The objective must be to produce biomass in a cost-effective way somewhere in the world. It doesn't have to be in Europe. I will work with Minister Cramer, responsible for Spatial Planning and Minister Koenders, responsible for development co-operation, on projects to assist developing countries in the production of sustainable biomass.

The question, however, is, to what extent will structural agricultural feedstock prices increase as a result of the additional demand on the feedstock market?

Leading research bodies like FAO, OECD and the Dutch Agricultural Economics Research Institute have studied the economic impact of bio-fuels on agricultural markets. Most studies indicate that the long-term effects on agricultural product prices will be relatively small. The conclusion is that other effects – like economic development in Asia and other regions – will have a much larger impact on the agricultural feedstock market. In the long-run, most studies forecast low real price increases. In real terms, agricultural prices on the world market have been stable, or even decreasing, for decades.

In policy terms, only 0.2 percent of the CAP budget goes into support for fuel crops on set-aside land. And intervening on the demand side of the market, by making the admixture of bio-fuels compulsory, means governments need not engage in enhancing supply: that is primarily the responsibility of the market. In our opinion Europe must not become a fortress to protect its own farmers from imports of SUSTAINABLE biomass, especially from developing countries.

Enhancing sustainability

The Dutch government is in favour of implementing sustainability criteria for biomass. We made proposals for these criteria to the European Commission through the project group 'Sustainable production of biomass', headed by my collegue Mrs Cramer, in her previous capacity as chair of this project group I would especially mention the added value in terms of reduced CO_2 emissions, and the prevention of negative impacts on biodiversity and food security.

But sustainability is not only an issue for the Dutch. The US also underlines the importance of sustainability. Robert Zoellick – until recently the US lead negotiator in WTO and presently the president of the World Bank – referring to sustainability, talked about 'an inclusive and sustainable globalization' – 'to overcome poverty, enhance growth with care for the environment, and create individual opportunity and hope'.

This approach will in time impact on the concept of 'like products', that has been at the basis of most WTO jurisprudence until now.

New opportunities

The demand for biomass and the development of bio-fuels present opportunities to developing countries. Thirty-eight of the forty-seven poorest countries are net importers of oil. It is estimated that some countries spend six times as much on oil as on health. In this light, the development of bio-fuels can offer an opportunity to developing countries. We can already see some of the results. For example, in 2006, Senegal and twelve other African countries set up the Pan-African Non-Petroleum Producers Association.

On a smaller scale, a Dutch business has been working with an NGO in Mali since 1999 to promote Jatropha as a raw material for bio-energy. This development offers a chance to break the dependence on oil and develop the rural economy. Another example is the proposed cooperation, supported by the Netherlands, between Brazil and Mozambique in producing bio-ethanol from sugar cane in the African region.

So there are opportunities. But when we consider the future use of bio-fuels, we have to make sure that they come from sustainable sources.

Ultimately the impact of bio-fuels on impoverished people will vary from country to country, and it will be different in urban and rural areas. Of course, the quantity of biomass available in the world is also a factor. In the coming years we need to look at how far fossil fuels can be replaced by sustainably produced biomass. I do want to stress here that biomass is not the only option. To achieve sustainability we need to make full and intelligent use of all available resources, including waste and residual flows. Fermented organic waste, for example, could be used as an alternative to first-generation biomass.

Biodiversity

I come to the third topic of this lecture: biodiversity. Biodiversity is important for the three Ps – people, planet and profit. We need biodiversity for all three. We also need ecosystems and the benefits they provide. However biodiversity is under heavy pressure from those same people, and the profit we hope to generate.

The Millennium Ecosystem Assessment, drawn up by 1,300 researchers between 2001 and 2005, makes it very clear: never in the history of humanity have species and habitats declined as much as in the last fifty years. And that decline continues. We use our ecosystems so intensely that we now have a scarcity. Our own actions have placed so much pressure on the planet and its natural functions that there is a real danger that ecosystems will not be able to address the needs of future generations. In this sense there is already a scarcity of biodiversity.

The scarcity of biodiversity is not only due to human activity: it is also linked to the way we have dealt with biodiversity around the world, without sound economic foundation. We do not generally have to pay for the services we get from biodiversity, and the gifts that nature gives us (including clean air, raw materials, food, cultivation, recreation, pollination). It is remarkable that we are not used to paying for something that is so important for all of us, and that we have simply taken it for granted.

As yet there is very little in place to counter-balance certain human activities to cancel out the negative effects on biodiversity. Therefore it would be useful to develop better mechanisms to compensate for the impact of our activities on biodiversity.

We have often failed to apply the precautionary principle to our use of biodiversity. We have not counted the costs associated with loss of biodiversity. And of course the costs are not just economic. Biodiversity satisfies many different requirements, including quality of life and a good living environment. Our cultural, social and religious values are also affected by the loss of biodiversity.

My policy therefore aims to improve the sustainability of international raw material chains; to create ways of paying for biodiversity, partly by means of compensation mechanisms, and to reduce the impact that our country has on biodiversity in other countries.

But a country like ours cannot achieve these goals on its own. International cooperation is essential, to support developing countries with a rich biodiversity and to strive for sustainable land use and management, and sustainable development. It is also vital to raise awareness among the business community and the wider public. I will do my best to gain national and international support for this approach.

Conclusion

I hope I have given you some insight into the dilemmas and challenges facing us concerning the desirable and necessary development of agriculture. In relation to the problems of scarcity, too, it all comes down to sustainability.

We must show that we can be good stewards, and accept responsibility for future generations. We must take a sustainable approach to biodiversity, both in use and conservation. We cannot continue to compromise biodiversity, while its many benefits are so vital to us. We have to realise that we cannot sustain socio-economic development at the expense of biodiversity and natural resources, which are the very basis of our existence.

We now finally understand that what we invest in agriculture, food, and bio-fuels also has a cost in terms of biodiversity, and that that is often seen as an obstacle to economic growth. We have to find a way to disengage our claim on biodiversity from the economic development that we also keenly desire. This requires sustainable agriculture, not just in the Netherlands or Europe, but on a world scale. And this in turn requires many different types of agriculture, suited to local conditions and capable of satisfying local and regional demand and local requirements.

Much needs to be done. We need investment, innovation and policy change, and the government must take the lead. We see this as an important task for the coming years. But we cannot do it alone: it's a matter of all hands on deck. Everyone must do what they can. Our success will require the cooperation of all responsible partners in society, including the academic community.

Bio-Fuels versus Food Production:Challenges and Threats for Developing Countries

Prof. Rudy Rabbinge, with comments by Kornelis Blok

'Food or fuel' is the subject of many important debates. To enable a fruitful discussion, we need to consider a number of factors related to this controversy. These factors are significant not only for politics and policy-makers but certainly also for scientists like myself. In the following essay I will try to contextualize the whole debate.

Agriculture and economic development

In almost all countries, economic development began with agricultural development. Obviously, when people need to spend all their time collecting food, no time is left for other activities and economic development cannot be initiated. A higher agricultural labour productivity is therefore key to economic development. As the basis for higher productivity, agricultural research and development also kick-start economic development. In this respect, investing in agricultural research and development is an investment in a country's future. This view is acknowledged in the World Development Report of 2008. Agriculture has played a major role in development and will continue to do so for a long time to come. This notion is also the basis for Dutch policies and is reflected in a joint statement of the ministries of Agriculture, Nature and Food Quality (LNV) and Development Cooperation (DGIS).

Agriculture was for a long time a localized activity. This changed rapidly at the start of the industrial revolution. In the nineteenth century, cheap cereals were produced in the rich soils of the New World and exported to Europe in steamboats instead of in sailing boats. This was the first time that the Old World was faced with

Figure 1   Global Food Production, 1960 - 2000

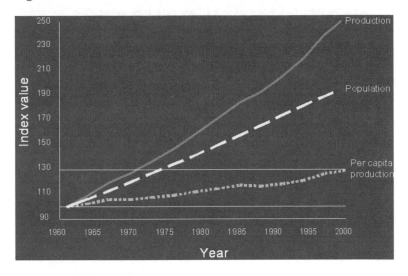

large-scale competition in agriculture. Grain prices dropped and Europe reacted in three different ways. The British reacted with liberalization. As a consequence, farmers went bankrupt and had to look for, and found, other professions in the production of all types of industrial products. Germany and France, with their feudalistic structure, reacted by protecting their agricultural sectors. Neither solution suited the Netherlands. Liberalization could not be the answer since around sixty percent of the population was still active in agriculture. Nor was protection the answer because the Netherlands, being a trading nation, could not simply close its borders. So innovation was the only solution and after 150 years this is still reflected in the Dutch agricultural policy. Agriculture in the Netherlands survived because of innovation, and responses to future challenges lie in new innovations.

At the end of the eighteenth century, Thomas Malthus warned for the first time of population outgrowing agricultural production capacity. He pointed out that where population tends to grow logarithmically, food supply will increase linearly at most, with the inevitable consequence that food supplies run short. Yet food production has grown faster than anticipated. Per capita, more food is currently available globally than a century ago. Population has increased worldwide considerably over the last forty years, but food production has increased at a higher rate (see figure 1). The main reason for this is much higher land productivity everywhere in the world, with the single exception of sub-Saharan Africa. In that region, the food situation is worse than it was forty years ago.

The enormous increase in land productivity is referred to as the 'green revolutions'. New technologies in combination with education and the right institutions have enabled vast increases in yield.

Figure 2   Discontinuity in production trends in the Netherlands, USA/UK and Indonesia

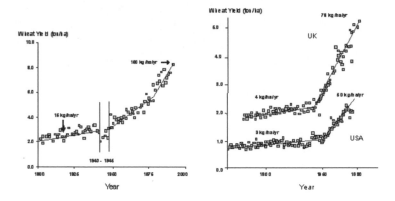

Figure 2 shows a few examples. It represents the discontinuity occurring in the Netherlands in the early 1950s, in the United Kingdom and the United States in the late 1950s, and in Indonesia and other parts of Asia in the 1970s. Before the Green Revolutions, yields tended to grow a few percent per year. Since the Green Revolutions, this growth is much higher. As a result, land productivity now increases much faster than it did half a century ago. However, sub-Saharan Africa has not been touched by the green revolutions for reasons beyond the scope of this essay. To improve agricultural productivity in Africa as well, Kofi Annan recently called for a green revolution in Africa. As a result, the Alliance for a Green Revolution in Africa (AGRA) was launched and will hopefully have an impact.

The role of research and development: seven mega-trends

In the previous section it was argued that research and development are key for agricultural and economic development. In fact, this is reflected in seven mega-trends.

1. As mentioned above, the first mega-trend is an increase in productivity per hectare, per man-hour and per kilogram of external input. Per hectare, productivity rose from 1,500 kilograms early last century in the Netherlands to 9,000 kilograms of wheat per hectare at present. Per man-hour, productivity early last century amounted to 250 hours per hectare, and now it is fewer than 8 hours. Productivity per kilogram of external input has also increased during the last three or four decades owing to, for example, precision agriculture.
2. The second mega-trend relates to the methods of agriculture. Nowadays, agriculture relies on industrialisation, as can be seen most explicitly in our greenhouses. The industrial approach allows us to optimise production.
3. The third mega-trend concerns chain and chain management. Productivity affects not only primary production but also all other stages of production from spade to plate.
4. The fourth mega-trend is the acknowledgement that there are broader concerns related to agriculture than productivity alone, namely the environmental effects of agriculture and the environmental responsibilities of those working in the agricultural sector.
5. The fifth mega-trend is a change in the knowledge model. The traditional linear knowledge system is being replaced by a participatory knowledge system. As a result, co-innovation is stimulated.
6. The sixth mega-trend relates to food, nutrition and health. To date, food is considered as a means to improve human health and to prevent diseases. A good diet and good composition of the food that we are eating are considered to be vital.

7.   Finally, and this might become the seventh mega-trend, there is increasing debate about using agriculture for the production of bio-fuels. In the sections that follow I will argue that it is unwise to take that route.

Agriculture and production ecology

Over the last one hundred years, we saw an enormous global population increase: from 1 billion to 6 billion people. By the middle of this century, the world population will have increased to 9 billion or 10 billion. Evidently, we need to produce more food to feed that population. Furthermore, the increase in wealth is causing a shift in diet. Higher wealth is directly correlated to the consumption of animal proteins. The richer people are, the more animal proteins they consume. With increasing wealth in Asia, the demand for meat and dairy products increases considerably. Animal production requires more cereals like rice, wheat and maize. To produce one kilogram of chicken meat you need three kilograms of grain; for one kilogram of pork you need five kilograms of wheat; and for one kilogram of beef you need at least eight kilograms of wheat. If meat consumption increases from a level of less than one ounce per day, as is common in many parts of the world, to four ounces per day, as is the case in the United States, there will be a dramatic effect on the demand for biomass. Hopefully this will not happen to this extent, but there will nonetheless be a substantial increase in meat consumption in the world. It is estimated that we need to double plant production by 2050 in order to meet the needs of an increased global population with an altered diet. This is the challenge the world faces for the coming decades. To do so, our best option is to further increase land productivity. The question is whether this is possible.

The production of all biomass is due to solar energy. Solar radiation is captured in photosynthesis, allowing the conversion of CO_2 and H_2O into biomass. Let us consider the energy efficiency of photosynthesis in relation to the primary production process of grains (see Figure 3). About 50 percent of the incoming radiation from the

Figure 3   Efficiency of energy

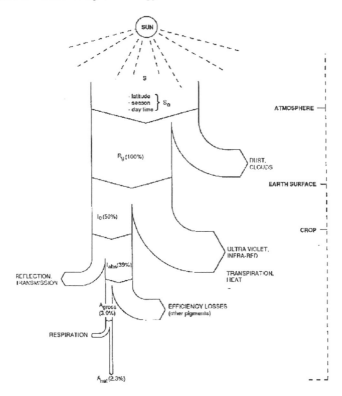

sun is photosynthetically active. Part of the energy that comes from the sun is lost in dust and clouds. Part of it is lost because it consists of ultraviolet or infrared rays which are not active in plants and are not being absorbed in plants for energy infra balance. Part of the radiation is reflected and transmitted to the soil. Furthermore, losses in efficiency are caused by a restricted active range of the pigments. There are also some losses due to respiration. So in the end, a maximum of 2 to 3 percent of incoming radiation is used by plants to produce proteins, fats, starch and so on, but also in the development of leaves, stems and other organs. Ultimately there is an actual maximum annual energy efficiency of between 0.5 and 3 percent. That is as high as you can get. To achieve even this efficiency in plants, sufficient water and nutri-

41

Figure 4   Actual maize yield in the EU an sub-Saharan Africa

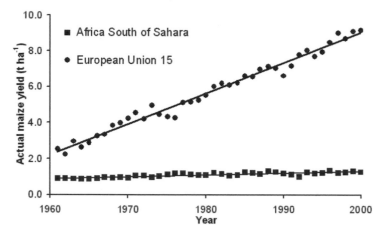

ents are needed; without these, plants will not grow. These are the basic principles of primary production.

These principles can also be applied to the global situation. Figure 4 illustrates the actual maize yield over the last forty years in different countries of the European Union and sub-Saharan Africa. In sub-Saharan Africa the productivity stays at a level of less than one ton per hectare while it reaches nearly nine tons in Europe. A major reason for this difference is that in Europe we have a better understanding of the primary production process and access to sufficient water and nutrients. Yet there is another reason for the large difference in productivity. Besides limiting factors, sub-Saharan Africa has to cope with reducing factors such as pests, diseases and weeds. In Europe, these factors are largely well controlled by the development of resistant varieties, healthy seed, adapted agronomic methods and the use of pesticides. Crop protection is still largely lacking in sub-Saharan Africa, indicating that there is still progress to be made in this important domain.

The impact of bio-fuels

As discussed, we need a considerable increase in plant production to feed the world in the coming decades. Applying the principles of production ecology will enable us to increase this production beyond its current limits. However, the bio-fuel discussion adds a new dimension to biomass production.

When considering the production of bio-fuels, a distinction between first- and second-generation bio-fuels is made. The first generation converts food into bio-energy. In this case, direct competition with food is apparent. The second generation makes use of agricultural 'waste' like straw and wood to produce bio-fuels. Although at first sight this does not compete with food production, it may do so indirectly. Grasses and wood that are produced for the second generation of bio-fuels will compete with food crops for scarce resources such as land, water and nutrients, and their production may indirectly affect the availability of food crops.

Figure 5   Energy consump[ion and income are linked

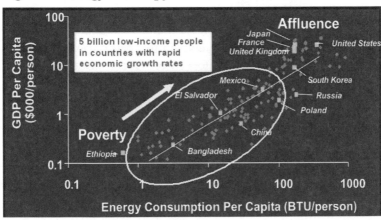

Source: Energy Information Administration, International EnergyAnnual 1998 Tables E1, B1, B2: Mike Grillot, 5/17/00 Gross Domestic Product per capita is for 1997 in 1990 dollars. Energy Consumption per capita is 1997.

A large-scale implementation of bio-fuels will have a huge effect on the demand for biomass. This is especially true when we consider the future energy consumption. Figure 5 shows that energy consumption increases with higher per-capita income levels. The average person in the United States consumes between 5.6 and 7 tons of oil per year, whereas the average Ethiopian uses less than 0.2 tons of oil per year. If economic development continues, the demand for energy will also increase.

The impact of bio-fuels is high because enormous areas of land are needed for energy crops. In energy terms, a tankful of bio-fuel is equivalent to food eaten by two people over a whole year. If the Netherlands wants to reach the target of a 5.75 percent bio-diesel composition of automobile fuel, as prescribed by the European Union, we need about 1.4 million hectares of rapeseed, the equivalent of about half the area of the Netherlands, in order to cater for our domestic demand of bio-diesel. This shows that even moderate applications of bio-fuels may have a large effect on food availability. So we need to decide: is it going to be fuel for the rich or food for the poor?

Some advocate that energy production should make use of marginal land to avoid competition with food production. However, marginal lands are by definition marginal because they require more inputs to yield the productivity possible on richer soils. As a consequence, to grow any crop on marginal land, as opposed to rich soil, higher investments yielding equal returns must be made, and so profits decrease. Therefore marginal soils are hardly interesting for the production of food crops. The same principles hold for energy crops. If the economic value of energy crops is even lower that that of food crops, an economically viable production of energy crops will not be feasible on marginal land. If, on the other hand, the economic value of energy crops exceeds that of food crops – be it because of world-market prices or because of subsidies and policies – the cultivation of energy crops will tend to compete with that of food crops for the more profitable rich soils. Therefore, the use of marginal soils will not be the solution for producing energy crops.

Another risk is linked to the use of marginal soils. If no agricultural inputs are used, irreversible depletion of the soil may be the result. This is already a big problem in some places in Africa, where the nutrient depletion in soil is due to overuse of the land. In Africa and in numerous other parts of the world, many people are caught up in what is referred to as an unsustainability spiral. Nutrient depletion through land overuse will yield infertile soils that become unproductive. Only by applying more inputs can the

Figure 6   Phosphorus lifetime of reserves

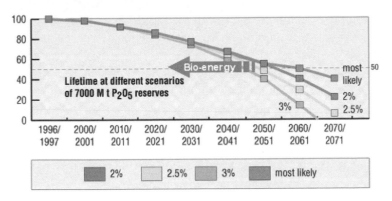

soils be saved for agriculture and food production. But inputs, such as phosphorus, are limited, as shown by figure 6, which shows that the lifetime of the remaining 7,000 tons of phosphorus is decreasing and will decrease even more quickly if we use it in the production of bio-fuels. Recycling phosphorus is therefore very important and needs to be actively pursued.

Another input, water, is also scarce. The majority of agriculture in the world is suffering from the scarcity of water. To increase the efficiency of water usage substantial innovations are needed, but it can be done. One kilogram of conventionally irrigated rice uses between 2,000 and 5,000 kilograms of water. If rice is grown via a more sophisticated precision-agriculture method, only 200 to 400 kilograms of water per kilogram of rice need to be used.

Living in a century of dreams

The twenty-first century is the century of dreams and stories, so the reversal of the Maslow pyramid is probably possible. On the left-hand side of figure 7 the original Maslow pyramid has the meta-level at the top, followed by culture, social cohesion and food and safety at the bottom. On the right hand side the Maslow pyramid is turned on its head: meta-dreams and stories of virtual

Figure 7   Maslow's pyramid reversed

reality dominate at the top, while culture, social cohesion and food and safety are becoming less important.

Figure 8   The 12 Fs of agriculture

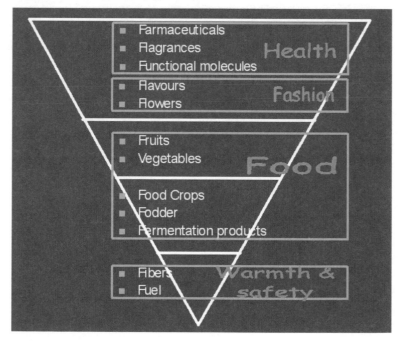

Figure 8 shows the '12 Fs', the different types of agricultural products that can be produced: flowers, flavours, fragrances, pharmaceuticals, functional molecules, vegetables, food, fodder, fibre and fuel. The land area needed to produce these commodities differs according to various factors. For example, only two square meters is needed to grow ten roses every week if they are produced in our glass houses in the Netherlands, while six square meters is sufficient to grow Nederwiet. Based on the consumption patterns of the average Italian, to feed a vegetarian for a year, 200 to 400 square meters are sufficient; for a meat diet comprising meat, such as the Western European diet-eater, 2,000 square meters are needed. To produce fuel, many hectares are needed.

From a bio-fuel to a bio-based economy

I hope it is clear so far that I am advocating a bio-based economy as opposed to a bio-fuel economy. In a bio-based economy, new products are predominant, including high-value products such as the 12 Fs introduced above. These are products such as pharmaceuticals, flavours, flowers, food additives and plastics which have high value in new markets. The basic process used to produce these is photosynthesis. Oil and gas are the results of photosynthesis of the past whereas plants now represent the photosynthesis of the present.

Figure 9   Natural resources: petrochemistry vs. biochemistry

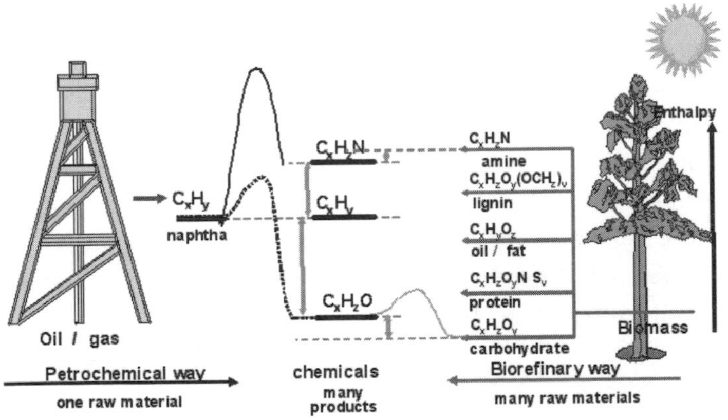

This brings new and exciting opportunities: plants are a much better source for many products than petrochemicals, because a large variety of basic products can be obtained from them directly.

Figure 9 illustrates how products can be made following the petrochemical route. The biochemical route is more useful for making highly sophisticated products via refined chemistry. However, this requires long-term investments, public-private cooperation, the right consortia and an environment that enables research and innovation.

Plants can produce pharmaceutical products, proteins, artimicine and specific oils like calendula oil. These are high-value products which are very attractive for a bio-based economy yet have nothing to do with bio-fuels. If we want to use plant components for direct energy production, we would do better to focus on solar cells, which exploit only the first steps of photosynthesis, the photochemical process, without actually producing the energy-demanding biomass. We can also use waste products to produce energy in a cascading system through bio-refinery, fermentation and gasification. It is already possible to directly produce hydrogen from biomass using phototrophic bacteria. Still another interesting option is the use of algae for food or fuel, as limited soil availability may not apply.

Conclusions

- Secure and sufficient food supplies can be attained with a growing population, even in combination with a diet change in the developing world. To achieve this, highly productive agriculture is needed and a productivity increase per hectare is imperative.
- The food situation in various parts of the world varies: Latin America is different to Asia, and sub-Saharan Africa is dramatically different to other places.

- Growing biomass for fuel production may have detrimental side effects because of the competition for land with food production.
- Bio-refinery methods of production and bio-based economies in which plants are used as 'factories' are desirable.
- Solar energy is the ultimate long-term solution to our energy problems; bio-fuels may play only a short-term role.
- If needed in the short term, we need to produce and employ bio-fuels with care, and we have to do so reluctantly.
- We need to recognize that policies that dictate that a certain percentage of bio-fuel be used in our gasoline are devastating for the environment and increase problems for both developing and developed nations.

Comments by Kornelis Blok

After Rudy Rabbinge's lecture, everybody now expects me to tell a more positive story about bio-fuels. I will start with a detailed look at the possibilities of bio-fuels, but I am also not blind to the problems. At the end of my lecture I will also pay proper attention to those problems

But first I would like to show you one of the possible futures under the limitations that climate change is posing us. Then I will move to the potentials of bio-energy. Thirdly, I will give some examples of interesting small-scale applications, and finally I will discuss the topic of sustainability.

Exploring the future

When we explore the future, our basic tool is scenario analysis. There are many of these analyses, and they are typically drawn together by the International Panel on Climate Change (IPCC). I will show you one example that comes from a study of the NMP, formally known as the RIVM.

On the left is a base-line scenario, showing conventional development, implying the use of a lot of fossil fuels. This scenario is probably not sustainable, and this not only because of the CO_2 emissions. After all, sustainability has not only to do with climate change, but also depends on other topics such as local air pollution and security of energy supply. In the energy policy area there are a lot of topics to deal with, of which climate change is only one. But climate change deserves our attention most at the moment and out of all the topics relating to sustainability, we can currently

Figure 1 Energy use in a 450 ppm CO_2-eq. stabilization scenario

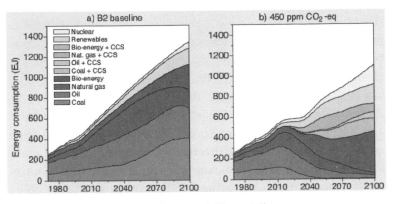

Source: D.P. van Vuuren, Energy Systems and Climate Policy,
           PhD thesis, Utrecht University, 2007

quantify its magnitude best, even better than security of energy supply issues.

What can be done about climate change? The picture on the right shows one of the most ambitious scenarios that has been produced so far. It aims for the stabilization of greenhouse gases at the level of 450 ppm CO_2 equivalent, which is about the level that we already have today. It is not unlikely that we will need to work towards that scenario.

What does the energy supply look like in that scenario? First you see that total energy supply is much lower than in the base-line scenario and that the supply comes from a larger range of different sources. In this scenario conventional fossil fuels are gradually phased out.

There is also a huge contribution of biomass. Then we have other categories to consider: fossil fuels but with sequestration of carbons, i.e. with underground storage of CO_2. On top we have the different forms of renewable energy, wind and solar and nuclear energy. This is the possible package that is suitable to allow us cope with climate change.

If you look at all these energy sources, there is none without debate. Even on the most obvious one – the one that you do not see, which is *energy conservation* – being probably the least problematic, there is also much debate. Is this scenario feasible? It implies that if we want to go for a more energy-efficient world, we need to make efforts in all parts of society. We need to convince people to behave differently and purchase more efficient equipment, for example. Is that do-able? I think it is do-able and probably more can be done. But it is under debate.

We are all familiar with the debate about *nuclear energy.* There is also a lot of debate on *wind energy.* All of you who live in rural areas have probably seen the meetings in all kinds of villages about whether wind turbines are acceptable or not. There is a lot of tension about that. My company, Ecosys, is now developing offshore projects and even there the debate is starting. Not only about the impact on the environment and the landscape, but also, or even more so, about the economic interests that you have at sea. *Solar energy* is not so much under debate, I must say, perhaps because it is not applied that much. One of the problems with solar energy is that it is very expensive, much more expensive then other conventional sources.

Then we come to *carbon storage*: that also is very much under debate. It is also important to know that there are limitations to the total amount of storage capacity there is on earth. The same goes for the other sources. There are also problems with *biomass*, but you have heard enough about that already.

This is the overall picture. We need a lot of options and we probably cannot do without any of them. It is not possible at this point to say, 'Well, let's just skip one of them.' In village discussions on wind turbines there are always people suggesting we forget about wind turbines and go for biomass and nuclear energy. I personally do not think we can skip over any of them. If you look at this picture above, it is *a package*; let us for the moment develop each type of energy source.

In the area of renewable energy there is one particular thing that makes biomass very attractive compared to the other main sources like wind and solar energy – there are a number of others like wave and tidal energy that I could mention – but both wind and solar energy produce electricity that is difficult to store and difficult to transport. The big advantage of biomass is that you can easily convert it. You can store it for the production of hydrogen or whatever, even if that is also very complicated and relatively expensive. So it is difficult to base the system purely on solar energy and wind, but it is possible to envisage having one based on solar energy, wind and bio-fuels.

What is the role of biomass for energy purposes ?

Figure 2 Amount of biomass needed for energy purposes

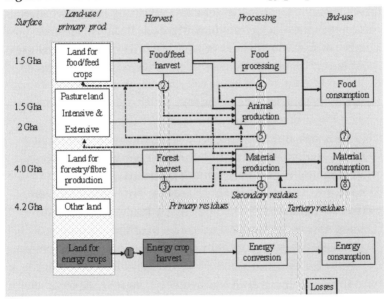

Figure 2 gives an overview of the total food and material production system based on agriculture and forestry. On the left-hand side you see the various sources and the number of hectares involved in production on a worldwide basis. One of the important things to note is that there are all kinds of residues in a cycle. Ultimately all this production is used for food or materials. Then you have primary residues in agricultural forestry, secondary residues in the processing industries and finally tertiary residues after consumption, like waste paper and waste food.

All these waste flows represent together an energy value of 5,200 exajoules, and you can compare that to the total energy consumption on earth, which is 450 exajoules. All this waste and these residues created in producing 450 exajoules can provide 5,200 exajoules. There is not much debate that this is a good path to pursue, although in a number of cases it could be argued that these residues are normally used to maintain soil fertility. So you need to take care, but it is clear that in most of the cases residues are a good source of energy.

The important question is, how much of the land can we use for direct energy crops? In Utrecht University an extensive analysis was carried out by a PhD student, Monique Hofwijk. She drew up a number of scenario analyses of what we can expect. As there are a lot of uncertainties to consider we need scenario analysis here.

Figure 3 Exploration of the ranges

- Present agricultural area
- **High** population growth
- Meat **intensive** diet
- **Low** agricultural intensity
- **High** demand for competing options (e.g. bio-materials, sinks).
  - High demand for agricultural land
  - High supply of residues

Barely any potential
(0)

- Present agricultural area
- **Low** population growth
- Meat **extensive** diet
- **High** agricultural intensity
- **Low** demand for competing options (e.g. bio-materials, sinks)
  - Low demand for agricltural land
  - Low supply of residues

Very high potential
(1100 EJ per year)

In her analysis she made a distinction between two different situations: on the left-hand side you see high population growth, a meat-intensive diet, low agricultural intensity and high demand for competing options. In this case there is not much potential to use bio-energy. In the other scenario, with low population growth and a less meat-intensive diet, there is much more room for bioenergy. The PhD study used the storylines of the IPCC in another scenario approach with two dimensions (see Figure 4).

Figure 4 Scenario approach

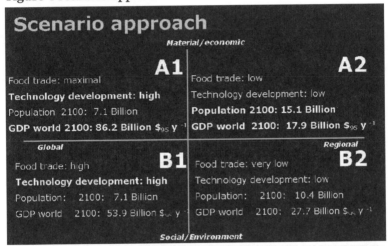

The vertical dimension is material/economic versus social/environment. The horizontal dimension is global versus regional, or scenarios with more attention to globalization versus more attention to regional approaches. These storylines include different rates of population growth, different technology developments and different rates of GDP growth, issues that are relevant for food consumption and energy production.

In a materialistic world you will have higher meat consumption, as in the A1 and A2 scenarios. In a more socially oriented world, the opposite would be the case. But what is important is the outcome, for example with respect to land use, and that is what you see in the next figure.

Figure 5 Land-use pattern changes

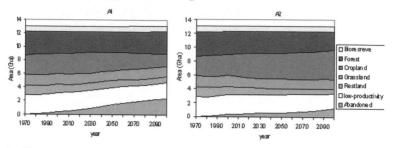

In Figure 5 you see the differences in land use in the A1 and A2 scenarios: for example in A1 you see an increase and in A2 a decrease in available crop land. In all scenarios technological development is taken into account, but you can imagine that technology is developing more quickly in a globalised world than in a regionalised world. What is important, however, is the outcome that you see at the bottom of the graph: abandoned land that, given the outcome of the calculations, is no longer needed for food production, is substantially larger in the A2 scenario with low technology development than in the A1 scenario with high technology development.

So you see that these two scenarios differ substantially. There are other types of land, such as land at rest and low-productivity land, but in the ultimate calculations it turns out that abandoned land, which is land that potentially has high productivity, is most important for the production of bio-energy.

In the A1 scenario, which is the one we are particularly interested in, it is assumed that we have high technology development and low population growth. In this scenario it is assumed that, as soon as you have produced enough food, you can take some land out of food production and make it available for bio-energy production. This results in what some call the new map of OPEC or BIOPEC. On this map there are a lot of such areas in all world regions, in particular in Russia but also in China, Latin America and Africa. These are areas with a potential for huge amounts of bio-energy production. The question is: where does all this lead us?

Figure 6 Geographical potential

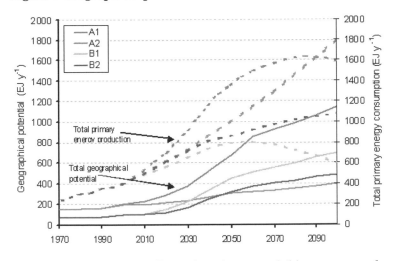

In this picture the solid lines show how much bio-energy can be produced in each of the four scenarios. This could be compared again with the 450 exajoules of current energy production. You see that in the most optimistic scenario bio-energy production could be even above 1,000 exajoules, while in the lowest scenario it is more or less equal to the current level of energy production. So the conclusion of this study is that bio-energy can substantially contribute to global energy supply. Many studies have been done since then, but this one was based on geographical potential; of course, other constraints should also be taken into account. The bottom estimate is, however, that in the lowest scenario 200 exajoules can be made available and this can be raised to 600 to 700 exajoules in the higher scenarios, which is quite substantial.

Some local examples

So this is the overall, global picture. Let us now turn to some local examples, and I do this also to honour Kees Jan Ouwens, who passed away last year, and who has been a pioneer in developing local bio-energy systems. Like many others in the world, he has cast his eyes on a particular plant called jatropha. It is a plant that is not edible and contains oil. The other interesting thing is that it not only grows on fertile land but also on lower quality land. Kees Jan Ouwens set up a project in Mali, which I find a good example of how the development of bio-energy can also contribute to the local prosperity of a village of 10,000 inhabitants.

He developed the jatropha project of 1,000 hectares. Pressing and oil storage was all done locally to feed diesel engines and supply electricity to the grid which was newly developed in that particular village. By doing so, the village became fully self-supplying. Alternatives were hardly available for the village because bringing in conventional energy is very expensive and will probably be even more expensive in the future. Kees Jan Ouwens still has a team working on the project and it will be fully operational early 2008.

So this is a good example and, to some extent, a completely different picture to the large-scale overview of world food production I showed earlier. This shows that you can do useful things locally in Africa, a continent that is sometimes considered to be a lost continent.

Kees Jan Ouwens worked on many other projects as well. He worked, for example, on seeds and reforestation combined with charcoal production. Charcoal is a very interesting fuel because it can be used for all kinds of applications, including iron and steel-making. He also worked on the production of meat, and on bio-diesel from fat that comes from pigs. I found this quite a surprising application. He worked too on anaerobic digestion, improved woodstoves and the local production of ethanol from waste streams, ethanol being a very useful automotive fuel.

From local to large-scale applications: issues of sustainability

These are some examples of projects that can be done on a small scale, but we will probably have more sustainability challenges if they are carried out on a large scale, which is the last point I want to talk about. If we are developing bio-energy systems worldwide we will see big trade flows and big companies being involved with very strong economic interests. In these circumstances it is very important to guard the sustainability of these systems. We have seen clashes already here and there, for example around palm oil in Indonesia and Malaysia.

When talking about bio-energy, there are a number of sustainability issues to consider. There are the regular environmental topics: soil, water and air pollution. Biodiversity is very important, especially conservation and the preservation of forests. Greenhouse gas emissions are very important because if you want to reduce the impact on climate change you should not have other impacts here and there. But other sustainability issues are also important, such as the rights of the local population, compatibility with national laws and, finally, the impact on the production and availability of food.

What to do? There are two important things. First of all it is important that certification systems are introduced for bio-energy. Many countries are now stimulating the production of bio-energy for electricity or as fuels, but it is important that in all cases biomass is produced and processed in a sustainable way. Some systems are already in place, for instance the FEC for wood, but also the RSPO for palm oil, and many more systems will probably follow.

It is also interesting that it is exactly through bio-energy interests that the systems are sometimes stimulated. Take for example palm oil: last year I was very much involved in a commission to advise Dutch electricity producers on the use of palm oil. Palm oil industry is growing worldwide strongly, and we know that tropical rainforests are cut down to build palm oil plantations. This is not due to the growing bio-energy demand but to the big demand of palm oil in general and in particular from countries like China and India, and that mainly for food production. All these palm oil users do not care about sustainability issues. While only a small percentage of palm oil was used for energy production, and even then we talk about the lowest grade of palm oil, the Dutch electricity producers were still the driving force in the sustainability debate.

So I see a very positive stimulus coming from the bio-energy world. Many sustainability issues can be tackled by certification systems, but one clearly cannot, and that is the impact of bio-energy production on food production. Food production is not a matter of one individual plantation or one individual processing plant. This is a regional and sometimes even a global issue. What we propose here is to implement monitoring systems to make clear what the actual impact on food production is. Such systems make it possible to take counteractive measures if necessary, or if the impacts are too strong or take too long. Then certain stimulating measures for bio-energy may be reduced or turned back.

It is also important to show that in a number of cases effects may occur that are not caused by bio-energy demand. I already mentioned the growth in palm oil production that in the popular media is often accounted to bio-energy use, though this is not the case.

Another topic in the sustainability debate that is difficult to tackle is displacement. For example, it may be that one company that has some sustainable plots, and at the same time in other locations is cutting down tropical rainforests. Monitoring is important here, but so too is making agreements with companies that they are only allowed to produce palm oil if they refrain from cutting down original rainforest.

Conclusions

Bio-energy is most likely necessary for a sustainable energy system. The potential for bio-energy is substantial. Bio-energy contributes to local economic growth and certification and monitoring is necessary.

Food and Bio-Fuels

Andre Faaij

The problem of bio-energy is not an easy one to solve. If you have distilled your information on bio-fuels and bio-energy from the media over the past eight months or so, then this is more or less what you may think: the greenhouse balance of this option is not good; you need endless subsidies to make it work; if you are serious about water and land, the potential is marginal; it is bad for food supplies and for farmers and there are much better alternatives to supply sustainable energy.

That is the picture that has developed in the media. However, I think that picture is quite exaggerated, because we already have scenarios from years ago, including the recent IPCC fourth assessment report – which is a scientific overview on mitigation that was referred to already by Pier Vellinga in his chapter – that says that bio-energy is a very important option, on the one hand to mitigate climate change and on the other hand to provide a large part of our future energy supplies. So where is this mismatch coming from?

Bio-energy and bio-fuels

Let me begin by saying that bio-energy is not the same thing as bio-fuel. I will give you a view figures on this. About 10 percent of current global energy demand today is covered by biomass. That makes it the largest renewable energy resource. Immediately I have to add that a large part of that fraction is non-commercial and non-modern, i.e. the typical kind of cooking fuels that you see used on a large scale in developing countries. Part of this biomass is definitely not sustainable.

Then you have the so-called commercial or modern component, for example in the production of electricity, in power plants, i.e. the production of so-called process heat in various industries like pulp and paper and sugar. And then you have the bio-fuels, to the amount of about 8 million exa-joules of energy on an annual basis worldwide.

Ten percent is not a very big share of total energy demand, but that is what we are looking at today. So the main controversy that has developed in the public debate is focussed on the bio-fuels proportion, which is still a minority share of bio-energy use. In fact, the use of biomass for power and heat is largely undebated and is also very effective in reducing greenhouse gas emissions. Here we talk about way streams, wood residues and forest residues, where modern technologies are used that are quite well established.

The bulk of the share that consists of bio-fuels comes in the form of ethanol from sugar and starch. Sugar cane is a rather effective crop from which to make bio-fuels. In Brazil sugar cane is not subsidised; it is a very productive crop and it gives a high yield per hectare. It is also a crop and a system that delivers high net greenhouse gas reductions compared to gasoline and diesel. This is, for example, not the case for corn, which is the key crop in the United States for bio-fuel production and which is, so to speak, a moderately behaving operative system, similar to the use of rapeseed for bio-diesel production in Europe. So that is the fraction of the bio-energy that the discussion is focussing on.

To put things in perspective

Let me present you with another little fact to put the figures in perspective. At this moment we use a little more than 20 million hectares of land worldwide for producing crops for bio-fuels. So that is the sum of land for the production of sugar cane, corn, rapeseed and a couple of other such crops. Compare that to the total of 5,000 million hectares of arable and pasture land that we use today to secure our food supplies. This simple figure makes me wonder why the World Bank manages to say that 75 percent of the price increases in the world food market have been caused by bio-fuels over the past year. That was a remarkable piece of economic analysis!

That does not change the fact that in the present situation we do not only talk about peak oil. We are also confronted with peak soil, peak water, peak population, even peak wealth. As a consequence we see unprecedented biodiversity losses together with a number of problem areas that are interconnected and that we have to solve: there is the issue of climate change; we have a crisis in agriculture; we need to secure our food supplies in a sustainable way; there is the issue of energy security, of biodiversity, but also very much the necessity to abate poverty and secure development for the world's poor. Many of these issues are interconnected and we are in a hurry to resolve many of them. So we need options that can deliver in the coming decades.

A role for bio-energy

On the matter of bio-energy, some people say that we would do better to focus on solar energy and energy efficiency. But I think, and this is common knowledge among energy experts and also climate mitigation experts, that we need *all* the options that we have to cover the future energy demand, looking at the current order of magnitude of that demand. There is no either/or choice or option: we need them all. And bio-energy has a role to play in that context. The discussion should be about how large a role it should play, and in this lecture I will focus on that question, because we do not have the luxury to choose; we cannot afford to overlook bio-energy, nuclear energy or carbon capture and storage, otherwise very little will be left of our total strategy to combat climate change and secure future energy supplies.

Agricultural land use

When we know that we will need a lot more food, protein in particular, then the way we use land and the way we produce food are major issues. Up to 2050 we may be looking at a doubling of primary food-crop production. At the same time, in order to protect the world's forest, we don't have to and we don't want to use a lot more agricultural land. We also know from very good analysis by FAO in its millennium ecosystem assessment that agriculture and livestock today are the main threats for biodiversity. Also, together they are one of the key sectors emitting greenhouse gases, larger in total than world transport.

Those are problems that need to be tackled anyway, irrespective of bio-energy. In addition we see that, being very crude, agricultural problems, unsustainable land use and land-use management are strongly interlinked with poverty. Seventy percent of the world's poor live in rural regions, and with that also comes very low productivity in many of those regions: typically one ton of useful product per hectare per year in subsistence farming compared to about ten tons in countries like the Netherlands and the United States. A ten-fold difference: that is a tragedy.

Those agricultural practices without availability of fertilizers and without market access allowing farmers to earn money and reinvest in the land lead to large-scale unsustainable land use, erosion, loss of forest cover and so on. That is the tragedy that we see developing for example in sub-Saharan Africa. Poverty and a lack of investment are key drivers for unsustainable land-use management. This is an extremely important conceptual point to consider.

Uncertainties about biodiversity

In terms of biodiversity we still have very significant and real uncertainties and questions that we should not underestimate. Water is a key issue in the management of biodiversity and the interactions in competition with conventional markets in, for example, food and forestry.

We have to make sure that there is proper accounting of greenhouse balances and land-use management and that there is a balance in the macro- and micro-scale of economic development.

If you think that bio-energy is a complex issue in relation to all this, you are absolutely right. The modellers, and now I am talking about the best modellers that we at the Copernicus Institute have in the world, do not have a fully integrated and coherent set of modelling tools that can address all the questions that are asked in the current debate. Some of the economic models that play a role in the analysis of what bio-fuels, for example, do to food markets are not capable of tackling a variety of effects. For example, if you forgive the technical terminology, regarding price-induced use increases: what happens to agricultural production at the moment that prices are structurally higher than they used to be for decades? We think that, if you look at it in detail, this will have an increasing effect on yields because it is more worthwhile to invest. The macro-economic models are usually not very good in actually simulating those effects.

Second-generation bio-fuels, based on wood crops and grasses, are not part of the presently available economic models. So we have gaps. But nevertheless, attempts have been made to assess the best available knowledge and look at what happens to this biological outlook if we take all those interlinked issues into account. I will now focus on a couple of scenarios that we have on the table today.

Lessons from scenario analysis

We have underpinning information to show what the technical or theoretical levels could be in 2050 for biomass production in the long term, knowing that we will have 9 billion people that all have to eat and will need their protein, and assuming that we are going to work on raising agricultural productivity and also livestock management. An outcome of this technical analysis is that, in theory, it is possible to squeeze our food production to one fifth of the land we use today to produce the food demand in 2050. This is all explained by the technical capabilities that we have at this moment or that we can develop in the coming period. Will this happen? Of course not. It just shows how important efficiency in agriculture and livestock management really is.

Even if we acknowledge that this is not exactly how this will develop, we still have to think about possible development pathways: which one do we choose? We don't know yet. Different scenarios can result in different futures, different economies, different trade regimes, but also in different land-use patterns. So the projections we are talking about have been made in quite a high level of detail in the context of these scenarios.

Let us start with the A2 scenario of the IPCC, which, to a large extent, is the path we follow in terms of emission profiles. This is a very unpleasant scenario in terms of population growth and of remaining large differences in wealth between the North and the South. There is very limited technology transfer in this scenario and trade is not really open. One consequence is that modernisation in agriculture stalls in large parts of the globe, which means that the increase in food production is just covered by the increase in agricultural land use. The result is that the category of abandoned cropland is increasing at the expense of forest land, and you will see that abandoned land is probably going to be depleted and destroyed and become degraded land.

On the other hand, there is the B2 scenario that assumes rapid technological progress and will lead to a rich world with a lot of energy consumption. One result is that modernisation in agriculture takes off, especially in developing countries. If such a trend continued during this century, the net result would be that agricultural land use could be cut in half in a gradual fashion. In this scenario there will be much more abandoned land and it is expected that good quality land will no longer be needed for food production and so may be used for other purposes. This is to highlight that we can still choose different pathways and the net result can be incredibly different.

What crops to choose?

At the moment if we have land available and think we can use it, we have to decide what to plant on it – food crops for bio-fuel like maize and rapeseed, for example. To make decisions, you may compare some very basic figures on what different crops produce in terms of net energy yields in bio-fuels produced. For wheat and corn, which are also used for ethanol production today, the typical result is about 50 to 60 gigajoules per hectare per year. If we assume that we will have technology available to convert wood or grasses to fuel, the energy yield per hectare for these perennials, as we call them, is about the same on degraded land as for food crops: between 30 and 120 giga-joules. But on good-quality land those same crops have a net energy yield that is much higher than the food crops currently used for bio-fuels.

So there is far less competition in this case, which means that on the one hand with perennial crops net energy yields are about three times as high as with traditional food crops, and on the other hand the land area needed for producing those crops is three times larger. So there really is an order-of-magnitude difference in potential bio-fuel production between food crops and perennials, and therefore a fundamental difference between so-called first- and second-generation bio-fuels.

Scenario analysis of biomass production potential

To understand what this could mean at the global level, a simple translation has been made from those different scenarios in terms of exa-joules produced, keeping in mind that at the moment primary energy production is roughly a little lower than 500 million exa-joules worldwide. The different scenarios have been translated in terms of biomass production capacity compared to food demand. There is a wide difference between the various scenarios. In the unfavourable scenario, A2, wood bio-fuel potential would be lowest, with still a lot of marginal, degraded land being used, while in the other scenarios there would already be presumably more surplus productive land available.

We also have to take into account that there are limitations in terms of water and land degradation and also biodiversity. Very simply put, if we look at the different scenarios with the limitation on water, limitation on land quality, and so on, all incorporated to make corrections to the potential biomass production, then we arrive at the following overall result: there is a wide range of scenarios of what biomass could do for the future world energy supply, a very wide bandwidth that is especially explained by the various definitions of potentials that we use. The highest estimate goes up to about 1,500 exajoules per year. More pessimistic estimates give figures between 300 and 800 exajoules, and the low range is between 0 and 300 exajoules. In addition, there is a new assessment made on the basis of biomass residues and waste, amounting to a sizeable total of more than 100 exajoules. Then there is an amount that may be developed in the timeframe that we are talking about, from now until 2050, without serious constraints on land. Finally, there is a part that may be developed as soon as we are able to utilise the marginal and degraded land that has become available.

On top of that, if we go to the more optimistic scenarios, and if we are more progressive about increasing efficiency in agriculture and livestock management, biomass may contribute an extra 300 to 400 exajoules per year, which is a very large share of that also rapidly increasing future energy demand.

So, crudely speaking, taking all those issues and some of the serious limitations into account, for example water and biodiversity, I still dare to say that biomass could be developed to the extent that it contributes about one third of the world's future energy supply. However, the largest part of that supply does not exist today; it needs to be developed, and that comes with a large number of preconditions like the integration of agriculture and livestock management. We also have to work on further modernization of agricultural management. We have to choose second-generation biofuels. Water has to be taken seriously into account. And we need to be successful in using degraded lands. All those things matter. It is not an easy option, not at all.

Investment in agriculture is key

Investments in agriculture and livestock development are essential to make this work. Some people have called this the second green revolution and maybe that is not a bad term at all. I think technically and also economically this is feasible, and also necessary to abate some of the problems that we see in land use and agriculture today. With that also comes the need for increased efficiency of water use, which is a very important finding of recent assessment work. Water-use efficiency in current agriculture is low up to dramatic, and the moment you start to invest in agriculture you can also make increasing water-use efficiency a target. This is not only necessary in terms of resource management, but it can also generate better incomes and improve soil management, which is essential for food security.

The key action that I am willing to plead for is that the emerging markets invest in rural regions and go for solid biomass production for bio-energy and make money out of it. That is the difficult intertwined nature of, on the one hand, developing bio-energy and, on the other, linking that to rural development. That is the crucial knot that we have to untangle in the coming years. If we are successful, the result might be that in the first half of the century areas like Mercosur, Eastern Europe and also sub-Saharan Africa could become major producers and exporters of biomass and bio-fuels and thereby contribute to the total supply.

The certification debate

But this does not come about without controls. If you do not steer development, if you do not set the right preconditions, matters could still develop in the wrong direction. That is why the certification debate, which is another area of rapid development, is so incredibly important. The debate about bio-fuels, as negative as it has been, has also triggered a lot of positive activity.

Various governments, but also market players, NGOs and so on, have become involved very quickly and heavily in thinking about sustainability criteria, certification schemes and so on. This is far from perfect, but it is an extremely rapid response to the current debate. There are discussions in Round Tables on various commodities such as palm oil, sugar and soybeans, and there is even a functioning Round Table on bio-fuels. That is a very promising development as far as I am concerned.

And then we have a Dutch proposal, known as the Cramer Criteria, which is still one of the leading examples that we have in the international debate, on sustainabillity listing the key areas of concern including the greenhouse-gas balance, the issue of competition between food and bio-fuels in land-use, the issue of biodiversity and concern for social issues and the environment. What is very important is the notion in this proposal, which is worthwhile reading, that we will not be able to secure all of this tomorrow. We have never had such criteria for conventional agriculture, for example in land-use change. So we had better look at this as a process, as a pathway, in which we can start with minimum safeguards and then, on the basis of experience, gradually go for full-blown certification with a couple of brand new themes. So in various fields we will see, as part of a learning process, what will have to be done to develop this further.

I think that this is something to be very positive about. It takes hard work, but it is the first time that governments have tried to set sustainability criteria for individual commodities, and this is almost a paradigm shift. It has a spill-over effect as well to conventional agriculture and forestry. So far we have, for some reason, not really bothered about setting criteria for our food supplies. Keeping in mind still the 20 million hectares for producing bio-fuels against the 5,000 million for food, setting standards is in fact far more important to land use in general than for the production of bio-fuels alone. This also refutes the suggestion that bio-fuel production is the cause of all deforestation.

This process takes time: we should allow for learning, and concerns differ for the most debated individual commodities like palm oil, soybean and corn, and for others like residues and wood that are already largely approved. There are areas where it is complex and other areas where we may say that we simply don't want some of the bio-fuels. But there are also areas, for example in relation to forest residues and the production of trees and grasses, where the discussion is far less heated, where we have positive experiences and where progress is being made.

There are still methodological issues to be resolved, for example, competition and biodiversity, and there is a need for priority setting and leadership to achieve global convergence, dialogue, collaboration and also, hopefully harmonisation of our efforts. Nobody is served by having dozens and dozens of labels on the market. This really is an issue that should also get policy priority.

The example of sugar cane and palm oil

We still have to better understand what these criteria imply for different places, for different bio-fuels, and ultimately also for crop management, costs, yield and land availability. All these relationships still have to be better understood. But we have some preliminary estimates on the net impact of the application of sustainability-criteria on sugar-cane based ethanol production in, for example, Brazil, showing that the additional costs may be manageable and can also be compensated by improved management in the future. There are partly historic and partly projected estimates for sugar-cane based ethanol in Brazil assuming continuous effectiveness, efficiency and cost decreases. The basic response from the Brazilian partners we have worked with on this topic is to let the criteria come: we can provide a higher value product, they say, we can carry out better management in our country; and we can absorb the additional costs that come with compliance with the various sustainability criteria compared to the reference situation. That is a very interesting and promising development.

Another example is the case of palm oil, which is truly the black sheep of bio-energy and bio-fuel. Palm-oil producers have been accused of nearly everything that is wrong with bio-fuels. But there is a very recent analysis of what actually happened to land-use change in Indonesia, which is really the hot spot for this type of development. The study definitely confirms the absolutely dramatic loss of forest cover in the last decade. But what they also found is that palm-oil production, with current and immature palm oil taken together, can never be the sole explanation for the change in forest cover if you look at the size of the area for palm-

71

oil production. There are far more important factors explaining the forest-cover loss in Indonesia. So even if there is a relation between palm-oil production and forest-cover loss, other factors make up a much larger share in explaining this loss.

What is also clear is that the category of degraded land is far larger than the current land use for palm-oil production in Indonesia. There is a fundamental difference between planting palm oil on tropical rainforest land after first cutting it down, and then emitting a lot of carbon (and this practice has, for very good reasons, been in the press a lot) and cutting down forest on the peat land and then draining the peat land, which leads to much higher greenhouse gas emissions. In addition, cutting down forest and draining peat land causes more emissions per kilowatt-hour than using palm oil from those types of land. If you compare that to the situation with palm oil produced on degraded lands you even see a negative result, i.e. a substantial reduction in GHG emissions per kilowatt-hours of electricity produced.

This is possible although it is hardly being done at the moment because it involves slightly higher costs and requires a little bit more governance, a little bit more steering, which has to do with unravelling the existing complex of forest companies in Indonesia, addressing the illegal logging that is going on there and so on. But in principle it is possible to have fine yields of palm oil on those degraded lands and in fact see a huge carbon benefit at the same time.

So it is not justified to overlook even palm oil, because this could be a serious option for providing income for farmers and the smallholder parties that desperately need income if they are to be prevented cutting down more tropical forest. This is one of the issues that will be investigated in the pilot project that has been started by the Copernicus Institute in Indonesia.

Expected changes in Europe

We have also looked at Europe and the historic development of its yields, which have over the last decades been growing faster in Western Europe than in Eastern Europe. We assumed that those developments would simply continue in the future and that it would be quite modest to say that Eastern Europe would catch up to some extent with Western Europe. That is in fact already happening at a very fast pace.

So we have based our analysis of the potential yields in Europe on those historic developments, and looked in particular to what the trends are in Eastern Europe. We did not assume all kinds of incredible changes in agricultural yields but were rather just sticking to those historic trends.

One result is that, with the spatial cost distribution of biomass production in Europe in 2030 developing on the basis of these assumptions, especially in the new member states in Eastern Europe and in Ukraine, a very large amount of land could be mobilised for biomass production, and that biomass could also be produced at a very attractive cost level. If we choose between annual crops and perennial crops we see a large difference again: the ultimate result could be that Europe, in a timeframe of about three decades, could produce enough energy from biomass to cover its whole oil demand. That is about the order of magnitude we are talking about here, in this particular case. We are not talking about exotic science-fiction-like changes in agriculture, we are basically following the trends, pursuing further modernisation in agriculture, especially in Eastern Europe, and gradually incorporating the biomass crops. First we gradually phase out the first-generation crops and then we introduce second-generation biomass: this could also very well be the economically most attractive pathway.

Final remarks

Bio-energy is definitively not a given. To make this happen, resources need to meet a broad range of criteria, including macroeconomic criteria. The resource base needs to be diversified and shifted from food crops to perennial crops and from cultivated to marginal and degraded lands. We still have very little market experience with that, so we have to experiment, especially in developing countries and in rural markets and investments. Sustainable international markets need to be established and provided with certification techniques. Much word needs to be done in this field as well. We need international collaboration and harmonization on those criteria and standards and all that has to be done under the condition of stable and coherent policies. We also need to consider bio-energy as a range of options and not just look at bio-fuels. That would be a big mistake, which has already been made with the policy choices made at the end of the 1990s which were just pushing bio-fuels. The power and the heat markets, which are the silent work-horses and success stories of bio-energy, are in fact the stepping-stones for the second generation of bio-fuels because they use the same kind of feedstock. This success can be drawn upon for the basis of a new plan.

In the meantime, we have to push very hard for the technologies that can be used for second-generation bio-fuels. That is also why I love the idea of coal gasifiers that we discussed earlier. Coal gasifiers can be one of the stepping-stones for getting biomass into the energy system with tomorrow's economies of scale.

There are also niches in the ethanol market. To make use of those we need to learn that reduction of costs involved in conversion and in the supply and the production of biomass is important. Again, that comes with stable and coherent policies. Look at the Scandinavian countries that have demonstrated how to do that.

To conclude: bio-energy is really at a crossroads of land-use, development, energy and climate. That is also exactly the reason why it is so difficult to develop policies in this area. This is not just about energy, not just about pushing wind turbines. However much I might like wind turbines, this is more complex. It is more difficult because we have to realize that we should aim for more benefits at the same time. We have the bio-energy options to achieve those synergies, but people can also make the wrong choices, as we have seen over the last few years. Governance in cross-departmental fields is key and that is where I think the main challenges lie.

Global Energy Competition and the Third World War

Michael Klare

E nergy is the most pressing, the most difficult, the most
dangerous issue facing the world community today and for the
rest of the twenty-first century. It touches virtually everything in
international affairs, from war and peace to the global economy,
and especially the global environment and global warming.

We cannot have peace and stability in the world without global
economic growth, and we certainly cannot overcome the problem
of global warming unless we solve the energy problem. Although
government leaders have spoken of bold plans to overcome this
crisis, none has yet come forward with an effective blueprint of
how to do so. Moreover, the global economic crisis will make it
more difficult to finance such efforts. Therefore we are currently
facing the future without any sign that international leaders are in
a position to solve this problem.

Why energy is so crucial, central and dangerous

To begin with the obvious: it is worth repeating that energy is
absolutely essential for the successful functioning of the international economy. We take it for granted, but bear in mind that –
notwithstanding the present economic crisis – this is a period of
unprecedented growth in terms of demand for energy, and this is
going to be an enormous problem for the world economy.

On one hand the mature industrial powers – the United States, the
European countries and Japan especially – expect to continue
using high levels of energy, as they have in the past, and anticipate
even an increase in use of energy. At the same time newly indus-

trialising societies, especially China and India, are growing at a very rapid rate, and in their growth and industrialisation expect to use vastly more energy than they have in the past.

Just to put some numbers on this: the US Department of Energy predicts that in the next twenty-five years world energy consumption will grow by 50 percent, from approximately 475 quadrillion British Thermal Units (BTUs) today to about 700 quadrillion BTUs in 2030. Arguably there has never been a time when world energy consumption was expected to grow this rapidly in such a short period.

The question is, where is all this additional energy going to come from? We would like to think first of all that it would come from environmentally friendly renewable sources. But that is very unlikely. According to the US Department of Energy, approximately 85 percent of it will come from fossil fuels – oil, natural gas and coal – the sources of energy that are responsible for most of the carbon dioxide and other greenhouse gases that are heating up the atmosphere. Maybe another 5 percent will come from nuclear power, and another 5 percent from traditional fuels, wood and animal dung. The final 5 percent will come from renewable sources of energy, including hydropower. Maybe there will be some changes in this, but that is the current expectation: 85 percent of energy from non-renewable fossil fuel.

Where, then, are these fossil fuels going to come from to supply this increase in energy consumption? Can we assume that the world energy industry is capable of supplying a 50 percent increase in fossil fuels between now and 2030 and then of continuing to grow beyond that? Can we have any expectation, any confidence, that the world energy industry is capable of supplying this additional energy to satisfy both the old industrial societies and the new? I believe we should have absolutely no confidence in this possibility and will briefly outline why.

The lifecycle of fuels

All three of these fossil fuels – oil, natural gas and coal – are finite substances, and they all follow an extractive lifecycle. That is, after their commercial development they follow a curve of production. The curve begins with a rapid burst of production and rises quickly as entrepreneurs are motivated to find the most easily developable sources of these energies – the most productive fields; those easiest to detect; the biggest pools of oil, coal and natural gas; the richest ores; those closest at hand – and to develop them as rapidly as possible. Typically, production rises quickly for a period of time until a point at which the most valuable, most productive and largest fields are completely exhausted. Then begins the hunt for the less rich, less easily extracted and smaller fields, and production ceases to rise rapidly, slowing down until a peak in sustainable production is reached. That peak may last for a while as a plateau and then, eventually, no matter how much money is spent, all of the rich sources of that fuel or resource will have been exhausted and production will go into decline.

This is true of any commercially developed extractive resource. Of course, in terms of individual fields, such as oil fields, some are developed later then others: at any one time, looking around the world, there are some oil fields that have been completely exhausted and some that have only recently been developed or are on a rising curve of development. So the question is, where does the world supply of oil, gas and coal stand at this moment?

It appears that we are very close to the moment of peak oil production worldwide, that there are more fields approaching decline than there are fields rising in production and that in the next five years or so, we may very well reach that historic moment at which the world oil industry will not be capable of producing additional supplies of conventional oil. It is possible that the world oil industry will be able to supply oil from unconventional sources, such as oil from Canadian tar sands, Venezuelan extra-heavy crude oil and arctic oil. There may be other expensive and environmentally risky forms of petroleum substitutes that will stretch out this peak moment for another decade, but it is highly unlikely that by 2030 we will have more oil then we do now. The greater likelihood is that we will have fewer petroleum liquids.

The strongest evidence for this is that we are now using and relying on more oil discovered twenty or thirty years ago than we are adding to the world supply; in fact, it has been thirty years since the world oil industry added more new oil to the world supply than the amount consumed. That peak in discovering new oil fields is now in decline. Since 1980, we have been drawing on previously discovered oil, and the rate of new discovery has been falling with each subsequent decade. We are running out of oil.

What about natural gas? The extraction of natural gas was developed a little later than that of oil, so we are less far along the curve of production. We probably have a decade of two before we reach the peak moment of natural gas production. Reports suggest this may be somewhere between 2020 and 2030, but then natural gas will also reach its peak sustainable limit and begin to decline.

And coal? Coal is relatively abundant but comes in different forms. Many of the world's richest, most abundant and most productive sources of coal have now been depleted. Yes, there is a lot of coal left in the world, but the environmental costs of mining it will be increasingly prohibitive. In the United States, the Bush administration adopted a rule that allows coal producers to blast the tops off mountains, reducing some of the most beautiful mountain chains in the Eastern Appalachian chain to rubble, because traditional mining techniques are no longer effective in reaching the richest coal supplies in the eastern United States. In the western United States, strip mining is the only effective way of getting at coal. And eventually coal production too will reach a peak, probably between 2040 and 2050, though there is less certainty about this.

Supply versus demand of energy

It is very clear that the supplies of these fossil fuels are not going to increase to the magnitude necessary to satisfy the increasing energy demands of consumers.

What are the implications of the fact that the world energy industry is unlikely to be able to supply energy at an affordable price in order to sustain global economic growth? The most obvious are the economic consequences – in 2007 and 2008 very high oil prices caused extreme hardship for farmers, airlines and the automobile industry, then very low prices caused hardship for oil-producing nations. Such price volatility is likely to be a continuing characteristic of the energy industry.

The geopolitical consequences

As energy becomes more scarce with respect to demand – that is, as the supply falls short of this huge increase in demand – competition between consumers will begin to intensify, and this is going to manifest itself politically as well as economically. Already, China, anticipating a huge increase in its needs, is competing with Japan, the United States and Europe to gain control over sources of supply in places where it has never before sought supplies of foreign energy, and it is beginning to collide with these foreign powers. The United States has to increase its imports of oil because domestic oil production is dropping rapidly while demand is increasing. This is happening simultaneously with another critical development, which is that there are only a few countries left in the world that still have the capacity to increase their oil production. All the consumers are therefore focusing their attention with greedy eyes on these countries, of which there are only a dozen or so. These include the five Persian Gulf countries: Iran, Iraq, Kuwait, Saudi Arabia and the United Arab Emirates. There are also five countries in Africa: Algeria, Angola, Libya, Nigeria and Sudan. There are two in the Caspian Sea basin, Azerbaijan and Kazakhstan, and finally there are Russia and Venezuela. These are the only countries which have any potential to satisfy the total growing thirst of the consumer countries, all of which are trying desperately to secure as much of what remains of these producing countries' surplus oil. Worryingly, the competition for this is taking not only diplomatic but increasingly military form.

Forms of competition

Of course, there are the diplomatic forms of competition, such as state visits. In early 2007, for example, the president of China, Hu Jintao, paid a visit to Africa – this was one of numerous trips to

Africa by senior Chinese leaders – to woo the leaders of Africa's oil-producing countries by promising them enormous amounts of development aid in return for a promise to open up their oil industries to participation by Chinese companies and provide additional supplies to China. Angola is now China's leading foreign oil supplier; it took over Saudi Arabia this year as its main supplier. Meanwhile, Nigeria – a frequent host to top American leaders – is expected to become one of the United States' leading oil producers. There is a rush for Africa's oil.

But in addition to more traditional methods of wooing oil-producing countries, the United States and China are also competing with each other in the military arena, using arms transfers, military aid and other military services to form military alliances with these countries. These methods are akin to those used by both the United States and the Soviet Union during the Cold War, when, in the pursuit of allies and clients in the developing world, arms transfers were used as the principle instrument of influence. Now, in pursuit of oil, the United States is stepping up its military aid to Nigeria, Angola and other potential oil suppliers in the region, while China is doing the same thing in Sudan.

Both China and the United States are also supplying weapons and military technology to oil producers in the Caspian Sea and the Persian Gulf area. This year, for example, the United States announced a US$20 billion arms package to Saudi Arabia and the other members of the Gulf Cooperation Council. This is just one of a long list of huge arms packages introduced in an attempt to solidify the United States' ties with the governments of Middle Eastern oil-producing nations in order to ensure American access to their oil. Now China is copying this behaviour, for example by becoming one of the leading arms suppliers of military technology to Iran. Introduction of these arms packages has taken on a competitive aspect, and this is true not only of arms but also of military support, training, instructors, advisory services and intelligence. So there is an influx of military personnel into these areas.

The strategic position of Africa

In 2008, for example, the United States established a new military command for Africa: the US African Command, AFRICOM. This is the first new overseas regional command of the United States to be established since the creation of Central Command, or CENTCOM, in 1980. Central Command was set up explicitly for the purpose of protecting Persian Gulf oil under the Carter Doctrine of 1980, which states that the United States will use military force when necessary to protect the flow of Persian Gulf oil. This is the basis upon which the United States intervened in the Gulf in 1990 and 1991 when Iraq invaded Kuwait. I believe that the United States' invasion of Iraq in 2003 follows directly from that initial intervention in 1990.

The establishment of AFRICOM in 2007 represents an historic turning-point from the United States' perspective. The United States never paid attention to Africa before. Why should it do so in November 2007? And why now? The only reason that seems to make sense strategically is that the United States expects Africa to be its leading supplier of oil. By 2015, twenty-five percent of oil imported to the United States is expected to come from West Africa. The Defense Department, I should say for the record, will deny this officially. But if you ask people off the record, they will confirm that oil is a key reason for the formation of AFRICOM. They will also deny officially that China's interest in Africa has anything to do with this. But if you ask them off the record they will say, of course, that they are worried about China's penetration of Africa. Africa has now become an area of geopolitical contention between US and China.

The Caspian Sea basin

The same thing is happening in the Caspian Sea basin, where the United States and China are competing for influence. Here China has taken the lead in providing military services, under the auspices of the Shanghai Cooperation Organisation, the SCO. This was set up originally as a counter-terrorism and border-protection organisation, but has now taken on a larger politico-military function. Its acts include calling on its members to prohibit the United States from establishing military bases in the region, and it has also provided a cover for China to supply arms and military services to member states. And so China, like the United States, is extending its military presence into an area of geopolitical competition where energy is crucial, and where the United States and China are competing for access to energy supplies.

But what makes the Caspian situation so dangerous and so important is that Russia is also competing for geopolitical influence in that area – not for the same reasons as China and the United States, because Russia does not need the energy of the Caspian Sea basin for its own use, but because Moscow wants to control the transportation of energy from the Caspian Sea to Europe.

The European Union has the intention of securing an independent source of natural gas that bypasses Russia. The Russians don't want Europe to have any independence in this regard. So Russia is determined that all natural gas coming to Europe from the Caspian basin comes through pipelines controlled by Gazprom. Mr Putin has been extremely active on the diplomatic front in the past year or so, travelling repeatedly to Kazakhstan, Turkmenistan and Uzbekistan to ensure that future gas production from those countries travel by Gazprom pipelines via Russia, rather than by any other independent pipelines that bypass Russia.

Europe is trying to persuade the Turkmens to build a future pipeline underneath the Caspian Sea and through Azerbaijan, Georgia, Turkey and Southern Europe – something the Russians seek to prevent – so Moscow is also militarising its geopolitical presence in the region using the CSTO, the Collective Security Treaty Organisation, and the SCO, the Shanghai Cooperation Organisation (of which it is a member). It has established a base in Kyrgyzstan, where the United States also has a base. There is now a Russian base and an American base forty miles or so apart.

Though much more can be said about the energy competition in the Caspian Sea region, this gives a flavour of the degree to which competition has been militarised, troops are being deployed and arms are being imported in these areas which are inherently unstable. The pursuit of energy does not only have economic effects, but also makes the world more dangerous.

Other dangers

Consumers are competing with one another for the pursuit of energy, mainly in the form of oil and natural gas, from the handful of countries that are capable of providing a supply. But this competition and the flow of money into these countries have a secondary effect of increasing the likelihood of conflict within them. Why is this the case?

It has to do with what is sometimes called the 'resource curse', for the most part because these are poor countries to begin with. They are not like Norway, Netherlands and the UK, countries that were already wealthy when oil and natural gas was discovered in the North Sea. There wasn't a risk of a military *coup d'état* in an attempt to take over and capture all of the oil rents or the revenues from natural gas production, nor were monarchs going to control all of this, keep the profits and give it to their friends and cronies, because these countries are robust democracies and have many other sources of income.

But in Nigeria, Angola, Kazakhstan, Azerbaijan and Iraq, there are few sources of income aside from oil or natural gas. In these countries it is the state that collects the rents or revenues from the production of energy and decides how these are allocated. And as the price of energy goes up, the revenues increase. Whoever is in control of the government is in possession of fabulous wealth, while typically everybody else lives in poverty. So there is a huge incentive to stay in power indefinitely and pay off the people in the military and the police to ensure that no rival parties come to power.

It is estimated that the current government of Nigeria – there have been several of them – has collected US$ 200 billion from oil revenues over the last forty years. Meanwhile, the income of an ordinary Nigerian is around a dollar a day. A large part of that $200 billion has never been accounted for. There are similar situations in Azerbaijan, Kazakhstan and Angola. In these countries a very large percentage of profits from energy is going into the pockets of the ruling faction, whatever it is. Under these circumstances those in power have very little incentive to hold democratic elections and allow for the possibility that another party or faction will take power and pocket the proceeds. The discovery and production of oil in these developing countries has lead to authoritarian governments, and that means that any rival is going to have no other choice then to rely on the force of arms to change the government. So these countries typically have a history of military rule, authoritarian governments, *coups d'état*, assassinations and insurgencies. Moreover, in many cases the national boundaries of these countries were drawn by the imperial powers to meet their own convenience, often incorporating ethnic minorities that do not accept the legitimacy of the central government, which typically keeps all of the wealth and excludes the minorities, who sometimes occupy places where the oil is actually produced. This therefore creates high resentment against the central government and leads to insurgencies by ethnic groups often wanting to keep the oil revenues for themselves. There is therefore a natural inclination towards internal and separatist violence in all of these so-called petro-states dominated by the production of oil.

Nigeria

In Nigeria, the recent drop in oil production is one of the factors that have driven up the price of oil. The oil is largely produced in the Niger delta region where Shell, a partly Dutch-owned company, has been a leading producer. The local people, who are considered a minority by the central government, have borne the brunt of the ecological damage caused by oil production and yet have never seen more then a penny from the oil rents that are collected by the elites in Abuja, the capital. They live in extreme poverty. They have been promised again and again that they will see a greater trickle-down of the oil wealth, but they have never, never really seen any

of this and have risen in a series of increasingly violent and diffi-
cult-to-control insurgencies against the central government.

The United States has chosen to ally with the central government,
increasing its military aid in an effort to suppress the insurgencies.
The United States is on the verge of becoming involved in another
counter-insurgency in Africa, another reason why it seems that
AFRICOM is certain to be at least partly driven by strategic concern
for oil.

Iraq

The modern nation of Iraq is an invention of the British Empire, a
nation created after World War I for a couple of purposes. One
purpose was to help protect the lines of communication of the
British Empire to India. But the main purpose was to facilitate the
extraction of Iraq's oil by the British. To do so, the British took
three provinces of the former Ottoman Empire – Mozul in the
North (the Kurdish-dominant area), Baghdad in the centre (the
Sunni area) and Basra in the South (the Shiite-dominant area) –
and said, 'From now on you live in the Kingdom of Iraq, and by the
way, we are going to bring you a king, somebody brought in from
Medina. He will be your king. Now obey your king.' Not surprisingly, there was considerable resistance to these moves from the
people of the three former Ottoman provinces. There were insurgencies that were brutally suppressed by the British.

Eventually, after World War II, the kingdom established by the
British was overthrown. Then Saddam Hussein – there were some
others in between – inherited this system and continued the
British policy of suppressing the regional insurgencies by brute
force and bribery, using oil revenues to finance the repression. The
United States – or rather George Bush, in his supreme wisdom
refusing to listen to any advice from his professional advisors –
destroyed this system, and is now facing an increasing drive by the
North and South to re-establish themselves as separate states.

The key factor is control over oil rents. The Kurds are determined
to create their own state in the North to be financed by the oil of

Kirkuk, the oil centre of the North, and the Shiites want to create a mini-state in Basra, which is also an oil-producing area. Both are perfectly happy to leave the Sunnis, in the middle, to their own fate without any oil whatsoever; after all, as they see it, the Sunnis lorded over them under Hussein. The Sunnis, needless to say, find this objectionable, and this to a large extent is the reason for their refusal to support the current government and their sympathy for the insurgents. And so conflict over oil rents is a driving force behind the political chaos in Iraq today. Of course, there are other influencing factors, but this conflict serves to highlight the way in which oil distorts these societies, escalates and exacerbates the internal divisions and increases the risks of violence.

Concluding remarks

To sum up, increased competition from the outside is intertwined with the tendency of oil to exacerbate and heighten internal divisions within the oil-producing countries. For those who have studied world history, the situation may seem very similar to that of the colonial world and the Balkans in the early 1900s, another period when external geopolitical struggles intersected with explosive internal forces.

To say that we are heading towards a third World War is probably stretching things a bit too far. But George Bush used this expression last month when he said that the United States' conflict with Iran, which seems to be essentially about who will control the oil flow from the Persian Gulf, could lead to World War III.

The essence of this peril lies in the overlap of the external competition for energy and the internal dynamics in the oil-producing countries. And so I want to finish where I began: that energy is the most difficult and dangerous issue facing all of us in the twenty-first century and one for which nobody has yet devised an effective solution. We need to radically rethink our energy behaviour and aim for totally new approaches.

The European Response to the Russian Challenge

Jonathan Stern, with comments by Catrinus Jepma

In this chaper[1] I will try to introduce some thoughts about European energy security, and in particular the role of Russia in this regard. While the majority of modern academic energy researchers are working on climate change, renewables and the hydrogen economy, we at the Oxford Institute for Energy Studies are some of the last academics in Europe working on the very old-fashioned topic of fossil fuels, which still account for 85 percent of global energy supplies. There are so few academics still publishing regularly on fossil fuels that the subject may disappear altogether from universities within a decade. In this brief article I am really able to touch on only a fraction of the work that we have done in this area, and I urge anyone interested to look at our website and our more detailed work. I will begin with some observations about European energy import dependence and confusion surrounding its importance and then discuss in more detail the energy situation in Europe and Russia, focussing on gas in Europe, which I think is an interesting case-study of the problems that we are facing.

Energy policy issues and problems

A traditional European energy security lecture starts with Europe's dependence on imported oil and gas supplies, and then gives some numbers from the International Energy Agency or the European Commission which show that Europe's energy dependence will grow from about 50 percent to about two thirds and then to about 80 percent over the next twenty years or so. I have no quarrel with these projections, but I do not find presentations (and indeed analyses) that spend a lot of time on how much energy country x or region x will import from country y or region y terribly interesting. They place much emphasis on what I call 'dependence arithmetic', in other words, percentage estimates of dependence. However, we have mostly been wrong about the extent and timing of these developments in the past, and are unlikely to be any more correct in the future.

I am happy with the generalisation that much of the additional oil that Europe will have to import will come from the Middle East and North Africa, and much of the gas will come from these regions and also from Russia. The conclusion that is always drawn is that this has already led, or will in the future lead, to over-dependence, and that in turn this will leave European countries open to commercial and political blackmail. The other common argument is that politically unstable regions and conflicts between countries will lead to supply disruptions. These are the traditional arguments about the problems of fossil-fuel dependence and hence energy security.

There are not many compensations for getting old, but someone like me, who has carried out research on fossil fuels for over thirty-five years, has seen these arguments come up again and again; they are very old arguments. We in Europe have been hearing them certainly since 1973 and probably before. The question that I would pose is: have we got anything new to say about energy security? The only new issues, as I speak in early 2008, that I see is what we all see: oil and gas prices at over a hundred dollars a barrel and rising; a lot of oil and gas producers unable, and in most cases unwilling, to increase their production and export capacity of oil and gas dramatically; and a lot of OECD leaders and the IEA complaining that these producers are not investing in new production capacity. At the same time, China and India have become determined to attract increasing quantities of new oil and gas supplies toward their economies.

My feeling is that the urgent question we face, particularly if the people who say that oil and gas prices will continue to rise to US$150/bbl are correct, is: can Europe obtain adequate oil and gas supplies in the 2010s, and if so, how much will it need to pay to obtain those supplies? My observation is that we have a number of security issues which have been periodically discussed over the past several years, but that we are fundamentally confused about whether the main problem is increased import dependence, or whether the problem is Europe's ability to obtain the oil and gas supplies it needs. The reason we are confused is that, as I mentioned at the beginning of the lecture, the majority of the research community, certainly the academic research community, but increasingly the wider research community, is focussed on the carbon emissions problem. Essentially it is the view that the basic problem facing the planet is that the burning of fossil fuels creates an unsustainable climatic situation. If you believe that the future of the planet is at stake, then issues such as 'From where are we going to get our gas supplies and are these countries going to cut us off?' pale into insignificance.

My suggestion is that we as Europeans, and particularly European politicians, have to try to prioritise the important energy questions; I will come back to these questions at the end of the presentation.

Europe, Russia and energy

Europe has a very long energy history with the Soviet Union and Russia. If you look back at the historical literature, you find Europeans in the 1920s talking about the 'red oil menace'– in other words the dangers of importing oil from the then new state, the Soviet Union. So Europeans have been talking about this issue for a very long time. And what I am going to present to you here is just some very recent history, to give you a flavour of the current landscape.

Figure 1 tells you that, in terms of oil products from former Soviet countries, and mostly this is from Russia – there is a little from Kazakhstan and Azerbaijan, but not much – imports are significant, but if you look at the shape of the curve you can see it is levelling off. At the bottom of the chart are the overall figures in terms of percentages of imports and percentages of demand of oil products coming from these countries. Although people like to have

Figure 1   OECD European oil product imports from the former
            Soviet Union countries, 1990–2006

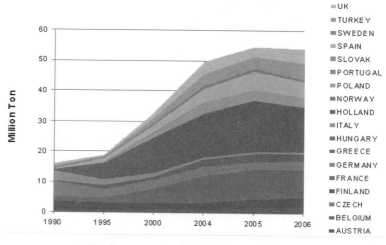

18% of imports and 8% of demand in 2006

Figure 2   OECD European crude oil imports from FSU
            countries, 1990–2006

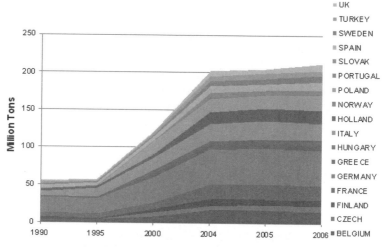

35% of imports and 32% of demand in 2006

these figures, in my view they are almost completely meaningless and thus you should not pay a lot of attention to them. More detailed study shows that some countries are highly dependent and others (not on this chart) are not at all dependent.

Figure 2 is a chart of crude oil imports. Notice the shape of the curve and the fact that Europe is much more dependent on *crude oil* imports from Russia and the former Soviet Union countries then on *oil product* imports. I mention the shape of this curve because you can see that imports since 2000 have been flattening off. In the past few weeks, we have seen a lot of angst in the press from organisations such as the IEA and major energy consultants about the decline in Russian oil production as well as criticism about the lack of investments and an inadequate tax regime.

It is important to understand that nobody in Moscow is worried about a possible decline in oil production. Why not? Well, because they are earning five times as much money from these exports in 2008 as they were in 2002 and, frankly, they have so much money that if oil production and exports decline somewhat, it will not be a big problem. They have other much more important things to think about in relation to how their economy is going to evolve.

Figure 3 **OECD Europe steam coal imports from Russia,**
1990–2006 (thousand tons)

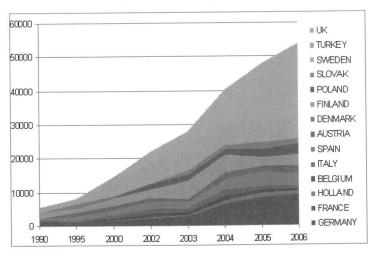

So in our press we constantly focus on issues that are of concern to *us*, but are not really of concern to energy producers. To complete the picture, Figure 3 shows the coal import situation. There has been a huge increase in European coal imports from Russia since 2000, much of it to my own country, the UK. Obviously this is not, in terms of absolute numbers, nearly as important as oil and gas and also not terribly welcome in carbon terms.

Russian gas and Europe's needs; past, present and future

Figure 4   Russia gas exports to Europe, 1990–2006

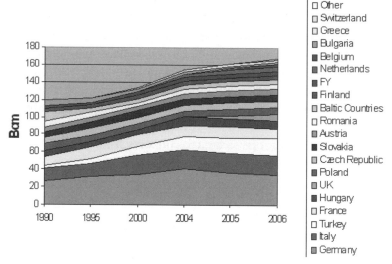

27% of 'Europe 34' demand in 2006

Figure 4 shows the shape of Russian gas exports to Europe and demonstrates that in the post-Soviet period they have increased significantly, but at a relatively slow rate. Notice, once again, that these exports are not evenly spread around Europe. The UK is one of the biggest gas markets in Europe but only a minor importer of Russian gas; the Netherlands also only imports small volumes from Russia. So it is not an even spread and a figure of 27 percent of demand in 2006 does not really give the sense that Finland, for example, is completely dependent on gas imported from Russia, whereas Spain and Portugal, for example, import no gas at all from Russia.

With that as the general picture I want to talk in a little more detail about the landscape as we look further into the future. In the middle of this decade, around 2004 to 2006, without a great deal of publicity, virtually all the large-volume contracts between Russia and west European countries were extended.

For those of you who are unfamiliar with gas contracts, this is a very old-fashioned business. Companies still sign contracts for between twenty and twenty-five years, something that hasn't happened in most other forms of business since the 1960s. The European gas business, however, and to some extent the gas business in other parts of the world, still signs these very long-term contracts. These contracts are legally binding arrangements under international arbitration with liquidated damages. So they are not the kind of pieces of paper where companies suddenly wake up one morning and say, 'Sorry, we discovered we haven't got any gas to export to you even though we said we would.' They are serious financial and legal documents which have been ongoing in Europe for most of the last forty years and will stretch out for most of the next twenty-five to thirty years.

Russian gas and European energy security

The basic problem with Russian gas in terms of European security, in other words the continuity of gas flowing to Europe, has been that with the break-up of the Soviet Union the countries through which the gas flowed between Russia and Europe became independent. The major problem has been the corridor through Ukraine (see Figure 5). About 80 percent of the gas that Russia exports to Europe goes through this corridor; about 13 percent comes through Belarus and Poland; and the remainder arrives in Turkey via the Blue Stream pipeline or goes by a direct line to Finland. During the post-Soviet period, there have been enormous problems with Ukraine, which came to a head in the first couple of days of 2006. This was widely reported in the European press as Russian energy-blackmail against Ukraine. Having myself followed this story for a long time, I would suggest that it was the logical culmination of the Russian government and Gazprom trying to move all CIS countries to European market prices; a complicated subject and almost that of a separate lecture.

Figure 5   Existing pipelines taking Russian gas to Europe and North Stream

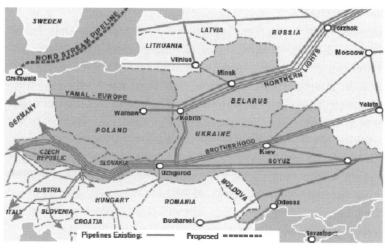

This is a little too simple, but in essence, and baldly stated, by 2006 most CIS countries were paying Russia a price for gas that was about one fifth of the average price paid by European gas companies. To talk of 'subsidies' is overly simplistic because it is not just gas supplies that were involved in these transactions. Nevertheless, the resistance by CIS countries to paying much higher prices and the indebtedness of those countries to Gazprom, particularly Ukraine, but also Belarus, led to this crisis. And then there is the question of whether it is possible for Gazprom to solve its transit dependence on Ukraine, and if so, how. Their response has been that they would like to build two new pipeline corridors to avoid Ukraine, as is demonstrated in Figures 5 and 6.

The first alternative is the North Stream Pipeline (seen in the top left-hand corner of Figure 5), which would go through the Baltic Sea to Germany, and then either physically or by displacement from there to the UK. There has been a huge resistance to this pipeline from the Baltic countries, Estonia, Latvia and Lithuania, and also from Poland, because their feeling is that avoiding Ukraine and also avoiding their countries is a political issue. They are keen that a pipeline be built on land through their countries, which is of course something that Gazprom does not want, the whole idea of bypass pipelines being to avoid countries that may cause problems.

The second alternative is the Southern route (Figure 6), which is in two parts. In the early 2000s Gazprom built, with Italian help, the Blue Stream Pipeline, which avoided expansion of the western pipeline route to Turkey created in the 1980s. Blue Stream is a direct route to Turkey, and Gazprom considered expanding this route by bringing another pipeline through Turkey to south-eastern Europe. Owing to its concern about the behaviour of the Turks, it replaced that idea with the South Stream Pipeline, which is intended to go straight across the Black Sea to Bulgaria, with three branches ending in Greece, Italy and Austria.

Figure 6 The Blue Stream and South Stream Pipelines

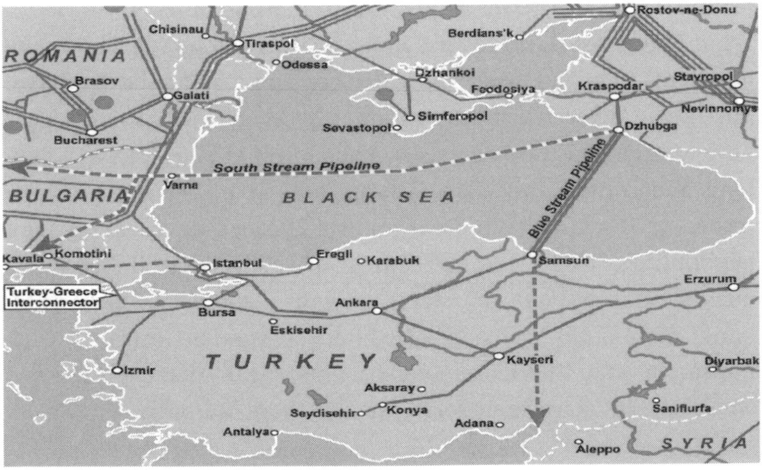

The European press has interpreted these pipeline projects in two ways: first as the dumping of massive additional volumes of Russian gas into Europe and secondly as an attempt to exclude other gas principally from the Middle East and the Caspian region. In my opinion, both views are completely wrong. The majority of the capacity of these pipelines, as and when they are built, will not involve additional gas imports. The pipelines will simply take gas out of the Ukrainian corridor to the same countries by other routes, such that by 2015, if these projects go ahead, Russian gas will have three routes: a central route through Ukraine and Belarus, a northern route and a southern route, with Gazprom able to arbitrage between them. It will still have the problem of the lack of an international transit regime, and this relates to story of the Energy Charter Treaty and its transit protocol.

What I have told you so far is a story of Russia's gas export to Europe. But Russia has other options. What the Russians would like to do is to export LNG from the Shtokman field in the Barents Sea via a terminal in Murmansk, mainly to the US. But that option is going to take some time, as it will be very complicated to build such a large facility under Arctic conditions. So the first element of Shtokman will be to feed the second North Stream Pipeline (mentioned above) and only in the second phase will it begin to export LNG. The Russians say that this can happen by 2014. My feeling is that it will not be possible to move so quickly.

What about Asia? There is a great deal of discussion about the possibility that if Europe does not cooperate with the Russians, Russia will divert all its gas supplies to Asia. This is something I have written about in a book published in mid 2008. To cut a very long and complicated story short, there is no agreement with respect to Russian pipeline gas going to China, even after very long negotiations. There is an agreement to export Central Asian gas, but I'll come back to that later. Despite a potentially promising hand, there is no 'China card' which the Russians can play with Europe in Asia. There are long-discussed deals that we expected would already have been done, but they have not been.

Will there be enough Russian gas for Europe?

So let me come back to the question of Russia and Europe's energy security: will Russia have enough supplies for Europe? This is a subject of another rather different lecture specifically on Russian gas, but to give you the conclusions from that lecture: Russian gas supplies will be tight from about 2010 to 2015, until their new supergiant Yamal Peninsula fields come on stream, but the main impact of that tightness will be felt in the Russian market and also in the CIS market. That is why what happens between Russia and Ukraine, and Russia and Belarus, is very important.

I believe European markets will be less affected, but my feeling is that the consequence of this tightness and the problems the Russians will have in the next few years is that they will sign no new long-term gas contracts with European companies and that their supplies will be limited to the commitments they have already made: 180–200 bcm (billion cubic metres) a year, compared to about 160 bcm, which they exported in 2006. So, in my view, the Russians will honour the commitments they have made. But we can already foresee the peaking of Russian gas supplies to Europe around the early 2010s, and I think there won't be substantial additional supplies from Russia until the late 2010s, if at all.

What about other suppliers?

If that is the position of Russian supplies, what does the European gas situation as a whole look like? Again I have resisted the temptation to put up a lot of reserve numbers and compare a lot of countries' reserve-to-production ratios, but believe me, there are tremendous reserves around Europe. For those of you interested in the thesis that world oil production will peak, my view is that whatever the oil situation, there is definitely no shortage of gas reserves. It is not the availability of reserves, but the intentions and the capabilities of suppliers and their motivations and relationships with Europe that will determine what will happen in the future.

Figure 7   Projected decline in European gas production 2005–17

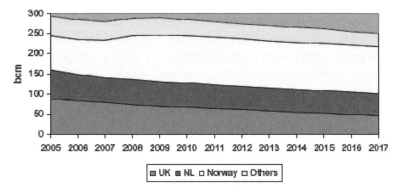

Figure 7 shows the projected decline in European gas production over the next decade. Norwegian production will increase a little and then flatten off. Dutch production will decline somewhat. UK production will decline significantly as will production from other continental European countries. So before we say anything about increasing demand, Europe is going to have to replace its falling domestic supplies with imports.

Figure 8   Availability of gas supplies from Africa, the Middle East, Caspian and Central Asia

- ALGERIA: major exporter, no major growth beyond currently contracted volumes
- EGYPT: sold out – minor growth potential
- LIBYA: major LNG growth potential but could take 10 years
- NIGERIA: NLNG Trains 1–6 achieved
  - NLNG 7/8 + Brass River + OK LNG delayed
  - domestic (power) demand will take priority over additional exports
- EQUATORIAL GUINEA: minor growth potential
- ANGOLA: some growth potential
- IRAN: highly unreliable gas exporter, major domestic demand requirements + political instability + conflicts with the international community create major problems; any significant gas pipeline exports will be to Pakistan (India?)

- AZERBAIJAN: around 15 bcm of Shah Deniz gas from 2015(?)
- TURKMENISTAN: huge reserves, offshore prospects consider-able but not before late 2010s?
- KAZAKHSTAN: dependent on availability of Kashagan gas, and probably not until late 2010s

Figure 8 shows a range of countries from which Europe does get and could get additional gas supplies. Africa is a very important source of gas for Europe. Algeria and Egypt are already major suppliers, but with limited growth potential beyond currently contracted volumes. Let me stress again: that is not a judgement about reserves. Most of these countries have plenty of reserves, but they are constrained in bringing them into production because of their upstream policies, and they are constrained in expanding exports because of the increase in domestic gas demand. The two big hopes for significantly increased African exports are Libya and Nigeria. In Libya there is enormous growth potential but it could take a long time to realize and the Libyans are not in a big hurry. Europe already imports a lot of its LNG from Nigeria. But new projects are suffering substantial delays, mainly because of political instability. This is partly a protest against central government, where local communities with no access to gas (and often electricity) supplies are protesting against their resources being exported to rich countries as they don't receive any benefit from the resulting revenues. Finally in Africa, Equatorial Guinea and Angola are becoming significant exporters of LNG, but with limited growth potential.

Let us then look at the Middle East: the Caspian Sea region with its huge potential gas availability, and the difficult problems of Iran, a country with huge gas reserves, enormous gas demand requirements, marginal gas exports to Turkey and Armenia which have been extremely unreliable, and major conflicts with the international community over almost anything from nuclear power to the existence of Israel. In relation to gas exports to Europe, Iran remains a question mark. I should mention that I am the author of a paper published in 1975 in which I said that by 2000 Iran would be a bigger gas exporter then the Soviet Union; twenty-five years later Iran was a net gas importer! The country has a huge number of pipeline and LNG export projects which have been well advertised in the press, but which have made very little progress.

There are big hopes for exports from Azerbaijan, which currently delivers around 6 bcm of gas per year, not much of which gets beyond Turkey. It is difficult to see more than about 21 bcm of gas exports being available starting around 2015. Ideally, up to 15 bcm of gas will flow through Turkey to Southern and possibly Central Europe. But the problematic part is what role Turkey will play.

Then there is Turkmenistan, which has huge reserves of gas but uncertain timing for development, and is currently focussed on exports to Russia and China; Kazakhstan is in a similar situation with not quite such large resources. Exports to Europe from either of these countries will depend on a resolution of the legal status of the Caspian Sea. In other words, will it be possible to build pipelines across the Caspian until its legal status, and therefore the ownership of the sectors, has been established? Some people say yes, others say no.

For European politicians, and in particular those in Brussels, an enormous amount of hope has been invested in the Nabucco Pipeline from Caspian and Middle East countries to Europe through what is known as the 'fourth corridor'. But it has proved very difficult to find sufficient gas to fill a 30 bcm per year pipeline prior to 2020. It has not been well publicised that at the end of 2007 and the beginning of 2008 Turkmenistan cut off gas exports to Iran which did not recommence until around March, as a result of which Iran cut off Turkey (the third winter in a row that they had cut Turkish supplies). Turkey then cut supplies to Greece and Greece had no gas for the first two months of the year from that source. That left Gazprom to supply the gas shortfall along this route, and this is the route by which politicians want to diversify supplies away from Russia. The moral of this story is that diversity does not always equal security.

There is an even bigger issue here, which is that Central Asian gas is not yet a European game. The Chinese have a different commercial way of operating than OECD countries. Once they sign a memorandum of understanding with a producing country, jumbo jets full of Chinese workers and Chinese equipment arrive and within about three months they are drilling wells. So they don't sign treaties, they don't wait for due diligence, they don't need complicated financing plans, they don't spend years negotiating Production Sharing Agreements: they basically get on with it. And they have agreements to import up to 40 bcm per year of gas from Central Asia. But the 'great gas game' in Central Asia – and I personally don't like that phrase – if there is one, is between China and Russia. Europe is not yet part of this game, but might be in the future.

LNG and European energy security

European LNG supplies are really the subject of a different lecture. Figure 9 shows the terminals which have already been built and are under construction in Europe, while some of the ones which have been proposed, like the terminal in the Netherlands and a few others in Northern Europe and Italy, are shown in white. Spain is in a different category to other European countries because two thirds of the country's gas is imported in the form of LNG. It is important to remember that LNG constitutes not yet a global market, but a globalising market. Europe will increasingly have to compete not just with the US but also with the Pacific for LNG. So, unlike the old days of fixed and rigid contracts, today and increasingly in the future, the LNG which a country thought belonged to it may not in fact belong to it unless that country is prepared to compete for it. In the future, LNG supplies may go to the highest international bidder. But LNG has become a highly competitive and globalising market and the term 'security' will increasingly be about money rather than gas availability.

In summary, I would say that in early 2008 producers and exporters are not expected to increase exports as rapidly as expected. They are focussed instead on increasing domestic demand for gas. For exporters it is no longer extremely important to increase export revenues, because high prices mean they already have so much more revenue then they were expecting.

Figure 9   European LNG terminals

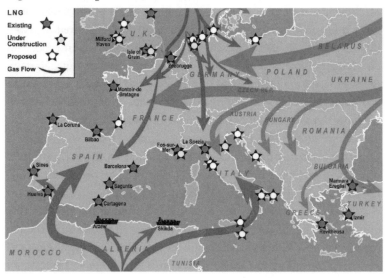

In that context, exporters are increasingly likely to consider LNG preferable to dedicated pipeline gas supplies to Europe. They give exporters greater arbitrage possibilities, which means that they need to be less concerned with what US and European politicians think about their domestic policies. They want to have the freedom to export their LNG to China, India, Latin America, or wherever they want. And if Japan or Korea is paying a higher price this week, and Spain is paying a higher price next week, that is the flexibility they want to have. Increasingly, they do not want to lock themselves into long pipelines going across a large number of countries, all of which have the potential to make trouble. All of these issues are much more important than the real or imagined threat of a gas cartel, a so-called gas-OPEC.

Conclusion

The key question we are facing in European gas markets is, from where we are going to get substantial additional gas from after 2015? Not where *could* we get it from – we know that – but where *will* we get it from? At present, not from Russia or other current major suppliers. That means Europe faces more long-term supply uncertainty. Unlike those rather tiresome op-ed pieces in newspapers or blogs on the internet, I do not think this is a great disaster. It does, however, raise very important questions, coming back to the beginning of this chapter, about the future of power generation and carbon emissions. If Europe is not able to obtain substantial incremental gas supplies around 2020, many countries will have to develop alternatives which will include renewable energy, nuclear power and coal-fired power stations. Because of problems of acceptability of nuclear power, and limits on the potential for renewable energy, the consequences of those decisions may result in the building of additional coal-fired power stations. I am not a climate-change sceptic; I have no reason to doubt whatever anyone says about climate science. I am, however, a target sceptic. I doubt that targets which say that the European Union or its individual countries are going to reduce emissions by 20 percent by 2020, or are going to introduce 20 percent of renewables by the same date, are possible to achieve. But the main policy that I can see that might result in achievement of those targets is a combination of renewables and gas: as many renewables as possible – there is a question of commercial viability but that is a different topic – with gas to balance the load. If that is going to happen, we have to change the present gas outlook relatively quickly.

I spend a lot of time talking to journalists about whether Europe can trust the Russians and other gas exporters, and whether Europe should limit future Russian gas supplies. I am not saying that Russian supplies are totally problem-free; they can be problematic. I am not saying there are no serious issues and no worries about Russian supplies. But to me much more serious issues include determining from where are we going to get our gas after 2015 and deciding how we should try to develop successful relationships with Russia and other suppliers instead of telling them, 'We don't like you, we don't trust you and we would rather not have to deal with you.'

If we fail to resolve these problems, or to improve our relationships with Russia and other gas suppliers, what will be the consequences for European energy and carbon balances? I fear they may be very bad.

Comments by
Catrinus Jepma

I liked very much that in his opening remarks Jonathan Stern said
that it is now very 'sexy' for scientists to talk about climate
change, carbon trading, the role of renewables and so on, but that
in academic circles there is relatively little attention any more for
energy security and supply issues. It is definitively true that there
is very little appetite in general to focus on the traditional classical
fossil-fuel markets. As Stern said, there are only a few people still
focussing uniquely on this particular subject. As a researcher, I
myself started from the climate debate and began dealing with
climate issues and related research twenty-five years ago. Only
during the last five years have I moved towards issues such as security of energy supply. So some people do make the reverse route.

I agree that security of supply is an underrated issue, probably not
in policy circles, but definitively in the research community. The
key issue that Jonathan Stern addressed is the question of whether
there is some reason for concern, particularly in Europe and the
European Union, as far as the Russian supply response is concerned.
Should we be worried about that? Should we be prepared for this,
yes or no? That is the bottom-line question to be addressed.

My basic conclusion is that there is some basis for concern: at least
a number of contracts are due to expire in the next five to ten
years. But many of the long-term contracts with a duration of
about twenty years still stand, and for the time being they provide
a legally very stable pattern of supply from Russia. If you look at
the historical facts, I fully agree with Jonathan Stern that long-
term contracts with Russia have always been honoured. Even
during the Cold War period in the 1960s the Russians never went

back on their long-term contracts. So for the next five to ten years there is not much concern, particularly also because, even if the production of the most important Russian fields may decline, in particular in Siberia, they do not decline to such an extent that there would be substantial risks of the supplies from Russia creating problems.

Of course there were the political problems with Ukraine in 2006, but I think those were minor problems. They were basically intra-political issues in which the Russians tried to make clear to Belarus and Ukraine that they had to accept living in a world where they did not any longer get the domestic Russian price, which is about one sixth or so of the price that the West is paying for the Russian gas. So major adjustments need to be made in Ukraine and Belarus and this question has been played out on the political front.

Along with Jonathan Stern, I also think there is no serious problem between now and 2015, but I think that in the period after 2015, until 2025 or maybe 2030, there are a number of problems that may be very serious. One, which I don't think Jonathan Stern dealt with sufficiently, is the production decline in Russia. The decline is already there. In the most important gas production fields in Western Siberia, production is actually declining. There is some serious concern that the investments that are needed in Russia to maintain production up to levels of about 200 bcm of exports to Europe in the period up to 2015–2020, and double that amount for the domestic market, are at the moment not really being made. Those investments amount to 30 to 40 billion US$ per annum, needed only to maintain that level of production. At this moment, real investments are falling short of those figures.

Of course there are huge promises. The Shtokman field is to be developed, 'hopefully', the Amalk field is going to be developed, 'hopefully', the North Stream Pipeline will be a transport corridor, 'hopefully' ready by 2015 or so. Well, these are all plans and it is very well possible that the developments will be much slower than people anticipate right now.

I am afraid that the Russian investment in oil exploration is going to fall short of what really is required to secure the supplies to the rest of the world. I think there is a serious concern there, which makes me believe that after 2015, until 2030 or so, we cannot be a hundred percent sure that the projected gas supplies from Russia will be delivered.

That creates challenges for Western Europe, because when there is uncertainty there everybody tends to turn to other suppliers of gas –Iran, Kazakhstan, and so on – and all those sources have problematic aspects for at least the next ten to fifteen years. So if Russia wants to play its game right, and wants to get the most out of its gas resources, then it has the period between 2015 and 2030, that is fifteen years, to play the game, if you like, and try to restrict supply. It could very well be that Europe will be going to pay for it. This is the main point we should focus on: that if the production during this period is less then we anticipated, at some stage Russia will have to face the decision as to whether it meets its own domestic demand and the demand of CIS countries, or whether it meets foreign, including European, demand. What choices are they going to make?

An essential question in this regard is the timing of the convergence between the export gas price level on the one hand and the domestic gas price level on the other. At this moment, as I said, the domestic price level is 15 to 20 percent of the export price level.

The Russian authorities have indicated that this is of course something that needs to be changed, but the actual practice is that, if we look at the gas price development in Russia, as compared to the export price level, the convergence is occurring very, very slowly. Inflation in Russia is close to 10 percent, while the annual gas price increase is somewhat, but not much higher. The process of price convergence that is required in Belarus and Ukraine, which are the main transit countries, but also consume a lot of Russian gas, is very slow as well.

So I am not convinced that the price convergence in Russia and the CIS countries will by the period 2015 to 2030 have come so far that demand elasticity is actually going to work. Demand elasticity estimated for Russia is relatively low: 0.5 or even 0.3, which basically says that the Russian people will not reduce demand drastically if the price increases. So if it is true that the Russian authorities will be slow in increasing gas prices in the future in Russia and the neighbouring states, it could well be that in the period from 2015 to 2030 there will simply not be sufficient gas to be delivered to Western Europe to meet the demand over there.

I think that the basic issues are what the domestic policy is in this respect within Russia and what we can say about the demand elasticity. The transport infrastructure is, in my opinion, a secondary aspect. Of course Russia is right not to focus only on the middle corridor but also to develop the Northern and the Southern connection in order not to be extremely dependent on Ukraine, which is now, I believe, transporting about 80 percent of Russian gas. It is good strategic advice not to continue to be dependent on Ukraine in this regard. But for the security of supply to Europe, the domestic measures to be taken within Russia itself are what is ultimately important.

Finally, what can Europe do? It should not make itself extremely dependent on Russian gas and should look for other countries of supply. But I think that for the Netherlands, the debate is going to be quite a different one: to what extent are we going to reintroduce coal? The big discussion in Europe could very well be that if we do not want to be overdependent on Russian gas, if we limit our imports from Russia to between 200 to 250 bcm, if we are not extremely successful in getting gas from Libya and other suppliers, and if we still want to increase our power production as scheduled, which is in the 1.7 percent increase over the next 20 years, then we have to reintroduce coal again as a relatively abundant and classic fossil fuel.

As we see already in our own country, the big challenge will be how that increasing use of coal can be combined with meeting the greenhouse targets that have been set at a 20-percent reduction by 2020 and continuing the trends of greenhouse-gas reductions.

And if we are going to reintroduce coal, perhaps alongside some nuclear power and renewables, another big challenge for Europe is whether we can succeed in developing carbon-storage technologies and facilities, and whether we can develop them relatively quickly. As the problematic period is going to be between 2015 and 2030, the restriction of its dependence of Russian gas could very well be one of the main strategies for Europe.

ANSWERS BY JONATHAN STERN

The production of new gas in Russia on a large scale is hotly debated. On the one hand we have Gazprom, which has said openly and repeatedly that production will start from the Yamal fields in 2011, and they have given an estimate as to what production will be. For those of you who do not focus on Russia: the Yamal fields are not speculative, they are confirmed as some of the largest remaining gas fields in the world with the potential to replace Russia's existing declining fields. Many of us, including myself, have said, 'Well, we have seen the reserves, we are not clear that we have seen investments so far, and we also have questions about technical aspects of opening up those fields.' But Gazprom knows more about this than anyone else, and to give you a sense of how confident they are, they have said that they will produce 7.9 bcm of gas, not 7 or 8, but 7.9 bcm in 2011.

Let me move on to the domestic demand issue. I published a book a couple of years ago, called *The Future of Russian Gas and Gazprom*. In that book I included a long discussion on prices and price elasticity. Although I still believe that this is very important, I now think that there is something much more important. Due to the disastrous decade of the 1990s, the Russian economy is basically operating on Soviet-era capital stock. We know that when the Soviet Union collapsed in 1991, it was probably the most energy inefficient economy that the world has ever seen. Eighty percent of that capital stock remains today. It has not been replaced.

Much attention is focussed on the question of raising prices and the commitment that by 2011 they will be at European levels (whatever that may mean). But much more important is whether old energy-inefficient, very energy-intensive industries will replace their plants, as we already see in Ukraine. It has been estimated that in virtually every energy-intensive sector in Russia they could, with not even the most modern but just generally available equipment, cut their energy usage by 40 percent for the same level of production. How quickly will that happen? We are not sure. How quickly can it happen? How long does it take to replace 80 percent of the capital stock of a huge country?

To follow on from Catrinus Jepma, pricing is extremely important. A criticism that could be made of the Russians is that they are charging CIS countries much higher prices, yet have no plans to charge their own citizens such prices. Prices are going up dramatically in Russia, but, to give you an example, by 2011 the Russians only plan to charge industrial customers US$125 per mcm. This year the Ukrainians are paying US$180 per mcm. Next year they may be paying over US$300 per mcm. So the Russians are relatively timid about price increases for themselves and that gives an answer to the question as to how quickly they will be able drive down domestic demand. However, the bigger debate in Moscow between my counterparts in the academic world is the question of how Russia can have a modern economy with Soviet-era capital stock. So this is not primarily an energy question, it is also a general question about the economic future of the country.

Let me just finish by commenting on Catrinus Jepma's observation about the reintroduction of coal and nuclear power. I don't have the information about the Dutch situation and am more informed about the British situation; but we have done a lot of work on power generation in Europe, all kinds of power generation. The conclusion of all that work is actually relatively simple: it is a fact that, even in a country where nuclear energy is possible, it would not be possible to build substantial numbers of nuclear stations before 2020 at the earliest. And even being very optimistic about carbon capture, that technology would not be available on a large scale until after 2020. There will be a few demonstration plants before then, but even the companies that develop carbon-capture technology and storage have no expectation that they would be able to introduce large-scale commercial plants until after 2020. So if we are going to meet our 2020 targets, we are going to have to meet them without nuclear power and without coal with CCS.

Note

1   This lecture was delivered in April 2008, when oil prices were over US$100/bbl and rising; before the global economic downturn was visible; and well before the January 2009 Russia-Ukraine gas crisis. All of these events have significantly changed the short-term outlook compared to what was envisaged in the lecture.

In for a Bumpy Ride?

Oil Turbulence in the Next Decade

Coby van der Linde

I n this chapter I would like to see if we can get little more on top of what is currently going on in the world of oil, in the middle of one of the most turbulent times we have ever experienced. I just arrived back from Surinam where I had been for only two days, and I discovered on my return that the oil price had gone up by US$25 per barrel in my absence. That is not really fair, because I want to be there when that sort of thing happens!

Oil and finance are becoming more and more intertwined. In the past nine months and in the last couple of years, we have seen an increase in oil prices that is fairly consistent with the depreciation of the US dollar. At least that was the case until March of this year, when that relationship was broken somewhat while oil prices continued to increase. Of course, then it came back after July when the price was at its peak at US$147. The oil price collapsed to US$90 a couple of weeks ago and went back to US$120 this morning, 24 September 2008. So I think I have a lot of explaining to do.

The global political agenda

If we look at the global political agenda for the years ahead, we see why we should be concerned about energy, linked as it is to the issues of climate change, terrorism, nuclear proliferation, democracy and nation-building, the rise of China and India and the relationships with Russia and OPEC. In short: security increasingly means security of energy.

This fits in with the new make-up of the geopolitical system and the fact that American bankers, if in trouble, fly to Beijing or the Persian

Gulf to see if they can save their banks. What will happen and has already been happening for the past year is a change in ownership. In fact, we have seen a change in ownership in oil since the 1970s. As I will show you later on, quite a lot of energy, in particular oil, is now at least under the safe guardianship of states. This is the case not only with OPEC countries for oil but also with Russia for oil and gas. Particularly for Europeans the Russian discussion is very interesting, and this is not a new discussion, as the tendency to diversify away from Middle Eastern oil towards Russian oil and gas has already been around for quite some time. Of course now we are crying wolf for doing that though it seemed like a very sound policy at the time. For the purposes of our discussion, Russia means gas, but in this lecture I will not deal with gas unless you ask me to.

Are we on the right track?

If I look at the big issues, at oil and at policy-making, then I sometimes have the feeling that everyone is thinking about and discussing things as if we already live in 2030 with quite a lot of the current problems already resolved; as if we are already clear about what is going to be the transition path and that we know what we want. The European Union has formulated its 2020 policy, in the Netherlands we have the policy paper 'Schoon en Zuinig', which, if allowed, we want to push a little bit further. So we feel very comfortable that we are now on the right track and will resolve all our problems.

What I am really worried about is that the discussion at present is not about transition problems. That means that there could be a very nasty mismatch in time, when all those new energies are available and when, with shortages in our traditional fossil-fuel markets, whether it is oil, gas or coal, there is also some constraint on the value chain – this could plague us in the next fifteen years. That is possible because the demand for energy, despite the current turmoil in international economics, is still increasing, particularly in China and India and other developing countries that will continue to show strong economic growth. Also, reserves are more and more concentrated in only a few countries that are hesitant to invest in new capacities, and the solution that we had in the past after the first and second oil crisis by beginning to exploit reserves in the North Sea and in Alaska is no longer available. There are not that many options at the moment unless we go to the really expensive stuff in the very deep offshore areas and in the Arctic circle. We cannot pull off that trick one more time.

So while production outside OPEC will be declining, our dependency on OPEC, as well as developing countries' dependency on OPEC, will grow in the meantime.

Power shifts

So the OECD countries will diminish their position as the most important consumers and give way to developing countries. Since we are part of a world system, of course that will also be part of our own reality. At the same time, as we looked to the future in the early 1990s, we thought that we would be able to benefit economically from our international relations. Globalisation was going to be the answer. Private investments, international trade, that would be the driving force behind all our actions. We could forget about the state: that would actually diminish in importance.

Of course what we have seen is almost the opposite. We see an increase in bilateralism as an alternative for globalisation and multilateralism. We see that governments, particularly in the energy sector, but also, after last week I would like to say, in the financial sector, play an increasingly important role. Nationalisations and state interventions are back with a vengeance and this changes the outlook on how the world will work. It will also have an impact on how, for instance, the negotiations go in Copenhagen on climate change next year. These things really matter.

Our geopolitical relations and the world system and its underpinnings in economic terms are changing rapidly. The southern wealth funds are now the main actors that we have to take into account, particularly when it comes to investments needed to make this transition into sustainable energy happen. I would say that the southern wealth funds from the Middle East and China are the ones that would be able to foot this bill because we in the industrialised world are beginning to become pretty poor, particularly if you look at the United States.

World primary energy demand continues to increase, supply lags behind

World primary energy demand, consisting of coal, oil, gas, nuclear, biomass and other renewables will, according to the International Energy Agency, continue to grow. This is business as usual. If you look up some more recent data you might find a somewhat lower number than the 160 million barrels per day – which is the number the Agency was expecting in 2007 – but from the oil industry there have been a lot of signals that say that 160 million, or even the 120 million of the year before, is an unsustainable level to supply, not so much because the geology would be a major constraint but because there are problems above the ground.

We could have energy demand growing very rapidly in developing countries, but we ourselves in the industrialised world are also still addicted to oil and gas. It will take a long time for us to transition away from fossil fuels. In the meantime, we continue to consume these fossil fuels despite dwindling supplies because we do not have the investments at the moment in capacity expansion that we would need to fend off supply constraints in the next decade. Investments would have to be done today: they are simply not being done at the right level and at the minimum cost in all provinces in OPEC countries. So there is a major problem.

What drives demand? Population growth and lifestyle changes. The number of cars sold already in China this year makes this clear. Even if these cars were driven only from home to work, that would already have a huge impact on oil demand! Also the impact of China and India on coal demand is very large and, from the point of view of sustainability, very worrisome. It will make a discussion on CO_2 reduction all the more difficult. But the increase in oil demand and energy demand in general is worrisome and has a quite large impact on CO_2 emissions.

Price effect

I expected you to ask me how we reached US$147 per barrel earlier this year and what this meant. Well, we got there because the increase in demand from China and India, without an increase of supply capacity, of course means that very quickly we begin to use up the buffer capacity that was already in OPEC's hand, predominantly with the Arab Emirates and Saudi Arabia. That capacity had to be used on a daily basis just to satisfy daily demands. When this happens, you lose all flexibility, which means that even the smallest supplier has market power.

So if there is a problem in Nigeria or in Ecuador, or in fact if there are maintenance problems anywhere, then you can almost calculate what problems you are going to have in the market. If the Bonga oil field in Nigeria gets attacked and you know how may barrels are disappearing, you can calculate how long it will take before that oil is going to be back on the market. This inflexibility is a constraint that you will see reflected in the prices.

So what we have seen since 2004 is that the buffer capacity, in terms of effective spare capacity, as a percentage of production, is very low indeed in relation to increasing demand.

The question then is, will Saudi Arabia be willing to increase that buffer capacity, to the benefit of the entire international community, and to create some more stability in the market? Of course Saudi Arabia would *not* be totally prepared to do that, because it would be very costly. If you made this proposition to a private investor, he or she would say: why should I invest in capacity that I cannot use when I am not certain that, if there is peak demand, the price I could fetch will pay back my investments?

So the buffer capacity of the OPEC countries in the past has been a huge investment on the part of those countries for stability in the world market. In a couple of years' time, we will think back over the years of the so-called OPEC-ruled world and be grateful that they had created so much buffer capacity and stability in the market.

I expect the future will be a lot more volatile. If you want a definition of volatility, what we have seen between January and July: up by US$50 and then in two months down by US$ 50, and then up by US$25 over last weekend – *that* is volatility. How can anyone who has to deal with energy prices at the moment plan business in the face of this sort of volatility? Planning has become extremely difficult because every predictable factor is gone from the market.

The problem of lagging investments

With oil supply being constrained and with demand rising, the result is these huge price increases that we have seen in 2008. With oil reserves, the question is: where are they and are they enough? One of the main problems is that at the moment nation states are among the most important actors in the market. They are responsible for the pace of development of new resources. For the period that we are talking about there are sufficient oil reserves. With the prices of today, all the oil that is needed can be produced. So the bottleneck is in the relation with the desired pace of development. Apparently there are incentives in the oil market that prevent, for example, the OPEC countries from investing in extending their capacity.

Partly this is because the motive to invest is different for international than for national oil companies: for an international oil company the motive is to make profit; for a national company it is not so much to make profits as to provide income to the state which also has a social function. In addition, because of the turbulence in the financial markets, the state increasingly has to manage the underground wealth against the above-the-ground wealth.

If you produce oil and amass its wealth in US dollars, and if the dollar depreciates, you have a negative return performance on your capital. You would have been better off if your oil had stayed underground. That has been exactly the sort of discussion that we have seen in oil-producing countries recently. So the incentives in the market have been pointing in the wrong direction and, because of all these shifts, political problems have been increasing.

The marginal cost of supply is rising

For the next fifteen years we will see more concentration of reserves in the Russian shelf, the Caspian Sea and the Middle East, which constitute 72 percent of both oil and gas reserves in the world, while the distance between the producing and the consumer countries is increasing. For them, the era of 'easy oil' is over. In most OPEC countries and also in Russia and Mexico, for example, the availability of medium-cost oil is diminishing, and the cost of production has increased quite substantially. The cost inflation that has been impacting the industrialised countries in the last couple of years is now also prevalent in oil-producing countries. So they have produced their 'easy oil' and now they have to make a little more effort to get it out of the ground.

Let us say that they can produce against between US$30 and 50 a barrel. That should be possible. So that is one thing. But the cost structure for the IOCs, given their access to reserves, has changed remarkably in the past couple of years. Their marginal cost of supply has already increased to between US$70 and US$80 per barrel. The cost inflation of the marginal barrel has increased dramatically and therefore there is a bottom in the market for the IOCs, which will make them look again at their investments. If, like last week, the price goes down to US$90, they were probably already thinking about delaying certain investments, otherwise they would not measure out.

In order to build up oil prices, the cost of the marginal barrel is crucial. Usually, and that has been the case over the last twenty years, 75 percent of the oil price could be explained by the cost of the marginal barrel and 25 percent by all sorts of other factors, such as politics, but also the cycle on the market and, until March and probably now again, the exchange rate. If you take that into account, we would probably arrive at the price of around US$120 per barrel as a consensus price for various reasons. This is important for producing countries like Venezuela and Iran in order to balance their economies. They have a profound interest in not letting the price sink below that level. But the IOCs also have their interests.

What we see is that the old oil provinces are in decline and that production capacity needs to be replaced, but this is not being done quickly enough. Therefore there will already be difficulties over the next ten years to actually maintain supply at levels as we see them today, and that is really serious. Why? With all the delays in these big projects, such as the 2P project and other off-shore Brazilian projects, even if they began today, it would still take seven to eight years, in an optimistic scenario, to get oil from those projects to the market. So those new investments are not going to be the answer for 2015. We will suffer from even higher prices if we do not handle this carefully.

What happened to the price after July?

Given the market situation, why did the prices come down after July this year? There are various factors. For one thing, I think there is growing uncertainty about the world economy, coinciding with the fact that Saudi Arabia was prepared to produce a little more oil after the Jeddah conference of 23 June 2008, which I thought was a really important initiative. As there were a lot of countries experiencing very serious consequences, they wanted to create a kind of co-management of the high oil prices at that time. That may have made a contribution.

Also, demand, particularly in the US, may have been responding quite dramatically to the high oil prices. People were changing their behaviour. Whether they did that on a structural basis remains to be seen, but for the time being somewhat fewer SUVs might have been sold. If they have not yet taken to the road again, that might help a bit.

So demand really responded, particularly in the US, but also to some extent in Europe. Demand did not respond, however, in countries where oil gets subsidised, such as China and India, even if they had difficulty financing their subsidies. We should remember that about three quarters of the world's population is not consuming oil at market prices but at subsidised rates. So if the market price goes up most of the world will not respond by lower demand, even though their governments are struggling to make ends meet.

What also happened is that inventories were drawn upon quite substantially. In July inventories went down from above average for the period to nearly below average. What also had a major impact was that China had built up large inventories for the Olympic Games and once it was clear that they had enough, they started to draw upon those inventories. That might have been the explanation for the collapse of the oil price from US$147 in July to US$90 in September 2008. So there were a couple of temporary occurrences which made the market drop.

According to the short-term energy outlook in September 2008, expectations were that once nations stopped drawing upon inventory or the dollar actually began to slide again, oil prices would go up again. Everybody at the time put the expected price somewhere around US$120 because that seemed to be the consensus price at which producing countries would still be happy because they could continue to do what they were doing, and at which the IOCs did not really have much to complain about.

Where to find oil and gas reserves?

Government ownership of oil and gas reserves is becoming an increasingly dominant feature of the market. It will change the business models that we deal with. Sometimes, when we discuss energy issues in our Western societies, we tend to forget that perhaps the national oil companies should also be discussed, because they have become very important partners in supplying our markets because currently we cannot rely on bio-fuels as an alternative.

If bio-fuels become a serious alternative, however, our relationship with the oil-producing countries will change dramatically. That is exactly the reason why these countries are very reluctant to invest, because our answer to higher prices has been that we are going to transition ourselves away from dependency. If oil-producing countries were to answer our increasing demands by expanding their production capacity, by 2020, as the Western countries are on their way to become less dependent on oil-producing countries, the increased capacity of those producers would be beginning to arrive on stream. That is why the producing nations feel insecure about demand, even if, looking at China and India, demand seems so buoyant that you are inclined to ask. 'What is the problem?' But I guess that, contrary to what we sometimes believe, the underlying thought is that sometime in the future, China might actually experience a recession, and economic growth there will not continue infinitely.

Oil, the financial market and the role of southern wealth funds

Let us now look at the relationship between oil and the financial market. To start with, oil is to a large extent determining our balance of payments. As a consequence of price increases, balance of payments of the oil-consuming countries has really deteriorated. More worrisome, however, is the position of the oil-consuming developing countries which are in a much weaker position to fend for themselves.

But I think in this case the US is also a very interesting subject of study because it has a very large trade balance deficit and its capital balance does not look too good either. I guess it is to some extent understandable that the US Congress is looking at Poulsen's rescue plan more closely, not just for the impact it may have on the financial market but also because of the impact it will have on the government budget.

So what we have seen is a huge build-up of financial reserves, not official monetary reserves but reserves in sovereign wealth funds which have become very large, and important players in the world capital markets. But we do not really see them invest, understandably, in the energy sector. There is a certain reluctance for political reasons of course, but for them it would make sense to actually invest in our downstream markets to create that security of demand by vertical integration. But of course they have their doubts and do not feel so sure since China tried to take over the Unical Company (which did not succeed because the US Congress intervened). Perhaps these funds may change their minds now that the banks have come up for grabs, and maybe the oil companies will not be that difficult to get either.

What we are discussing here is that strategic industries that have played a very important part in our economies for a very long time are also coming under foreign ownership in terms of investment decisions. This is a political issue that will be raised on top of the 2020 discussion in the coming years. It is not just, for instance, that investments by Russian companies are already in the headlines in the newspapers and that we have great difficulties with them, but that the whole world around us is changing and other countries seem to be amassing the type of wealth that we used to have ourselves. And with that wealth comes decision power.

Effects on the structure of the energy market

I expect therefore that in the coming years we are going to have some very interesting discussions, amongst nations but also amongst companies, on how we are going to structure the future energy market. That also implies a discussion about the security of supply. I promised I would not talk about gas, but sometimes I think that it would be better to link discussions on the supply of oil and gas. For China, as well as for Europe and the United States, security of supply is an important issue to discuss.

For Europe, until now the discussion has mainly focussed on gas, but oil should also be part of it. Europe's position is slightly different from that of the others. Europe should therefore try to play this more strategically and be a bit more sophisticated and at least understand what its problems are. Europe at least should think three times before putting its lot behind, for instance, the United States, which is seeking trouble with Russia, when the European position with Russia is different to that of the US. Whatever happens, Europe is not going to get a different neighbour on this continent. Europe is sharing it, and will always share it with Russia, so Europe is forced to think about energy issues a little bit differently.

Europe should not write its energy agenda in a way that is thrown off course by American interests in this respect, because there does not exist a gas relationship between Russia and the US. That makes a big difference to the way to play this. The gas market is not as fluid as the oil market, so it is different and different solutions have to be found.

Conclusion

For the future all that I can see is that, even if we wanted to, we will not be able to get the energy issue off the agenda. We will have to live with much higher prices, not for the reasons that we think, i.e. temporary shortages. We will have them because we created a lot of mismatches in times when we were overoptimistic of what we could do and were ignorant or not paying enough attention to what we could do to manage this mismatch better.

So we should be wiser about seeing our limitations and that would be my last word on this.

Water for Food - but not for Waste

Jan Lundqvist

This essay[1] deals with the dynamics in the food chain, i.e. what happens between 'field to fork'. The purpose is to stimulate debate about the need for a fresh look at the concept of food security and what it means in water terms. Conventional analyses focus on production or supply of food. But the definition of the concept refers to consumption of food or, more correctly, food intake requirements for "an active and healthy life" (FAO, 1996). Few people seem to be aware of the huge differences between the amount of food that is produced, the amounts available on the market and the amounts that are beneficially consumed, i.e. the food actually eaten. About 50% of the food available at field level is lost, converted and wasted as compared to the amount of food intake (Lundqvist *et al.*, 2008)[2]. The situation looks different in different parts of the world (Figure 12). Households in rich countries roughly throw away a quarter to one third of the food bought (WRAP, 2008; Jones, 2004; Kantor *et al.*, 2005; Kader, 2005), most of it is "perfectly fit for consumption". In addition, losses occur between the field to the market. A proper analysis of food security should pay attention to undernourishment as well as over eating. Globally, the problems associated with overeating, i.e. overweight and obesity are much bigger in terms of the number of people affected, as compared to undernourishment.

In the literature, there is confusion about what may be considered as a reasonable and sufficient food intake and how it relates to production and supply. Food security refers to the level of food supply that is deemed necessary *at national level* to ensure that *individuals* get enough of food to eat. Naturally, aggregate food supply in society must be higher than the recommended food intake. A certain loss is hard, and quite costly, to avoid. Moreover, terminology tends to be fuzzy. Consumption, for instance, is generally used to describe how much food is bought or procured. But not all the food so acquired is eaten. Semantically, and for a proper understanding and analysis, it makes sense to distinguish between: the amounts of food produced, supplied, demanded or procured, the food intake, and the amounts thrown away.

The food that is lost and wasted has also consumed water and contributed to green house gas emissions and incurred other costs when it was produced. Reducing losses and waste is thus equivalent to reduce the pressure on scarce water resources and the vulnerable environment – *without* compromising food security. Alternatively, losses and waste could be seen as an opportunity in efforts to reduce undernourishment. A multiple win approach is possible: farmers will gain from reduced losses (no pay for losses), pressure on environmental/water systems is reduced, food security is enhanced and consumers would save money.

The world at a cross road

Let me first interpret some common figures and trends concerning food security and how they relate to the pending water crisis. Throughout history, the challenge to feed the world has haunted decision makers, scientists and, most tangibly, ordinary people in many societies. Hunger and food deprivation is dreadful for those who are affected. Not only is it a disgrace to society. It is also a threat to political and social stability. Food shortages and rising prices on food carry high political risks, something we have witnessed in recent months. A period of relative optimism about gradual improvements in food security can be noticed in the aftermath of the green revolution. For several decades, yields and total food production have been growing faster than the population increase. This development, however, has come at a cost in terms of a heavy pressure on water resources, especially the blue water resources (i.e. water in rivers, lakes and aquifers) and, generally the living environment. As shown below, Figure 1, water withdrawals from rivers, lakes and aquifers (i.e. groundwater) have been, and continue to be, significant in efforts to expand and maintain irrigated agriculture.

Many countries and the world at large are now at a cross road in several respects. Population growth continues, notably in areas where the natural resource endowment is meagre; the number of people who are undernourished is on the increase and so is the number of people who are overweight and obese; composition of diets among people who enjoy rapid increases in disposable income is shifting towards more water intensive food items. These kinds of trends signal an increasing pressure on finite and vulnerable water resources. At the same time, the possibilities to withdraw additional water for food production are limited; competition for land and water, both in rain-fed and irrigated systems to produce other commodities than food is stiff. Water provision for food is no longer a "privileged solution" to use an expression coined by Albert Hirschman. Climate change and global warming have negative repercussions on water availability including rates of evaporation and transpiration. A new era of resource scarcity, including water scarcity, combined with booming needs and demands is a characteristic feature in the world today.

It will not be enough to only aim for increased production to realize the goal of food security for all. If more food is produced, at high cost, but if a large fraction of it is not beneficially used, progress is thwarted. If those who are undernourished do not have the ability to produce more for their own benefit, the money to buy food on the market or the political power to get access to what they need, an increased production may very well only result in increased wastage, incidence of overweight and obesity and environmental costs. We do not want this kind of future. At this juncture of historical proportions, with a mix of complex issues calling for solutions, it makes sense to revisit strategies that could effectively address the food and water crises, which are intimately related to social and political issues.

Rapid and dramatic changes in food security

As indicated, the prevailing focus in analyses about food security has been on production and supply, e.g. how much water (and other resources) does it take to produce a certain amount of food in various climatic and geographic contexts. Recently, a thorough analysis summarized the experiences, trends and main challenges regarding water and food issues (Molden, 2007). That analysis provides a basically optimistic view about the possibilities to feed the world in the future, provided that considerable efforts are implemented (*ibid.*).

The difficulties of making predictions about the food situation have been illustrated time and again. A sudden and worsening food crisis received a lot of attention during the last year. In a short period of time, prices of most agricultural commodities increased substantially. During the latter part of 2008, they declined, but uncertainties and volatility characterise the price of most agricultural commodities.

An important feature influencing food demand, nationally and globally, refers to a strong economic growth. For instance, economic development in China over the last 30 years has been truly impressive. Since 1978, when the open door policy was initiated, China has had an annual economic growth of around ten percent. Comparatively speaking, this is much higher than its population increase. For China and other countries, the pressure on natural and other resources has to be interpreted as a combination of demographic and socio-economic trends.

Contradicting messages and real paradoxes

Stories about food price hikes and increasing difficulties to produce food have been discussed at highest decision making levels. A few examples may illustrate the vivid debate.

The UN Special Rapporteur on the Right to Food, Mr. Jean Ziegler, recently used very strong language when he compared increasing food prices with mass murder. Predictions of dramatic consequences of climate change are common. Lobell et al., (2008), for instance, argued that a substantial reduction in the potential yield – which should not be mixed with the actual yield – in Sub-Sahara Africa and South Asia of 30 percent by the year 2030 is likely in the absence of effective mitigation and adjustment measures. In contrast, the delegates at the World Food Summit in Rome in June 2008 were given an alternative vision. The UN Secretary General, Mr. Ban Kee Moon argued that world food production needs to rise by 50 percent by 2030 to meet rising demand.

But there are other aspects related to food security that warrant attention. An article in the New York Times, in May 2008, showed that an average family of four persons in the US throw away about 112 pounds of food, about 50 to 55 kilos, per month. BBC and other media have disseminated similar stories. Households in the UK, on average, throw away about 33% of the food that they have bought, i.e. paid for and carried home (WRAP, 2008). Most of the food so wasted is perfectly fit for eating.

With a growing world population with an improved disposable income and with water and environmental constraints, these features are worrisome. In 1900, world population was about 1.65 billion, while it amounted to more than 6 billion at the turn to the 21st century. In index terms, population grew from 100 in 1900 to around 380 in 2000. Figures for withdrawals of water are more dramatic (Figure 2). Available statistics show that about 580 cubic kilometres of water were withdrawn in 1900. Around 2000, they

Figure 1 World Population increase and Water Withdrawals, 1900 – 2000. Illustration: Britt-Louise Andersson, SIWI.

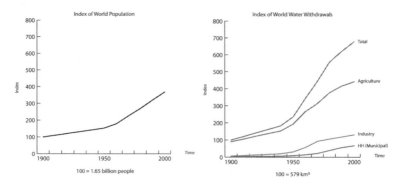

were in the order of 4,500 cubic kilometres (figures vary in different publications). In index terms, global water withdrawals have shot up from 100 to around 700. The graphs illustrate that the increase in water withdrawals was roughly 2 to 2 ½ times more rapid as compared to the demographic change during the last century.

As can be seen from the the graph to the right in Figure 1, the agricultural sector makes up the largest part of the withdrawals, followed by industry. Water for the municipal or household sector makes up a comparatively small fraction. For many people these figures may come as a surprise. Water requirements for "our daily bread" are significantly higher than the combined water needs for drinking needs, household and industrial requirements. It should be added that water use in agriculture and in the open landscape is to a large extent of a consumptive character, i.e. water returns back to the atmosphere as evaporation and transpiration. Water use in industry and also in households is generally non-consumptive.

The expansion of irrigated agriculture has given a boost to food production during the last half century. The amount of food produced in rain fed systems is, however, still much larger. In terms of quantity, rain-fed systems produce about 2/3 of the world food output and a bit less in terms of market value. As discussed at the end of this essay, the potential to increase food production in the rain-fed systems and in systems where supplementary irrigation is feasible, needs to get much more attention than full scale, conventional irrigation systems (Molden, 2007).

Figure 2 illustrates the very positive trends in food supply since the 1960s. Increases in supply are, of course, a reflexion of the increased demand, which in turn mirrors improvements in the ability of people to buy or procure more food. When income rise people first tend to demand more food. Gradually the preference is for more variety in the composition of the diet. When economic conditions improve for poor people, it is likely that they will spend a fairly large proportion of the increase on food. Unfortunately, the tendency to overeat and throw away food also increases. Indeed, development is a multi featured phenomenon with many contradictions.

Food supply, i.e. the food that is available in shops and in other outlets in society has increased steadily during several decades. For the world as a whole, supply of food expressed in energy terms increased from something like 2,250 kilocalories per capita, day in 1960 to about 2,800 in 2003. The graph in Figure 2 is originally published in Molden (2007) and in that report, 2,800 kcal per capita per day is seen as the threshold level for national food security. This does, however, not mean that the required intake of calories, on average, should be 2,800 per capita per day. Depending upon physical activity, age, sex, etc, it is generally much lower, or around 2,000 kcal person per day. The premise is that food supply in society must be higher than the recommended food intake requirement for the individuals to allow for a certain percentage of loss and waste.

The overall positive and stable trend hides huge differences between the developed countries, where the daily per capita supply is about 3,300 and Sub-Sahara Africa where it is in the order of 2,200. In addition, there is a problem with distribution and access within countries. As a consequence, roughly 830 to 850 million

Figure 2 Average, daily per capita food supply since the 1960s.
Source: Comprehensive Assessment of Water
Management in Agriculture, 2007.

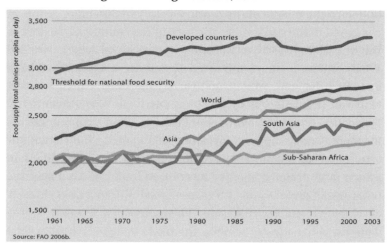

people were undernourished at the beginning of 2008. Due to very
turbulent changes in the food sector and in other parts of society
since then, the number of undernourished has increased and is
now well above 900 (end of 2008, early 2009). It is important to note
that undernourishment is not due to a lack of food. In most cases,
it is caused by a lack of access to food. Poverty, but also conflicts and
other circumstances reduce access. It is, for instance, often pointed
out that the rate of undernourishment among children in India is
among the highest in the world (The Hindu, 2007). This unfortunate
fact cannot be explained by the circumstances just noted.

Another very important circumstance is hidden behind the trends
shown in Figure 2. Roughly, 50 percent more people in the world
are suffering from overweight and obesity compared to the
number of people who are suffering from undernourishment.
With the recent increase in number of undernourished, this relation may have changed. But available information (beginning of
2009) suggests that overeating is still more prevalent than undernourishment, with significant social costs for both categories.

130

What about the future?

We have to assume that the population growth will continue. Analyses suggest that the world population will be about 9.5 billion by the middle of the century, i.e. about 50% more people as compared to the situation at the turn of the century. Compared to the situation in 1950, when world population was around two and a half billion, a staggering seven billion are likely to have been added to the table. About 200 years ago, when Thomas Robert Malthus published his book *An Essay on the Principle of Population* (1798), the world population was less than one billion. Most projections suggest that population increase will flatten out after 2050. Yet, demographic change is only one component in efforts to understand the likely additional demand for water and other resources.

To get a better idea of what is the likely demand for additional water in the future, it is relevant to compare information about population and GDP with water pressure. GDP gives an indication of the disposable income of people, which, in turn, provides a basis for estimating what amounts food and other goods and services may be demanded and how this translates into water requirements. Projections about economic change are uncertain but according to several reports, it is possible that global GDP may be 10 to 25 times larger in 2050 as compared to 2000. Compared to an annual population growth of about 1% or a bit higher, the socio-economic drivers are noticeable (Sachs, 2008).

At the beginning of 2009, a cautious attitude is warranted. To what extent the current economic recession is temporary or how long it will last and how deep it will be, is not possible to foretell. During the last few months, prognoses about the world economy have been increasingly pessimistic although formulations currently point at "glimmerings of hope". The psychological element in economic trends is strong. Both upwards and downwards trends seem to accelerate through overly pessimistic and optimistic expectations. Once the economy turns, the recovery process might be reinforced.

Many countries e.g. China and India, Vietnam and also countries in Africa continue to show high growth rates. There might be some wishful thinking behind economic projections, since we all hope that these trends will continue. People in affluent societies do not want to see their wealth eroded – indeed, we can ill afford it with widespread habits of high consumption, heavy loans on houses, etc. Equally important: commitments to alleviate poverty presume a continued economic growth. We want people to have a better life and be able to enjoy an increased income.

Colleagues at the Secretariat for Future Studies in Stockholm have studied the likely level of GDP in the future. In 2000 there were about 0.8 billion people who lived in countries, where the annual median GDP on a per capita basis was 10,000 US dollar or higher. According to their analysis it is likely that in 2050, 7 billion people or a stunning 80 percent of the world population may be living in countries where the annual median per capita GDP is 10,000 US dollar or higher (Malmberg, 2007; Lind and Malmberg, 2007).

Growth of the economies implies a tremendous historic opportunity. If financial resources would be spent on educational programmes, on improvements in transport, storage, water systems, environmental care, water management, etc., the boost to social and economic development and resources stewardship could be significant. To what extent the increasing wealth will lead to investments and opportunities for sustainable development activities and to what extent consumption will be the preferred choice is, however, a question far beyond the scope of this lecture.

Figure 3 illustrates how the level of GDP in different countries and in different regions of the world in 2000 was related to the supply of food (in the Figure, food supply has been translated into the consumptive use of water to produce the food supplied). Norway and the US have a very high level of annual GDP per capita, in the order $35,000 and Sweden is not far away. Generally, the OECD countries have a high position on the GDP axis and the "dietary water requirement" is about 5 – 6 tons of water per person per day (the Y-axis). This is the amount of water consumptively used for the food supplied in society. Countries in Sub-Saharan Africa, (plotted with triangles in orange; SSAF) have a low GDP per capita and also a low position on the Y-axis, about 1 to 2 tons of water per person per day, on average. Since a fairly large fraction of the population have a reduced access to food, some enjoy a diet that is much better than these figures indicate while others are suffering from a food deprivation.

Figure 3   Per Capita Consumptive Water Use for Food Supply (Y-axis) and GDP (X-axis), 2000 (Source: Lundqvist et al., 2007).

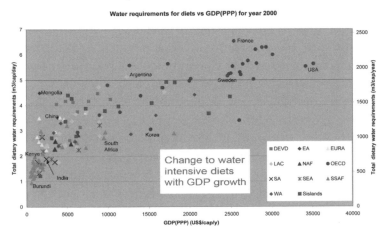

The graph indicates a clear trend towards water intensive diets at high levels of GDP, which however, flattens out in pace with economic improvements . We can also see a considerable variation in water intensity in countries at comparable levels of income. India (IND), China (CHN) and Mongolia (MNG) represent quite different types of societies but with a fairly similar level of GDP per capita in 2000. Their positions on the Y-axis are however quite different due to differences in the composition of the diets. India is mainly a vegetarian society while China has a high supply of meat, to a large extent pork. Mongolia has an even higher supply of meat.

Production of meat and dairy products differs quite a lot, depending on feed, relative reliance on irrigation, and similar factors. In Mongolia, for instance, meat and animal products come from cattle that are raised in rain fed systems or from feed that is produced in areas that are not suitable for ordinary crop production. In many developed countries, meat production is based on feed that comes from areas that could be used for alternative agricultural production and some of it comes from irrigated areas. These circumstances need to be kept in mind when interpreting the variation in the graph.

In OECD countries, the percentage of animal food items in the diets is quite high (Figure 3). Generally, the fraction of meat in the diet, or the demand, increases with increases in per capita income. Although supply is not equivalent to level of food intake, it should be noted that the availability of meat products is significantly higher as compared to what is motivated from a nutritional point of view for food intake (McMichael *et al.*, 2007).

The two graphs in Figure 4 compare meat and milk demand and GDP levels over the period from 1961 to 2000 for India, China and the United States. The increase in GDP was much faster in China as compared to India and the US. But the interesting feature is the difference in the change in the demand for milk and meat, respectively. In the case of India, which is mainly a vegetarian society, there was hardly any increase in the demand for meat but a significant increase in the demand for milk. In the case of China, the opposite trends are illustrated; there was quite a significant increase in demand and supply of meat products, but little change in the demand for milk. A noticeable preference for meat products in China, with significant implications for water pressure is also noted by Liu and Savenije (2008).

The world average annual per capita supply of meat was a little bit below 40 kg in 2003. This means that China is slightly above the world average while many other countries, including India, remain below the world average. The US is far above the world

Figure 4   Meat and Milk Demand & GDP growth, 1961 – 2000,
            in China, India and the US Source: Charlotte de
            Fraiture, IWMI.

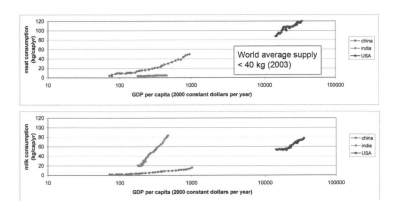

average with a supply of meat in the order of 120 kg per person and
year, i.e. about 3 to 4 hg on average per person per day.

Closed basins

Increases in water withdrawals mean that relatively less water
remains in water courses, including rivers. This is an inevitable
consequence since a large fraction of the water diverted for irrigation returns back to atmosphere in terms of evaporation and transpiration. Gradually, the rivers are being "closed" in the sense that
it is no longer considered possible to withdraw and allocate any
more water to meet additional demands (Figure 5). At the beginning of this century about 1.2 billion people lived in basins with
this predicament.
Based on data from the 1990s and the beginning of this century,
the map on Figure 5 shows "closed basins". The basins marked in
dark are, however, not continuously closed. Typically, the situation in any basin varies from one year to another and depending
upon location in the basin. In some rivers, the volume of water is
larger in upstream segments of the basin, whereas the situation
may be different in other basins. Precipitation in the catchment

135

Figure 5 An estimated 1.2 Billion people lived in "Closed Basins" at the beginning of this century. Source: Smakhtin et al. (2004).

typically varies between years, which also means that flow of water into reservoirs will vary as illustrated for a relatively large reservoir in a basin in Southern India (Lannerstad and Molden, 2008; Figure 6). Although 'there is no such thing as an average water situation' in a basin, variability is given surprisingly little attention in water resources analyses.

The huge variation from one year to another in terms of flow of water in Bhavani River and, thus, inflow into the reservoir does, of course, mean that water provision from the reservoir cannot be fixed (Figure 6). The water storage capacity of the Bhavanisagar reservoir, which was one of the first to be constructed in India after independence, is about 900 Mm³.The main purpose to build the dam and reservoir was to supply irrigation water to about 84,000 ha and to reduce the effects of recurrent droughts and a severe water scarcity as a result of failed monsoons. Historically, the unpredictability of the monsoon and the paucity of storage and poor ability to harness rain water at the time and place it fell resulted in a high number of famines (Lannerstad, 2009).

The need for storage of water from the monsoon period had been discussed for a long period, but it was only after Independence that president Jawaharlal Nehru started to turn words into physical structures for the harnessing and storage of huge volumes of water.

Figure 6   The first large scale dam and reservoir built in India after Independence, 1947, is located in Bhavani basin, Tamil Nadu. The graph illustrates that 'there is no such thing as an average'. Source: Lannerstad, 2009.

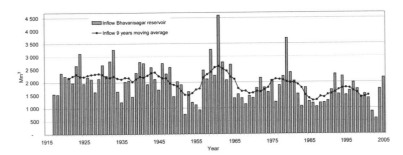

His perception of dams as the "Modern Temples of India" is famous. From the 1960's onwards, the building of dams storage facilities was given a boost in connection with the spread of the Green Revolution in large parts of Asia.

As discussed in Lannerstad (2009) and Lannerstad and Molden (2008), the situation in the Bhavani basin varies significantly between years and between upper and lower segments of the basin. For the farmer, but also for planners and development agencies, this variability creates huge problems and high risks. The example well illustrates that not only climate change but also climate variability is a tremendous challenge.

New demands for land and water

The demand for additional commodities from the agricultural sector has expanded very rapidly, for instance, the demand for biomass for bio-energy production. If current trends were to continue, the potential water requirements to produce more food and biomass for energy purposes might be at a similar level by the mid of this century. However, it is very difficult to estimate the water requirement to produce biomass for energy purposes in the

137

future. It is, for instance, likely that the second generation of bio-fuels will be introduced on a large scale and technical progress may change the conditions. A major question is also: on what land and with what water will food and biomass for energy purposes be produced? To what extent will areas that are now devoted to irrigated agricultural production be used for energy production and/or to what extent can biomass for energy purposes be produced with small or limited competition with food production?

With a business as usual approach and assuming that the trends that we can observe today will continue, we could expect an increase in the annual water requirements to produce food from about 7,000 to 11,000 cubic kilometres from the beginning to the middle of this century (Molden, 2007). As already noted, it is difficult to make valid estimates of water requirements for the production of bio-fuels. Depending upon feed stock and other circumstances, there are huge variations.

Increased demand for water will also come from other sub-sectors of the rural economy. The demand for cotton and other commercial commodities is on the increase as a result of economic growth, urbanisation and industrialisation. At the same time, the concern for the environment must be factored into the water policy. In a context of water scarcity and climate change and global warming, the water availability versus water supply equation becomes very difficult to handle. It is necessary to pay more attention to the potential of the precipitation, i.e. how to make a better use of it through rain water harvesting techniques and integrated land and water management (Falkenmark and Rockström, 2004).

Unresolved questions and challenges

I agree with those who, like Mr. Ban Kee Moon at the World Food Summit in Rome in 2007, argue that we have to give a boost to food production in the future. But since the effort and cost are high to increase production, it is necessary to also ask: who will get access to that food? The fact that some 950 million people currently are undernourished is not due a lack of food. Anybody who visits areas where undernourishment haunts people may easily note that food is available in shops and at market places. For people who have the money or who can exert pressure on authorities, food is accessible.

It is relevant to ask: how much food is or could be produced? However, a more pertinent challenge is: how can we best feed the world's burgeoning population, parallel with supply of other agricultural commodities, without inflicting serious harm to the environment? If a fraction of the food produced is lost and wasted and if overeating continues, the relation between production and food security remains poor. Increased food production should preferably be in areas where production and productivity are extremely low today and where food deprivation, food insecurity and poverty prevail. In large parts of Sub Saharan Africa, yields of about one ton or even less per hectare are common. Also in large parts of South Asia yields are quite low. Increased production is conceivable in areas which are well equipped with water and where cultivation conditions in general are favourable.

Magnitude of losses and waste

The point is that the food security challenge cannot, and should not, be handled only as a production and supply issue. It makes sense to analyse what is happening with the food once it is produced. The next graph, in Figure 7, is based on figures compiled by Vaclav Smil (2000). It illustrates that production of food, expressed in energy terms (kcal), is more than double as compared to the net amounts for beneficial consumption. Incidentally, the net availability of 2,000 is about what is considered as sufficient to meet the daily energy dietary requirements of food for an active and healthy life[3] (FAO, 1996). A large fraction of the world population does not have access to enough food, whereas an even larger fraction demands and consumes more or much more than what may be considered sufficient to 'lead a healthy and productive life'. Overeating and the consequences in terms of overweight and obesity cause huge problems and costs to individuals and society today.

Figure 7   Losses and Conversions: Production to Consumption. Illustration: Britt-Louise Andersson, SIWI.

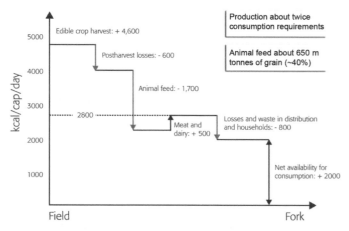

The level of 2,800 kcal refers to food that is available for purchase, for distribution at schools, hospitals, etc. But it is not the amount of food intake. Losses in the food processing, distribution, retail, etc, together with waste in the household sector, i.e. the throw away of food, is significant.

Losses and waste occur at different stages from the producer to the consumer and from the field to the fork. In line with the use of the terminology in literature, losses generally refer to stages between the field to the market/retail/similar. Waste refers to the throw away of food that is perfectly fit for eating and, generally, to consumer behaviour. Additional distinctions and concepts feature in literature. Spoilage, for instance, is often used to mean losses in transport and storage. To further illustrate the complexity and the *process*, it may be useful to distinguish between losses and waste in quantitative and in quality terms.

The situation looks quite different in the rich and the developing countries. In the developing countries the main problem occurs in the first part of the chain whereas in rich countries the challenge is much bigger in the latter part of the food chain, which is also a value chain. Waste of food that is processed, transported, stored, refrigerated, etc, implies a waste of money and resources. In addition to waste, overeating compounds the challenge.

Figure 8   Losses and wastage from field to fork. Illustration: Britt-Louise Andersson, SIWI.

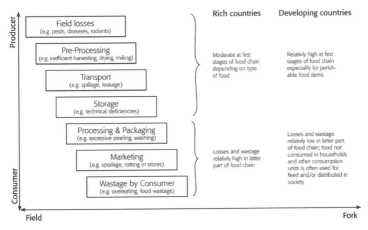

Three examples may illustrate this. A detailed study by the Waste Resources and Action Programme (WRAP) in the UK presented in 2008, showed that people in England and Wales needlessly throw away 3.6 million tonnes of food per year or 1/3 of what is bought, 60 % of it untouched, with an estimated retail value of about £ 10 billion annually of avoidable food wastage. In Sweden it is reported that a family with small children throws away almost 25 % of all food they buy. Close to half of all food produced is lost or wasted by households or before it reaches consumers. The Ministry of Food Processing in India says that a whopping Rs 580 billion or about 10 billion US Dollars gets wasted in India each year. The three examples underline the different character of the problem in OECD countries and in other parts of the world.

Apart from the waste that occurs daily, incidences of significant waste are documented. In the US, a recall of fresh and frozen beef in February 2008 got some headlines in the news. It represents a single event of amazing proportions (Rano, 2008). The recall of one hundred and forty three million pounds, about 65 million kg of raw and frozen beef, is probably the single largest meat recall in any country's history. The recalled meat has consumed in the order of 650 billion litres of water when the food was produced. In addition, the emission of green house gases and other production expenses should be added to the cost of production *cum* waste bill. Similar events, although of smaller proportions are reported from many countries.

Interests, indifferences and potential conflicts; benefits and costs

It will not be a tea party to meet additional demands for food and a range of goods and services that will be needed and demanded in a world of growing populations and expanding economies. With limited and erratically available water resources, which are subject to quality degradation and easily escape effective control, tremendous and complex development challenges are obvious. Irrigation systems have been perceived as a guarantee and as a means to overcome fluctuations in rainfall. But as illustrated in Figure 6, the amounts of water in reservoirs will also vary. It needs to be recognized that the main source of water is precipitation. Strategies are urgently needed to make best possible use both of the fraction of the rains that can be made available in the soil, the green water resource, and the water in rivers, lakes and aquifers, the blue water (Falkenmark and Rockström, 2004).

But, again, food security refers to adequate food intake, not to production or supply of food. It is logical and rational to consider how the best link production to consumption and *vise versa*. Given the huge problems to feed the world population, which are bound to increase, and in view of the huge losses and waste, how does it come that the latter category of problems are not given more attention? Several circumstances might explain the current indifference to these issues. A general challenge is that losses and waste occur in several steps, as indicated in Figure 8. A systematic strategy to deal with these issues is difficult to design and implement. Solutions may require changes or new forms of collaboration between different parties in the supply chain. Technical solutions may be difficult to implement and expensive and it is not always obvious who should and will cover investments and costs. A simple explanation is that the knowledge about the magnitude and the costs about losses and waste is poor and misconceptions are common.

Knowledge about the issues and the interests and preparedness to act probably vary between various stakeholder groups. Farmers, for instance, should be interested in the reduction of post harvest losses and to have access to better transport, storage and other means to safeguard the quantity and quality of the produce. Losing part of their crop implies loss of food or potential income. A primary objective, for farmer families as well as for society at large, must be to enhance the capacity of the rural communities to improve the food situation for themselves and for society. For improved livelihood and development in a broader sense, it is vital that agricultural commodities reach the market and that the farmers get a decent pay for their efforts. For a range of commodities, farmers have experienced a continuous deterioration in the terms-of-trade in relation to the cost of inputs in agriculture and in relation to goods and services from other sectors. Facilitating rural livelihoods must therefore involve better harvesting technologies, transport and storage. However, an increasing supply of staple crops may contribute to a downward pressure on the price paid to the producer. The challenge is to seize the opportunity in terms of the increasing demand for "new" agricultural commodities, as noted above. A suitable strategy must combine reduction of losses with efforts to diversify production.

Would farmers, food processing industry and super markets be interested in solutions that induce efforts by the consumers to reduce their waste and over eating? Isn't it in their interest rather that consumers buy three pieces for the price of two irrespective of how many pieces they need and actually consume? Household waste is a cost to the consumer and society at large but not to the commercial interests. With growing consumer consciousness about home economics and natural resource and environmental issues, a convergence of interest between various actors in the supply chain seems logical and reasonable.

In terms of policy, it is presumably more difficult to change the behaviour of consumers than that of producers. Consumption is part of our private life. In a democratic system you cannot, and should not, forbid people to eat what, and how much, they want. Educational and awareness raising campaigns are necessary but experience tells us that the results may be meagre. Moreover, if commercials convey a different perspective and message, campaigns about sound dietary habits may fall on "barren, infertile lands". For farmers and other producers, the situation is different. They are used to adjust to regulatory arrangements.

Impressive changes of human perception and behaviour

Human behaviour is not easily changed and consumer behaviour is no exception in this regard. Some interesting examples of changing behaviour should, however, finally be noted. In Malaysia, an initiative was taken in the parliament in early 2007 to reduce the incidence of obesity (http://iht/com/articles/ap/2007/0217/asia/AS-GEN-Malaysia-Fast-Food-Ban.php). It was argued that with 40 % of their population suffering from obesity – which is a surprisingly high figure – that a ban on fast food a "sin tax" on junk food are justified. An example of change that is actually implemented is the ban on smoking in most public spaces in the US (not in all States, though). Who would have believed that such a restriction would be conceivable in the country where the freedom of the individual is cherished?

In the political sphere, several examples can be quoted about a new course, sometimes sudden, often surprising. Fortunately, positive and big surprises of historic proportions have occurred; the fall of the Berlin Wall, change of political system in South Africa, a black president in the White House, etc. All of these changes have come about peacefully and with wide support of people. Shouldn't it then be feasible and possible to reduce losses and waste in the food chain?

Summing up

So where is the road ahead? There is a need for sensitizing the consumers and make them take their share of the responsibility. Very few people know of the ecological or water footprints of our diets. And they are not aware of the magnitude of their own level of waste and what it means in economic and resource terms. With increasing urbanisation people are further away from the places where food is produced, which is likely to augment resource illiteracy, as discussed by Amartya Sen, among others. Education and awareness programmes and campaigns have to be strategically designed and not be of a general nature.

But the blame should not only be put on the households and consumers. Food industry and supermarkets and, generally, commercial interests are playing a major role. A growing consciousness among colleagues in these sectors is noticeable. At the World Economic Forum in Davos in January 2008 and 2009, the mounting water scarcity and 'water bubbles' were firmly on the agenda. Representatives of the food industry and other related industries expressed concern about the water situation in the world. A fear for disturbances in the supply and value chain of commodities to the industry and supermarkets is noticeable and justified. Benchmarking in the food industry related to water is common. However, the concern is directed towards the link between primary producer and industry and market operator.

There is practically no concern for what happens in the entire food chain, including benchmarking to reduce loss and waste. It would be a sensible strategy for industries and supermarkets to introduce benchmarking also for other parts of the food chain i.e. not only for the first part of it.

Support to farmers is important. Small and medium size farmers often do not have the ability or get the opportunity to diversify and produce and bring more of demanded produce to the market. Programmes probably need to be designed for various groups. Transport and storage are, generally, huge problems. Finally, when we talk about food chain problems, there is another scarcity: data. We need basic data and information.

Notes

1   This essay is based upon a SID lecture, "Saving Water: From field to fork" held at Free university, Amsterdam, June 16, 2008. Thanks to Mr Bernard Berendsen who prepared a draft of this essay based upon a recording of the lecture. This article has also been published by Fundación Agbar in *Notes d' Aigua*. See also http://www.fundacioagbar.com/en/page.asp?id=24

2   It should be noted that a similar level of loss is also observed in other sectors, e.g. in the energy sector. It is important to identify major types of losses and waste and discuss ways and means to curb losses and waste and what are the efforts, costs and benefits from such measures.

3   The definition on food security may vary. The one that was formulated at the Rome Declaration on Food Security is useful: "Food secuirity exists when all people, at all times, have physical and economic access to sufficient, safe and nutritious food to meet their dietary needs and food preferences for an active and healthy life" (FAO, 1996).

References

Berndes, G. 2002. Bioenergy and water – the implications of large-scale bioenegy production for water use and supply. *Global Environmental Change, 12(4), pp. 7-25.*

Comprehensive Assessment of Water Management in Agriculture, 2007. *Water for food, water for life: A comprehensive assessment of water management in agriculture.* (Molden, D. ed.) London, UK, Colombo, Sri Lanka: Earthscan Publications, IWMI.

Djurfeldt, G., Holmèn, H. Jirström, M. and Larsson, R. 2005. *The African Food Crisis: Lessons from the Asian Green Revolution.* CABI Publishing, Wallingford.

The Economist, 2007. Cheap no more. December 8, pp 77-79.

FAO [Food and Agricultural Organization], 1996. *Rome Declaration in World Food Security.* World Food Summit. 13 – 17 November. Rome. http://www.fao.org/docrep/003/w3613e00.htm

Falkenmark, M. And Rockström, J. 2004. *Balancing water for humans and nature: The new approach in ecohydrology.* Earthscan publications, London.

de Fraiture, C., Giordano, M. and Liao, Y.S. 2008. Biofuels and implications for agricultural water use: blue impacts of green energy. *Water Policy, 10 (suppl. 1), pp. 67-81.*

Jones, T. 2004. What a waste! Interview: *The Science Show,* 4 December. http://www.abc.net.au/scienceshow/stories/2004/125017. htm

Kader, A.A. 2005. Inceasing food availability by reducing post harvest losses of fresh produce. Proceedings of the 5th International Postharvest Symposium. Mencarelli, F. and Tonutti, P. (eds.). *Acta Horticulture 682,* ISHS.

Kantor, L., Lipton, K., Manchester, A. and Oliviera, V. 1997. Estimating and addressing America's food losses. *Food Review, Jan.-Apr., pp.2-12.*

Lannerstad, M. *2009. Water Realities and Developmnent Trajectories. Global and Local Agricultural Production Dynamics. PhD Diss. Linköping Studies in Arts and Science, No. 475.* Linköping.

Lannerstad, M. 2008. Planned and Unplanned Water Use in a Closed South Indian Basin. *Water Resources Development, 24 (2) pp. 289-304, June.*

Lannerstad, M. and Molden, D. (2009) *Adaptive Water Resource Management – in the South Indian Lower Bhavani Project Command Area,* Research Report, 129. Colombo, Sri Lanka: International Water Management Institute (IWMI)

Lind, T. and Malmberg, B. 2007. Demographically based global income forecasts up to year 2050. *International Journal of Forecasting, 23, pp. 553-567.*

Liu, J. and Savenije, H. 2008. Food consumption patterns and their effects on water requirement in China. *Hydrology and Earth System Sciences, 12, pp. 887-898.*

Lobell, D., Burke, M., Telbaldi, C., Mastrandera, M., Folcon, W. and Naylor, R. 2008. Prioritzing climate change adaptation needs for food security in 2030. *Science, 319, (5863), pp. 607-610.*

Lundqvist, J., Barron., J, Berndes, G., Berntell, A., Falkenmark, M., Karlberg, L. and Rockström, J. 2007. Water pressure and increases in food and bioenergy demand. Implications of economic growth and options for decoupling. *Scenarios on economic growth and research development: Background report to the Swedish Environmental Advisory Council. Memorandum 2007:1, pp. 55-152.* http://www.sou.gov.mvb/pdf/ WEBB-%20PDF.pdf

Lundqvist, J., C. de Fraiture and D. Molden 2008. Saving *Water: From Field to Fork. Curbing Losses and Wastage in the Food Chain.* SIWI Policy Brief. SIWI, Stockholm. http://www.siwi.org/

Lundqvist, J. 2008. Where has all the food gone? Identifying and coping with food and water losses. In: *Förare, J. (ed.) Water for food. The Swedish Research Council Formas, pp. 23-35.*

Malmberg, B. 2007. Global income growth in the 21st Century – A comparison of IPCC, solow, and dividend models. In: *Scenarios on economic growth and research development.* Background report to the Swedish Environmental Advisory Council Memorandum 2007:1. pp. 9-32. http:// www.sou.gov.se/mvb/pdf/ WEBB-%20PDF.pdf

Rano, L. 2008. Industry concerns follow massive beef recall. *Food Production Daily.* February 19. http://www.foodproductiondaily.com/news/ng.asp?id=83362.

Rediffnews. 2007. *How much food does India waste?* March, 16. http://www.rediff.com/money/2007/mar/16food.htm

Sachs, J. 2008. *Common Wealth: Economics for a Crowded Planet.* The Penguin Press, New York.

Smakhtin, V., Revenga, C. and Döll, P. 2004. *Taking into Account Environmental Water Requirements in Global-scale Water Resources Assessments.* Research report 2. IWMI, WRI, and University of Kassel.

Smil, V. 2000. *Feeding the World. A Challenge for the 21*[st] *Century.* MIT Press. Cambridge, MA, USA.

The Hindu, 2007. *India's nutritional crisis.* March 2. http://thehindu.com/2007/03/02/stories/2007030203151000.htm

WRAP [Waste, Resources & Action Programme], 2008. *The Food We Waste.* http://wrap.s3.amazonaws.com/the-food-we-waste.pdf

Water as the New Scarcity

Michel Camdessus

W ater as a new scarcity?
Let me start with a very blunt statement. I am expected to speak about water as a 'new scarcity', but in fact I see water as an 'old scarcity'. And I also see the related MDGs having very bleak prospects of implementation, especially in Africa. Water, if anything, is a vital human need, the provision of which can only be made more difficult by the consequences of climate change.

Furthermore, we shouldn't lose sight of the fact that water is more than a commodity: it is a human right; it is more than a MDG: it is a prerequisite for the achievement of the other MDGs. This is why I think that I should insist on the uniqueness of the issue of water, and in particularly also of sanitation. For all potential actors it creates the pressing obligation of intensifying their efforts to fulfil the water MDG, knowing that whatever strategy is adopted to address climatic change will also have to complement this fundamental effort.

Working from this assumption, I will then concentrate on what continues to be the mandate of the members of UNSGAB: to work on how to achieve the water goal[1], keeping in mind the basic conclusion of the Panel of Financing World Water Infrastructure that I had the honour to chair in preparation for the Kyoto conference of March 2003.

Having told you that, I must hasten to add two last preliminary remarks.

The first is a piece of good news: the report of the 'Financing Water for All' panel, instead of being immediately shelved, has served its purpose as, soon after its publication, it was taken as a basis for important decisions, including the adoption by the G8, at the occasion of its Evian meeting, of an international five-year water action plan and the adoption of the Compendium of Actions – better known as the Hashimoto Action Plan – endorsed on the occasion of the Mexico Water Forum in March 2006. The second is more sobering. If it is true that action has been taken on the basis of these two agreements, we are still behind schedule in fulfilling the two Millennium goals for 2015 and in taking the required action following the basic principles and conclusions on which we agreed five years ago.

Five years after the publication of the report of our panel, the situation is such that its basic assessments remain no less pertinent than they were, and I feel obliged to repeat them at the outset of my presentation, as they are still the cornerstones of international water strategy.

Principles for achieving MDG

Water is a human right, indispensable for leading a life in human dignity, but this right is widely disrespected. More than one in three people in the world suffers hardship and indignity from lack of water. This person is much more often a woman than a man. This injustice is largely unspoken and is one of the most difficult to rectify, precisely because it is above all an injustice to women. Its root cause is our negligence and our resignation in the face of inequality. This silent injustice must be rectified.

Although water is the subject of only one of the goals contained in the Millennium Declaration, it is vital to achieving other goals, such as eliminating poverty, providing education and securing gender equality. To take just a few examples: providing segregated toilet facilities in schools is, in many societies, a pre-condition for the further education of girls; the availability of private toilets and water in-house or close by would make a big difference to the lives of millions of women; and irrigation is and will increasingly be a prerequisite to increased food production to feed the growing world population. Carrying water long distances and waiting at water sources waste the energy and time of women and children in particular, at the expense of family activities, education and productive work. Effective water-resources development and management are basic to sustainable growth and poverty reduction.

Although over the next fifty years more than half of mankind will be threatened by 'water stress', the dream of pure water for all is within reach of humanity. It can be attained by continuing, for a further ten years, the efforts to which we are committed from now until 2015. This is the challenging task for the generation of people now running the world! But we should make sure that water is no more an orphan of international organisations, and that proper governance and sources of financing are reserved.

In my judgment, on the basis of these fundamental principles, two recent developments deserve a particular emphasis: de facto priority to be given to the African case, and paramount importance to be attached also to sanitation issues, particularly noteworthy to mention in this UN year of sanitation. Allow me to concentrate on these two issues prior to drawing your attention to a few initiatives particularly worthy of your support.

The African case must get priority

As the international community was concentrating on the steps to be taken to implement the MDGs, it became increasingly clear that by far the most difficult case was Africa, and that the prospects for reaching them there were extremely remote.

The 2006 UNDP Human Development Report made several conclusions extremely clear. One is the good news: with strong progress in high-population countries such as China and India, the world is on track for access to water, even if off-track on sanitation. The second is more sobering: on a regional basis there is a widening gap between sub-Saharan Africa (SSA) and the rest of the world, 'fuelling wider inequalities in health, education and poverty reduction'.

In addition, the global water access/sanitation gap is set to widen. To be more precise: Latin America and Caribbean are on track, South Asia is almost there (sanitation goal to be reached in 2019), so too are East Asia and the Pacific (access-to-water goal to be reached in 2018). The case of Africa, however, is dramatic: the access target will only be reached after a full generation (2040) while the sanitation target will be reached after more than two generations (2076). This justifies this particular focus on Africa. As a matter of fact, the data available in mid 2008 are particularly worrying (AfDB). Compared with other continents, the situation of Africa is characterized by daunting challenges. The development and the use of the potential of water resources are extremely low: only 4 percent of the water that is available in the whole continent is used (2 percent in SSA) and less than 6 percent of hydropower potential is developed. About 54 percent of the rural and 19 percent of the urban population lack access to clean water supply, while about 76 percent of the rural and 58 percent of the urban population lack access to proper sanitation in SSA. Per-capita water storage is less than 100 cubic metres (compared to about 3,500 cubic metres in Europe and 6,000 cubic metres in the US); over sixty trans-boundary river basins dominate the African landscape, and weak regional cooperation reduces the effectiveness of water governance necessary for development.

At the same time we see steady environmental degradation, depletion and contamination of water resources. Pervasive poverty conditions, coupled with slow economic growth on the continent and high energy prices, inhibit investments in the development of water resources. In addition, according to Professor Pachauri, between now and 2020, climate change puts at risk the supply of water for 75 to 200 million people, while agricultural yields in regions depending on rain will possibly be reduced by half and the number of climate migrants will grow in amazing proportion.

Investments of approximately US$20 billion per year are required to attain the MDG and African Water Vision targets by 2025. Current commitments are far from adequate to meet these needs, and projected trends of financing are unlikely to be sufficient unless important reforms are carried out and available funds are used more efficiently. Constraints faced by foreign direct investment and international lending lead to the importance of making concerted efforts to tap national resources for investment in water infrastructure and, whilst large infrastructure investment programs remain critical of the realization of the AWV, it is clear that a strengthened enabling environment and new approaches are crucial in moving the sector forward.

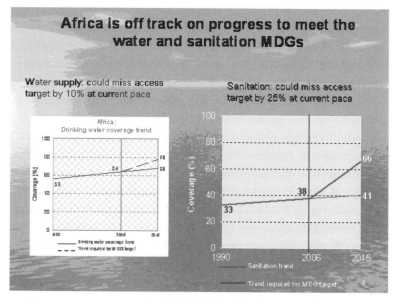

This very tragic situation has justified a particular concentration of the international community on Africa, and I see as particularly noteworthy the very special cooperation which has been established between the UN bodies, in particular the United Nations Secretary General's Advisory Bord on Water and Sanitation (UNSGAB) and the African Union. This cooperation has culminated in two very special occasions: the African Water Week, during which the African Council of Water Ministers (AMCOW) familiarised the UNSGAB with its work, and the preparation of the G8 and African Union heads of state summits, whose communiqués on water were jointly prepared by experts of the two bodies: a partnership very much in line with the Consensus of Monterrey.

After unanimously agreeing to support the AU Declaration of Charm el-Cheikh of 1 July, the G8 adopted the following text in its communiqué:

Water and Sanitation

47. *Good water cycle management is crucial in order to address the issue of water, which has a cross-sectoral nature. In this regard, acknowledging the need to accelerate the achievement of the internationally agreed goals on water and sanitation, we will reinvigorate our effort to implement the Evian Water Action Plan and will review it on the basis of a progress report prepared by our water experts by the next Summit. We will discuss with African partners the development of an enhanced implementation strategy. Moreover, we will promote integrated water resource management and the concept of 'Good Water Governance', with particular focus on Sub-Saharan African and Asia-Pacific, by taking necessary actions such as strengthening of trans-boundary basin organizations, sharing of water-related expertise and technology with developing countries, support for capacity building for water-related initiatives, promotion of data collection and utilization, and adaptation to climate change. We also acknowledge that ensuring adequate water supplies for human, industrial and environmental uses while minimizing the impacts of extreme hydrological variability are critical to protecting human health, promoting sustainable economic growth, and ensuring peace and security.*

(a) *We call upon national governments, in this International Year of Sanitation, to prioritize access to sanitation, building on the initiatives agreed at conferences on sanitation in Asia-Pacific and Africa. In this regard, we support the leadership role of the African Ministers' Council on Water and the action of the African Development Bank.*

(b) *We will support efforts to improve the governance of the water and sanitation sector with a view to ensure that monitoring and reporting, at the international and national levels, are improved and that institutions responsible for delivering water and sanitation services are more capable, accountable and responsive to the needs of users.*

Particularly noteworthy is the pledge of support of the two facilities that the AfDB has created to contribute to the realization of the water MDG. I will come back to that before concluding.

The sanitation year: 2008

I must report here on one of our most obvious collective failures. If the international community has been able to make some headway toward access to water following the adoption in September 2000 of the MDGs dealing with it, the progress remains dramatically insufficient as far as sanitation is concerned. We all know how difficult it is to capture public – and politicians' – interest on sanitation issues. Very emblematic of this is the fact that we had to wait for the Johannesburg/Rio-plus-10 summit to have sanitation added retroactively to the list of MDGs, with, as a matter of fact, very little consideration for the specificities of the case, including the magnitude of the investments involved and their financing, and the need for huge information campaigns to be launched and technical assistance to be mobilized.

One of the key problems presently is the de facto ignorance that water supply and sanitation should always be linked. Without substantially increased efforts, whereby equal attention is paid to water supply and sanitation, it will be impossible to achieve sustainable improvements in areas such as health, gender equality and education.

I would like to insist on a few basic data following closely a report of my colleague Dr Ushi Eid, Vice-Chair of UNSGAB, in an interpellation of the German Bundestag. The effects of dirty water as an obstacle to development are immense. Around 80 percent of all diseases in developing countries are caused by dirty water. Half of all hospital beds are filled by patients who are suffering from water-related diseases. Sanitation alone can more than halve child mortality. Water and sanitation are therefore the best preventive medicine. The UNDP has calculated that lost working days and spendings on health south of the Sahara, as a result of unhygienic living and housing conditions resulting from inadequate water supply and sanitation, cost Africa 5 percent of its GDP, and hence more money than the continent receives in development aid and debt relief. There is no doubt that investment in sanitation pays dividends: every euro invested in the sector, according to the Human Development Report 2006, generates an average economic return of nine euros.

Add to that the lack of sewage disposal that is having a severe effect on the shrinking supply of freshwater caused by rising consumption and climate change: 70 percent of industrial effluent in developing countries is pumped untreated into the environment. In the case of municipal effluent the figure rises to as much as 90 percent. More than 200 million tons of human waste are released untreated into the environment each year, polluting water resources and areas of human habitation.

So we are facing the sad reality that 2.6 billion people, or around 40 percent of the world's population, have no access to basic sanitation in the form of toilets and sewage systems. There is, therefore, a long way to go to achieve the sanitation MDG. This, obviously, calls for new types of initiatives.

New types of initiatives to be supported

In the area of sanitation we face an urgent situation, but this urgency runs the risk of being blurred at a moment at which so many other pressing objectives for national and international action are being identified. Let me point out a few priority actions which have been suggested to me by my work within the UNSGAB and under the chairmanship of Kofi Annan with the Africa Progress Panel (APP) and the Global Humanitarian Forum (GHF). On the basis of the six basic actions suggested in March 2006 by the Hashimoto Action Plan, I would particularly recommend the establishment of a water operator partnership to help the international organizations to improve their mutual cooperation under the guidance of the UN Water Forum.

With regard to sanitation, a special effort is required to generate more awareness and political will along with more capacity.

Concerted campaigns, in donor countries but with no less importance in developing countries, and particularly in Africa, are required to support the provision of financing, marketing, technology, and organizational assistance and guidance, using the momentum of the International Year of Sanitation to give incentives to national governments to implement concrete measures such as the designation of a focal point and the separation of the sanitation budget, and to review and increase the sanitation budget when it exists.

Finally, in view of the scale of the problem worldwide, a UN Global Sanitation Conference should be held well before 2015 to try to trigger the needed mobilization of human and financial resources almost everywhere in the world.

Time being short, I will not dwell on other important actions contemplated by this compendium, such as monitoring and reporting, integrated water resources management and the relation between water and disaster. Instead I will concentrate on the financing actions, even if it would serve their purposes poorly if the other initiatives were not fulfilled.

Financing

When addressing the financial issues of water in Africa, we must keep in mind two important statements. The first is the Africa Action Plan as adopted in Kananaskis: 'We will ensure that no country genuinely committed to poverty reduction, good governance and economic reform, will be denied the chance to achieve the Millennium Goals through lack of finance.' This was a pledge in our names. I cannot but deplore that it seems to have been lost from sight. No occasion should be lost to remind our leaders the promise they made on our behalf.

The second is the Evian Action Plan and the basic measures which were decided there:

1. promoting good governance;
2. utilizing all available financial resources;

3. building infrastructures by empowering local authorities and communities;
4. strengthening monitoring, assessment and research;
5. reinforcing the engagement of international organizations.

Under these five headings action has been taken following the two recent summits of the African Union and the G8, following also on the pledges of Gleneagles. Action will, I hope, be intensified in a number of directions, but I have understood that one of your objectives is to identify, among many others, actions of a special relevance to you. This is why I would like to conclude in telling you my particular appreciation for the so-called Rural Water Supply and Sanitation Initiative (RWSSI) of the African Development Bank.

In view of the particular intensity of the problem in the rural areas of Africa, in view of the certainty that these areas will be among the most severely affected by the climatic change, in view of the health and gender consequences and of the economic absurdity of not devoting more resources to this particular aspect of the problem, I value particularly this initiative in the framework of the AfDB, which is supported by the Netherlands together with France and Denmark, because it is designed to address squarely, and hopefully decisively, this crucial issue.

Rural Water Supply and Sanitation Initiative

The very daunting water challenges in Africa are particularly severe in the rural sectors: currently about 54 percent of the rural population lack access to a clean water supply and 76 percent lack access to proper sanitation in SSA. There are no words to express the human tragedies, which cannot be revealed by these numbers. The RWSSI is a well-designed instrument with the ambitious aim of tackling the main obstacles toward the MDG and the implementation, in 2025, of the African vision: namely, water and sanitation for all. From this perspective it is the intention that more than 270 million people are to be provided with water and about 295 million with sanitation by 2015, meaning 80 percent coverage by 2015. The RWSSI strategy involves the use of flexible mechanisms, innovative approaches and simple technology. It rests on a few simple principles, too frequently ignored so far. Firstly, that for such investments, grants rather than loans must be the basic instrument. Secondly, that a demand-driven approach is adopted, with user participation and partnerships at all levels. In-country systems will be used where appropriate.

The agreed initial financing program required investments of the RWSSI estimated in 2002 at US$14.3 billion. The African Development Bank is to cover 30 percent, the countries themselves 20 percent, and the donor community will have to provide the remaining 50 percent. Let me make a brief comment here.

These are important numbers and they call for a significantly higher contribution from the international community than so far provided. But may I invite you to compare these numbers – and particularly the total amount of US$14.3 billion dollars – with the annual cost for the African and international community, while being aware of the fact that we are far from having achieved the MDG. This cost is – annually, I insist – according to the WHO, significantly more than US$20 billion dollars. Is not that a formidable failure, not only of the markets, but also of the international community? For not investing over ten years an average of US$1.5 billion dollars every year, we suffer a yearly cost of $US20 billon.

I don't know many other examples where our lack of vision and generosity translates into such a waste of resources and human suffering. Sheer rationality – even leaving aside any sense of human solidarity – should suffice as motivation to give very high priority to the financing of such an initiative.

I must observe, nevertheless, that, owing mainly to the insufficient contribution of the community of donors, at the end of 2007 we had already accumulated US$1.35 billion dollars financing deficit (3.21 billion mobilized against a target of 4.56 billion).

I draw from this table a very simple conclusion that I hope you could agree with: the Netherlands and France, in particular, should continue and increase their effort but should take a joint initiative to convince several non-regional member-countries to join them in the replenishment of the RWSSI trust fund and in the full financing of phase two, now that we have seen the effectiveness of this instrument. A new pledging session, following on the initial one of April 2005 in Paris, should allow us to face not only the initial amounts programmed for phase two (up to 2010) but also the phase-one deficit and the increased unit cost.

I have particularly insisted on this instrument because after careful evaluation – and, in spite of a slow initial implementation – we can see it, and particularly RWSSI, as the most ambitious, but at the same time, the best-designed instrument to contribute to narrowing the gap between the MDGs and their present state of implementation. As we stress, nevertheless, time and again, financing is by far not the only decisive factor for that implementation. Among the other factors, the importance of which should not be underestimated, I would like to remind you of all the other headings of the Hashimoto Action Plan and, of course, all those which are very basic for the success of partnership for development on the side of the recipient countries; that is, the fulfilment of their own pledges to their own people, particularly within the framework of NEPAD.

Conclusion

Allow me to suggest that the Society for International Development, which I admire greatly, make some room in its conclusions for these very simple statements:

Water is life.
Water is a human right.
Water is a major gender issue.
We are committed to achieving the MDGs, but so far, we are behind in meeting the required targets as far as Africa is concerned.
It is not too late to reverse the trend, but it is more than urgent.
At the very least, let's join forces to make the best out of the initiative we have jointly launched to help the African people achieve, by 2025, their vision of water and sanitation for all.

Notes

1   Perhaps I should also tell from where my interest in water issues comes. For years, during my tenure at the IMF, I had time and again to remind international leaders of the importance of fulfilling their pledges, even before many of them were clustered among the Millennium Development Goals. This is why, having retired from the IMF, I couldn't refuse the invitation to chair in 2002 and 2003 the World Panel on Financing Water Infrastructure, which the two sisters organisations, the Global Water Partnership and the World Water Council, decided to launch in preparation for the Third World Water Forum, which took place in March 2003 in Kyoto. This was, for me, an occasion to continue to work for at least two MDGs for which the prospects of implementation were particularly problematic.

2   Climate change puts at risk the supply of water for between 75 and 200 million people between now and 2020, agricultural yields – in regions dependent on rains – being possibly reduced by half, and the number of 'climatic migrants' growing in an amazing proportion.

PART II

CLIMATE CHANGE

Political Ways and Means to Address Climate Change

Gurmit Singh

C oming from the South and having been deeply involved in the international debate on climate since 1990, I could address this issue of political ways and means to deal with climate change from a Southern perspective. I could also discuss it from a Northern point of view, but in fact I will do neither. I will not claim to look at it from any perspective but from my own, thoroughly coloured by my own personal experiences and prejudices.

There are a lot of contradictions in life. While many people talk about global warming and climate change, there are of course also some who insist we have global cooling. Instead of going into that,

Figure 1   Sources of the man-made greenhouse effect

Sources of the man-made greenhouse effect

10%   13%   12%   65%

Production and use of CFC gases, HCFC gases and HFC gases (CFC and HCFC gases are being phased out due to their destructive effect on the ozone layer).

Rice fields (CH_4) Chemical fertilizers (N_2O) Cattle farms (CH_4) Refuse dumps (CH_4)

Felling and burning of tropical forests (CO_2)

Burning of fossil fuels (CO_2, NOx,CO, CH_4, N_2O)

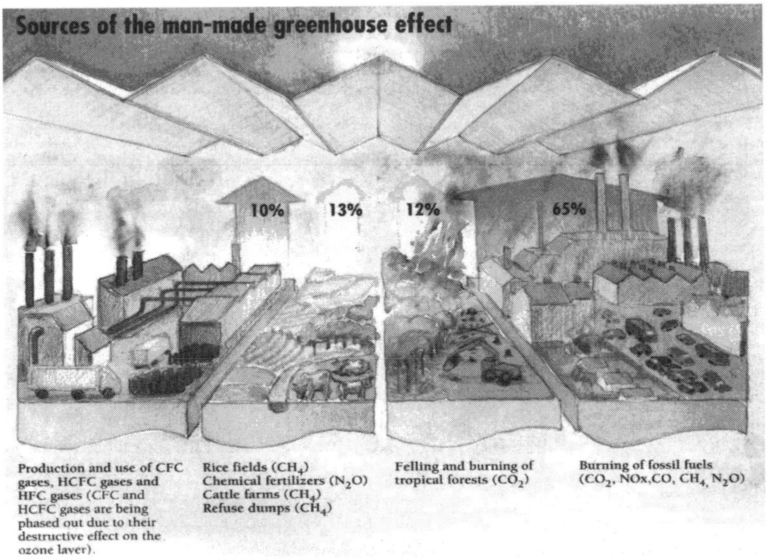

it seems pertinent to give a reminder about what the greenhouse effect is and why we are talking about it at this juncture. While a proportion of solar radiation is reflected by the earth and the atmosphere, another part is absorbed by the earth's surface and warms it. At the same time, some of the infrared radiation coming from outside passes through the atmosphere, but most of it is absorbed and re-emitted in all directions by greenhouse gas molecules and clouds. This has the effect of warming the lower atmosphere and the earth's surface.

Figure 1 shows the relative contribution to the man-made greenhouse effect from different sources. There is the production and use of CFC gases, HCFC gases and HFC gases (10 percent), rice fields, chemical fertilizers, cattle farms and refuse dumps (13 percent), felling and burning of tropical forests (12 percent) and burning of fossil fuels (65 percent). The percentages may vary: some people now say deforestation causes 20 percent of the greenhouse effect. I haven't found the scientific evidence for this, but it really depends on whether deforestation involves only logging. That is one of the issues talked about: when you log timber, the carbon stays in the furniture that is produced. Now, when you burn the furniture, to whom do you charge the carbon emissions? To the country in which the trees were cut or to the country in which the furniture was burned? This is one of the most difficult issues in the whole climate debate: who is the culprit? Very often the culprit is all of us.

Figure 2   Concentrations of greenhouse from 1 AD to 2005 (IPCC report, 2007)

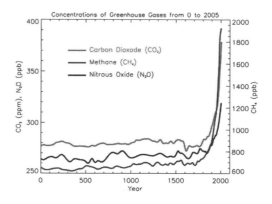

Figure 2, taken from the latest ICC report, is a reminder of the exponential increase in both carbon dioxide, methane and nitrous oxide in the atmosphere.

Global warming affects us all. No human or ecosystem is immune: we all contribute in many ways and all of us are starting to pay the costs, which will rise over time. But we must always remember: there are some who are more culpable then others, and therefore they should act now; this is the basis of the UN Framework Convention on Climate Change (UNFCCC).

Global warming impacts on health, agriculture, forests, water resources and aquatic life, coastal areas and species and natural areas. As a consequence, we see rising temperatures, more precipitation and rising sea levels. Factors such as air quality, ozone depletion, loss of biodiversity, deforestation, water quality and availability, desertification and the use of sulphate aerosols all contribute to climate change.

The UN Framework Convention on Climate Change

It is important to remind ourselves of the objectives of the UN Convention on Climate Change. They are: stabilization of greenhouse-gas concentration in the atmosphere at a level that would prevent dangerous anthropogenic interference with the climate system. The keyword is 'anthropogenic', which means man-made, not natural. We want the eco-system to adapt naturally, to ensure that food production is not threatened and to allow sustainable development to occur.

Many people forget the key words in the objective of the Convention and only argue about each other's positions and how much money they can make out of it. They forget the ultimate aim of sustainable development: food security – to ensure that food is available and that poor people are not denied it.

The underlying precautionary principle of, in the absence of scientific consensus, taking action when there is general agreement rather than waiting for absolute consensus has been undermined by the US and other nations which indeed want to wait for absolute consensus before acting. But on climate change there may never be absolute scientific consensus; therefore we should respond on the basis of common but differentiated responsibilities as defined in the Convention.

This is the reason why the Convention, when it was first adopted, was called the first equitable convention: it took into account the principles of equity with the fundamental point of common but differentiated responsibilities, meaning that those who have emitted the most must take action first and the others will follow. That is the whole basis of the Kyoto Protocol and the reason for having an Annex I and a not-Annex I country grouping.

The issue of historical liability is also tied to the earlier principle. Many people, especially in the US, conveniently forget the issue of historical liability, or the idea that they who have emitted most up to now must do something about it. It's difficult to expect China and India, who are beginning to emit greenhouse gases only now, to do the same thing as the US and the other industrialised countries that have benefited from the industrial revolution. This is the reason why the G77 and China are very reluctant to move when they see no action on the part of the Annex I countries.

Climate change is a global threat, but it is totally submerged in politics – one would say even in economics. In a way this is inevitable because its solutions rely on intergovernmental agreements. So politics is unavoidable, even more so because there is a whole range of vested interests at stake.

The number of vested interests of the Convention on Climate Change and of the Biodiversity Convention is vastly different. There are only two basic vested interests of the Biodiversity Convention: those of the biotechnology industry and those of the countries with a lot of biodiversity.

In the case of the Convention on Climate Change, there are all sorts of countries: rich countries, countries with high per-capita consumption, countries which are wasteful of energy, countries whose very existence is at stake if the sea level rises, and so on. Then there are the least developed countries. Those countries which are believed to suffer most from the impact of climate change are pitted against those considered to be historically the largest greenhouse gas emitters.

Also, and this is something that is often ignored or glossed over: there is a marked North/South divide. Like it or not, it has been there from the first day of the Convention. The divide is still there even if it has been obscured by some people. There is a divide between the OECD and the non-OECD, the Annex I and the non-Annex I countries. But even the G77 is divided between OPEC and the rest, the Alliance of Small Island States (AOSIS) versus China, India, Brazil and so on.

This was very clear when the first preparatory meeting was held in Berlin. AOSIS had a draft convention, a protocol actually ready to be negotiated, but it was totally torpedoed because China and India had not been consulted by AOSIS. So the whole process of negotiating what eventually became the Kyoto Protocol had to be restarted from scratch. But if either India or China had accepted the AOSIS Protocol, it would have been much better than the Kyoto Protocol.

The political stakes

What are the political stakes? Essentially, the question is: who will dominate and who will lose out? It all depends on whether this issue is looked at from the perspective of an individual country or from an international perspective. Very often the strong have managed to get their way, undermining equity in the process. People tend to forget that the US, a nation which talks a lot about climate change but does little to address it, actually dictated the final text of the Convention, prior to the preparatory meeting in New York.

At the committee meeting when the Convention was adopted there was a mutually agreed text which the US totally refused to accept. Largely because the EU caved in in order to keep the US on board, the committee gave up the original text and accepted the text proposed by the US word for word. So the Convention is American-crafted, and yet, the Americans refused to honour the Convention which they themselves drafted in 1992, while the EU and Japan were playing second and third fiddle.

But then – and this is what I have been telling developing countries for almost ten years now – there seems to be a second strategy, which is to delay implementing actual emission reductions until China, India and Brazil agree to do the same; their refusal is used as an excuse for current OECD members not to act, and in the meantime the world is frying while all the talk is going on: almost nothing is being done to reduce the emissions.

What is political?

In some countries anything that is critical of the ruling party is considered to be political and therefore anti-governmental and hence anti-national. In my country I experience this. In the past I have been invited to speak at the Lions' Club and told, 'Oh, we want you to talk, but please don't talk political!'. What do they mean when they say this? As an NGO activist I have to talk political: I have to take some position on what is happening. The Lions' Club worries about being critical of the government, but to me politics is the mobilization of the citizen's concerns and capabilities to govern and achieve sustainable development. Politicians are, in my opinion, mere agents for the achievement of the people's aspirations and not the masters they make themselves out to be. Many politicians forget that.

Figure 3   Annual CO$_2$ emissions in gigatons (2010 onwards is linear growth estimation)
Source: IEA, World Energy Outlook 2000

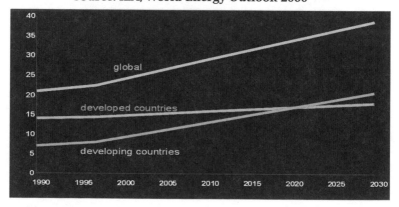

170

At the time of the early debates on climate change the South was expected to clean up the emissions from the North. But the reality is that the South cannot run away from the emission problem altogether: this is illustrated in the figures 3 and 4.

Figure 3 was produced a few years ago. It shows that in 2020 developed countries' annual CO_2 emissions will be equal to the growing emissions of the developing countries.

Figure 4   Cumulative CO_2 emissions in gigatons (2010 onwards is linear growth estimation)
Source: IEA, World Energy Outlook 2000

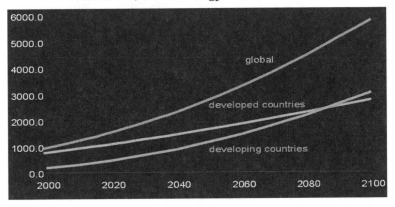

In terms of cumulative CO_2 emissions, the excess of developing countries over developed countries can last at most until 2085 or so. Therefore I keep telling my colleagues in the developing countries: 'We only have this luxury from now until about 2085. So we, the South, are the culprits ourselves, and we have to do something now! Forget about historical liability and all that.' Unfortunately, this is a very difficult sell to the politicians in the South, including those in my own country.

The International Panel on Climate Change, (IPCC) predicted what the future would look like and what the consequences of temperature increases would be at regional and global levels. The consequences are drastic, especially if temperature increases exceed 2°C, which is why in the current negotiations 2°C is used as a ceiling.

Previously, PPM concentrations were discussed. Now people have forgotten about them and refer to the 2°C ceiling. Among the various groups, I think the EU gives the strongest support of this 2°C ceiling, while other countries, in particular the US, are not letting themselves been bound by it.

The political drivers

Who are the political drivers? In the case of the EU, both the European Commission and the European Parliament seem to be the drivers, but a lot depends upon how much trust EU citizens give to both the Commission and the Parliament. In the European Parliament there are some progressive elements, but how much weight does the European Parliament have in decisions that are taken by the EU political leaders themselves?

What about the governments of AOSIS? It is worthy of note that Singapore has been the quietest of all AOSIS members. It is the richest member of AOSIS but the least active. In fact Singapore ratified the Kyoto Protocol only two years ago, but it should take a big interest because its survival is at stake.

The people of the Maldives are going to build a wall around their whole capital which occupies a single atoll. They will spend US$300 million in building a wall two metres high. Those are the desperate measures they will go to because the reality is that if the sea level rises by even one metre, many of the atolls will vanish. The renewable energy industry and the developers of mitigation and adaptation technology in the North see more profits from such moves.

In the early days of the negotiations we always used to be confronted with a notorious business sector which was led by the Global Climate Coalition. It was based in the US and was at that time made up of all the major oil companies. They were the biggest obstruction to any progress in the negotiations, with every intervention saying, 'Forget about climate change, it is going to cost us the earth.' That has slowly changed. Now the alternative lobby is coming from the renewable energy industry and in a way that means there is progress. Business is no longer totally opposed to action to tackle climate change, and we hope that the renewable energy industry will become stronger and stronger.

Global warming as an emergency

To me, the only way to see global warming is as an emergency. In fact, I would even say that it should be treated as a war. Climate change is a greater threat than any war the world has witnessed so far and in terms of the way I see history and the development of political issues, the only way to deal with it is to mobilise resources and shorten the time-frame in which to achieve the 80 percent greenhouse-gas reduction that is essential to avoid the 2°C temperature rise.

Furthermore, the 80 percent reduction was mentioned by scientists in the 1990s. Now, almost two decades later, we are again talking about 80 percent reductions, but only below our current levels, not the levels of the 1990s.

This war must be fought in a sustainable development context because we also have to eliminate absolute poverty globally. We cannot talk about climate change without simultaneously discussing global poverty. One of the criticisms levelled at the 1992 Rio Summit was that it did not adequately address the issue of global poverty. In talks about sustainable development and Agenda 21, one of the most important missing links is global poverty; the other missing link is that there is almost nothing discussed about the role of multinationals. The multinationals are free of blame in Agenda 21 while billions are being spent on military hardware. These billions should be redirected to technology transfer.

In Bali a Technology Transfer Fund was discussed, but that was already talked about at the Convention in 1992. Both the technology transfer and the financial mechanism to achieve this were already in the Convention, but almost nothing has been done about it since the Convention came into force. Forget about the Kyoto Protocol; technology transfer is already covered in the Convention on Climate Change and the US is bound by it. But the US gets away with it.

Is the EU a leader?

Is the EU a leader in all these issues? The European Parliament and the national leaders show potential but they tend to backslide, as I observed in Bali. Even within the G8 the EU tends to give way to the US and Canada. Germany was very strong on climate change before the G8 meeting in 2008 and in the end, almost with a whimper, it accepted whatever the US was able to dilute out of the G8.

Member nations of the EU show uneven commitment. This is even true of Spain, which is officially allowed to increase its emissions. So where is the driver? Is it possible for someone to suggest the equivalent of a Marshall plan for technology transfer? Is the EU willing to seriously consider this approach in solving the problem of technology transfer, which has been log-jammed for so long? Of course, the EU style of compromising internally and internationally weakens strong leadership. Compromises must have limits: the EU should not compromise itself into uselessness but should strike out for something that is really strong and take risks. The real test for political leadership of the EU is whether it will manage to decarbonise its economy; only then can it preach to China and India and ask them not to use more carbon in their economic development.

On energy consumption

Reducing consumption and making sacrifices boils down to two things: the affluent in all countries, including my own country, have to make sacrifices with the assurance that they can still have a good quality of life. My view is that it is possible to have a good quality of life without necessarily using that much energy per capita.

But the corollary to that situation is that those living in economically developing nations, especially in the vast countries of China and India, must also revise their aspirations for ever higher energy and resource usage while still having the promise of a better quality of life.

I remember a presentation by a Chinese delegate at the COP meeting in Milan. His talk was entitled 'Sustainable Development for China', and he began by saying, 'We Chinese do not want to make the same mistakes as the others; we want to have sustainable development.' But towards the end of the presentation he compared the number of kilometres of railway and road per capita in Japan with the number of railways and road per capita in China. At the end of the talk, I asked, 'If you want to have the same number of kilometres of railway per capita as in Japan, where are the resources? Your population is so huge; you know your resources will not be enough. You know what will happen as you are already suffering now: in terms of energy China is a big sponge.'

I attended a security discussion last year in Singapore where the focus was the threat to energy security posed by the hunger of China and India for more and more energy. Almost all the Asian nations were rebelling and asking whether there would be any energy left for them, oil and petrol energy especially.

On pointing fingers

But I must also say – and this is a point I keep saying at home – if we want to stop global warming we cannot go on pointing fingers. We must remember that three fingers will be pointing back to us and remind us that we need to act ourselves. Everybody needs to act, at the personal level, in our jobs, within our nation and globally. Sustainable development and sustainability will not occur if global warming worsens, especially if it exceeds 2°C.

At the same time – and this is one of the bigger things – we need to point out the inequity and stop being hypocritical, especially among the multinationals and the rich.

On the role of mass media and civil society

I want to touch a little on the role of the mass media and civil society in this whole thing. I would argue that the mass media have to monitor and report on how well emission reductions are being done, especially these days in developed countries, and later on in developing countries too. The media should also report more extensively on the scale of adverse impacts and local adaptation. When I was in the Netherlands seven years ago, I was interviewed by Dutch TV and was surprised to find out that the ordinary Dutch citizen did not care very much about climate change. I could understand this being the case in my own country, but not in the Netherlands. I am told that the situation has changed now – which I hope is true – and that the ordinary Dutch citizen is more concerned about the adverse impact of climate change and is putting pressure on the government and the politicians to act.

Civil society needs to expose shortcomings in political action to curb climate change at all levels. This is as much a challenge to those of us in the South as to those in the North. And campaigns to change our lifestyles must be lead.

I am actually about to publish a book called *Beyond-me-and-mine*, in which I try to put in layman's terms how ordinary citizens can really contribute to solve global climate problems if they only look beyond the me-and-mine-syndrome. Because in Asia – and I am sure in a lot of developed countries as well – it is this syndrome that is preventing a lot of things from happening.

Bali and beyond

To understand what was happening in Bali, imagine an elephant. This elephant represents the US and is being pushed by all sorts of people. In the front we are pulling and Yvo de Boer is crying as he pushes the elephant from behind. He is crying because he was accused, by China especially, of sabotaging the negotiations by allowing certain language that had not been agreed on but which made the text used almost devoid of any meaning. The final day of Bali was very much full of high rhetoric, with the American delegates also crying and leaving the meeting because they were so severely criticised by the developing countries.

In my opinion the Bali meeting did not result in very much of a breakthrough. Some people regarded it as an advance because the US agreed to discuss, in another ad hoc working group, the commitments described in the Convention, but they even didn't want to talk about those in the Kyoto Protocol.

Maybe I have become rather cynical. I have to wait and see what happens. In fact my NGO is going to organise a meeting in Malaysia to try to see what has really been happening since Bali. Beyond Bali the roadmap is just weak and vague. We cannot wait until yet another preparatory meeting (the fifteenth) in 2009 for effective action to be taken.

In the US, even under a new president, drastic action against climate change may not be taken. At every preparatory meeting in the past, it is either the president that intercepts or Congress that is not interested in any action being taken. Nowhere have we ever seen a president or Congress jointly interested in action.

And Australia, which has just come in, needs to move beyond saying only that it will ratify the Kyoto Protocol. It has to reduce rather than increase further emissions because, if you remember, in the Kyoto Protocol, Australia is the only country that has been allowed to increase emissions. And yet they initially refused to ratify it! In my opinion they ought to reduce and not to increase their emissions; they have already increased too much.

The next G8 meeting, which is going to be hosted by Japan, also has to move beyond Bali. It cannot just reiterate the bland statement that came out of that conference. And the biggest question of all is: has decarbonisation of the global economy begun?

Climate, Scarcities and Development

Jan Pronk

Introduction

Having chaired the negotiations that translated the Kyoto Declaration into a fully agreed text a decade ago, I have since stepped somewhat outside of the climate-change debate. But from this distance I have the impression that not enough has been happening. For instance, the conflicts in Sahel, where I have been engaged, have a notable resource scarcity component. If the balance between people with cattle on the one hand, and people with fertile soil and water on the other hand had not been so drastic, given the limited carrying capacity of the land, perhaps the disaster in Darfur would have been less enormous. I forecast there will be many such disasters in Africa in the decades ahead unless we do something about it. We need to focus on the consequences of climate change. For me, the IPCC report and the Al Gore movie are all inputs into the debate, but I do not want to touch on the issues they raise; instead I would like to look at the present policies and what we should do in the years ahead.

What do we know?

We begin by knowing that there is an annual capacity of the earth to absorb a number of greenhouse gases. Scientists are still debating what exactly the absorptive capacity is, but there is no question that it exists. Secondly, we have to assume that the carrying capacity will be reached soon. And it will be surpassed, indeed surpassed many times if the present trend continues. The present trend is a small annual increase of emissions in some countries, big increases of annual emissions, in particular in the US and in Asia, and, as a consequence of economic growth and industrialization, also in Africa.

If we foster economic growth in developing countries – even if economic growth is not all sustainable development is about, we know that economic growth is necessary for development – then carrying capacity will be surpassed very soon. And emissions of greenhouse gases will be higher than the level that could be labelled safe or sustainable by any standard.

We also know that these consequences will be borne by people in developing countries. And finally we know there are uncertainties: about the relation between climate change and biodiversity; between climate change and oceans; about whether climate change is a gradual process or a series of jumps. Indeed, the issue of climate change is extremely complex and solving it in a scientific way will create new uncertainties.

The road after Rio: the precautionary principle

The world decided in 1992 at the Rio de Janeiro Summit on the relation between environment and development to base our policy in the future on the precautionary principle. In my view you have to know the precautionary principle by heart: 'We will take precautionary measures to anticipate, prevent or minimize the causes of climate change and mitigate its adverse effects. Where there are threats of serious and irreversible damage, lack of full scientific certainty should not be used as a reason for postponing such measures . . .' (Framework Convention on Climate Change, 9 May 1992, 31 ILM 849)

The principle can be applied beyond the field of climate change when you deal with uncertainties from a political and ethical point of view.

The precautionary principle was embodied in specific international treaties. When I was Minister for the Environment in a debate on Genetically Modified Organs, we were able in a European context to have the principle enshrined in the pre-amble of the bio-safety protocols which we negotiated in Montreal. Whether the Europeans, who at the moment under a lot of pressure from the US, are still able to live up to that principle is another question. But it is a political question upon which citizens and political parties have to build their policy choices.

You know the uncertainties, but you also know the ethical principle, then: you need a worldwide agreement to stabilize the concentration of greenhouses gases in the atmosphere, because it is a global problem. And stabilization means reduction, and not just a simple reduction. We know that the reduction of the emissions has to be drastic.

We have to think about a reduction of 70 percent in about 100 years, or 40 to 60 percent in the year 2050. Even then the concentration is 70 percent higher than in the pre-industrial period in which there was a certain degree of – I would say – sustainability at that time, before the trend was changing.

It is quite a target because a reduction of 70 percent in a period whereby you have, say, 2 percent economic growth means, on a one-to-one growth and emission basis, that each year you have an accumulative increase in the gap between the calculated growth in emissions and the reduction you have agreed upon. So there is a huge gap between the trend and what you have to accomplish. This requires major changes in technology application and major changes in economic behaviour. The targeted reduction requires a major transformation of the world economy and a major transformation of the technologies to be applied, and all that has to start in particular with those countries which did have in the past the highest emissions.

The nature of the problem

Firstly, climate change is *the* global problem and secondly, it is *urgent*. Solving it cannot incur delays. It is that urgent. Thirdly, you have to understand that climate change is the result of past activities as well as of present activities. Economists would say climate change is an *external effect* of economic behaviour. We know what that means: the consequences of such activities are not incorporated in the price and in the costs on the market itself. Climate change is *the* example of an external effect. This is the only external effect of any economic behaviour which is *global*, which has consequences everywhere in the world. This effect is mass, it is global, it is also *long-term*. It is an external effect which is not taking place in the same period as the economic activity itself; it has a very long time-lag. The change in the atmosphere at this moment is the result of economic decisions about the application of technologies decades ago.

This means that it is an external effect not of a flow variable but of a stock. Consequences for the atmosphere are consequences of the stock of greenhouse gases. At present the stock is changing because of the flow of present additions, but the major consequences are the consequences of the past flow which is still in the atmosphere. The past flow and the present stock are to a very great extent the result of activities of countries in the North, of countries which had an economic, political and power advantage in the past. That means it is necessary that those countries in particular start to act on the basis of the principle of preferential treatment. This is a very well-known principle in international trade policies and international development policies in which you give preferential treatment to countries which are behind in order to reach some equality in the future. You have to go for a global, coordinated approach because this is a problem which can never be solved by individual countries alone and, because it is so global and long-term and urgent, it is not possible to deal with it on a voluntary basis. You have to deal with it on the basis of binding policies.

So, what can be done? Firstly, you have to put a number of these principles – the precautionary principle and the principle of common and differentiated responsibility – in agreements so that policies really can be based upon them. You have to set concrete targets in relation to these principles: not vague, not qualitative; you have to be very precise because otherwise you will not meet your aims.

This is very complicated because you do not know everything and things are changing. That means that in terms of instruments you have to be creative, flexible and innovative. You adjust yourself to new insights and new phenomena on the basis of binding law which excludes the possibility of free riders, which guarantees implementation and which includes both incentives and sanctions, so that all peoples, countries, nations and states, would see this as just, fair and equitable.

Kyoto and beyond

Those were more or less the ideas underlying the negotiations. We reached an agreement on the Kyoto Protocol and now we have to continue. So what did Kyoto mean? Kyoto embraced an integrated approach. It accepted quantitative targets, the principle of common but differentiated responsibilities, approaches and efforts, as well as preferential treatment on the basis of the common but differentiated responsibilities. The Protocol spoke about mitigation in order to reach that reduction target, but in the Kyoto Protocol there is also a lot about adaptation: there will be climate change, there always has been climate change, and we have to adapt ourselves to it. It is already in the Kyoto Protocol itself. Because of climate change everybody, at a certain moment, has to mitigate and to adapt. The Protocol also spoke about support for capacity building, a new element in the developmental policy because development means that you have to be sustainable and you have to be able to meet problems in the world, indeed also the problem of external threat to you. The Kyoto Protocol talked about support for capacity building. It also touched on absorption of greenhouse gases, in particular in the framework of forests.

In the Kyoto Protocol there was already talk about mitigation across borders, which meant that the negotiations had to include elements of joint implementation and the clean development mechanism. Also in the Protocol were elements about emission trading as a complement to what countries can do at home. And there were sanctions: not very harsh, but mild and, what is more interesting, they included a relation between what you did not accomplish in the present period and the burden of mitigation which you had to take upon yourself in the next period. So you had to top up the mitigation efforts in the present period with what you did not do; a shortfall in the earlier period could lead to exclusion from international consultations on the policies of the future. In the beginning the elements in the Protocol were very vague but the subsequent Conferences of the Parties laid out very detailed terms in order to arrive at a legal text without any loopholes so that it could function as a basis of joint international policymaking.

Why was Kyoto successful?

Still, Kyoto was successful, and that is important to state because the success of the past also may be a guideline for the future. Why was it successful? First, because at the time there was worldwide awareness of a global threat. It was replaced later by preoccupations with another global threat: security, homeland security, Al-Qaeda, and so on. So nobody was speaking about climate anymore. Secondly there was a joint political climate, leading to a global coalition between politicians and experts and bureaucrats and NGOs. Everybody came together for a while and it created dialogue among people with different insights and different interests, and it created a common aim to succeed. It was short-lived but it did work. Thirdly, there was – which is important – full agreement on the process. This meant acceptance by everybody of the IPCC, which meant you had a worldwide independent secretariat; full agreement on committee structures; on the agenda and on the step-by-step approach.

There was that joint atmosphere, and when Bush said Kyoto is dead, everybody said, 'That is not up to you Mr Bush, because it is a multilateral process and one party cannot pronounce unilaterally that the outcome of a joint initiative is dead.' We were not able to define the outcome and that helped a lot, including to keep the US tied to the process. It was important for the future to say that it was an outcome and a process that was concrete, ambitious, integrated, equitable and efficient, both in terms of market-orientation and in terms of the possibility to foster technological innovation. It was binding but at the same time it was flexible and to that extent you may say it was quite unique.

Because we agreed on a legal text at Marrakesh we got our rectification process and the whole thing became operational, but there was a time lag before implementation started.

So, what do we know today?

We are living in a very different world now. First, there is much higher growth in the world, in particular among very populous countries such as China, India, South Africa and Brazil, and a number of other countries have much higher growth and increases in national income per capita, as well as much higher consumption per capita than we thought would be the case ten years ago. We have higher emissions than we expected ten years ago and agreed in Kyoto. Thirdly, we know that the whole mechanism is much more complex. The uncertainties are now understood better by scientists and we know that the consequences in terms of the natural physical consequences are greater than were outlined ten years ago by IPCC in the early reports. Consequences for warming, extremes and biodiversity and rise in sea level are in physical terms greater than expected ten years ago. We also know that the economic consequences of the physical consequences are more complex, for instance with regard to food production, the availability of water, migration streams and other factors. There are more disasters.

And there is an additional factor leading to greater inequality: globalization, which is in itself a major threat for stability. There is greater potential for conflict now than ten years ago because of resources, because of climate, because of environment: greater than we thought and also greater in practice. Climate change aside, there is a much greater-than-expected shortage of fossil fuels for energy utilization. The era of low-cost energy, gas, coal and oil is over. There is not enough uranium for nuclear power in the next decades for the world as a whole and everybody who is betting on nuclear is betting on something which is not at all technologically feasible. There is also a much greater problem of energy security. Globalization means global markets, and it is not at all certain that there will be enough energy for them. That also has in itself a great conflict potential. Look, for instance, at the major problems between Europe and Russia and the fact that individual countries are trying to establish their own relations with the Russians.

Is there something positive from the last ten years?

On the other hand, first of all, we do know more, in terms of the outcome of scientific research, so on that basis you can expect better policy. Technological research in private industry has taken multiple directions, so technological change could yet help provide an answer. The positive decisions taken by the European Union to play an international role through target setting is broadening emission trading so that the specific mitigation target for the year 2020 is positive.

But there remain some big question marks. The first question mark is over the United Nations Climate Change Conference held in Bali in December 2007. Some were happy with Bali, but if you read the outcome objectively, it is not a road map: it is perhaps the start of a journey, but so far it has no direction. It was an agreement to talk and that talk ought to have begun already. It is an appeal: nobody has promised anything, nothing has been binding. There are some positive elements: there is more emphasis on adaptation than ten years ago. There is also emphasis on the need to avoid deforestation.

The second question mark hovers over bio-fuels. I share the concern that the first-generation bio-fuels will not be sustainable and will have major consequences for water and energy use for production, but also in relation to food availability, food pricing and deforestation.

Conclusion

In terms of the present political situation around climate change, it seems countries are still just blaming each other. They are failing to implement and I am very concerned that non-implementation of Kyoto creates the argument for the non-Annex 1 countries to say, 'No, we are not participating because you failed to keep your promises.' It is not certain at all that the Kyoto target of minus 5.2 percent is going to be met. There is an implementation gap. It is always 'next time, next period, not yet'. Where is the urgency of feeling? Why is there still the focus on procedures, institutions and the financial question of who is going to pay? The power question is still determining the conversations, which leads to a focus on secondary approaches in order to avoid mitigation. We have reached a situation where there is too much emphasis on, for instance, avoiding deforestation; too much emphasis on adaptation, drawing attention away from necessary mitigation and wrongly leading to compensation tactics. So rich people fly and pay a couple of dollars extra in order to compensate for some trees somewhere and then later on they will be cut. It is lip service. There needs to be more emphasis on a core approach to mitigation. All other approaches will not do the job. The attention on bio-fuels is an example of this. It is necessary to think about long-term targets of equal emissions per capita, of all inhabitants, of all countries in the long run. Without taking such a path we are risking a major disaster.

Note

1 This article is based on the speech 'Climate, Scarcities and Development' given by Jan Pronk on 17 March 2008 at the SID Netherlands Chapter Lecture Series 2007–2008 on 'Energy, Water, and Food: Global Scarcities and Power Shifts – a new world map for international cooperation'. http://www.sid-nl.org/index.php?a =lectures (accessed on 21 May 2008)

The Urgency of and the Political Ways and Means to Address Climate Change

Pier Vellinga

Two Statements

L et me start with two statements. Firstly, the risk of irreversible climate change is too great for it to be allowed to happen. Only drastic action to reduce emissions can adequately reduce this risk. There is no certainty it will work. But given the state of science, in particular the recent progress in understanding climate changes of the past, a business-as-usual approach is unacceptable.

Secondly, it is technically and economically quite possible to avoid the major part of the projections of climate change presented to us by the International Panel on Climate Change (IPCC). But it will be a race against time between global success to control emissions and the reactions of the earth, some of which are already visible. In fact, as Minister Heemskerk, the Netherlands' Minister of Foreign Trade, has said, international cooperation will be the bottleneck in addressing climate change. I believe it is an ultimate test for international cooperation.

Where do we stand in the debate on climate change?

Let us look at what is happening in the world around us. We have the IPCC report presenting a clear message, accepted by governments. However, there still is a hard core of scepticism, in the Netherlands and elsewhere in the world. As the economic interests are great there is continuous media exposure of this scepticism.

Within the science community this is completely fair. That is the business of science. But when it comes to policy, and there is an established theory by IPCC, supported by thousands of scientists, the scepticism should not have an effect as large as it has today. This continuous noise in the background makes actors who should invest in greenhouse-emission control measures uncertain about their actions.

Therefore I will begin by recapping the theory. The greenhouse theory was established more then a hundred years ago by a Swedish professor, Ahrenius. The sun warms up the planet through shortwave (white light) radiation. In turn, the planet re-radiates the energy in order to balance energy flows towards and from the earth. The re-radiation is in the form of infrared (longwave, invisible) radiation. The greenhouse effect is the phenomenon in which CO_2 and other greenhouse gases partially absorb and thus hamper this outward infrared radiation, while not affecting the incoming shortwave radiation. With the same amount of energy coming in, the earth will by necessity be warmer than it would be without greenhouse gases in the atmosphere. The warming trend measured over the last thirty years confirms the theory. The earth is warming up and the pattern that we measure clearly reflects the greenhouse theory.

By using fossil fuel, but also by some other practices in agriculture and forestry, we are adding to this layer of greenhouse gases. As a consequence, the infrared radiation has more difficulty leaving our planet. The earth will have to become a little warmer in order to push away the energy from the planet. I can illustrate this by an example: when I put an extra blanket on you while in bed, your body will warm up because it takes a warmer body to get rid of the same amount of energy.

The radiation theory and the effect of so called greenhouse gases on infrared radiation is well established on a laboratory scale: if you take a tube with CO_2 in it, and you have a source and a receptor of infrared energy, the more CO_2 you put in the tube, the hotter the source needs to be to transfer the same amount of energy. This effect works likewise at the planetary scale.

The question often posed is: are these greenhouse gas concentrations really increasing, and if so, is it because of fossil fuels? Well, they have been measured in many places in the world: the concentration is growing steadily. In pre-industrial times the average emission amounted to 280 parts per million (ppm), and now we are at a level of about 400 ppm. It is even possible to see the seasonal fluctuations that represent autumn and winter in the northern hemisphere, where there is more land and vegetation and thus more natural seasonal breathing of CO_2 than in the southern hemisphere. Why is it taking such a long time for the theory to be accepted? It is because there are a few big question marks. One is the question of how the emissions relate to the natural breathing of the earth. The natural breathing of carbon dioxide of our planet is about twenty times higher than the amount emitted by human action. We knew that already. Humans only represent a tiny group in this world. Just look at the deserts and the oceans, and you would not believe that humans would have a measurable effect on the planet. Indeed, the natural flows of CO_2 are in an order of magnitude larger than what we cause as a human species. The oceans, for example, breath in and out 90 megatons of carbon per year; vegetation, trees and soils breath in and out 120 megatons. We as humans, through the use of fossil fuels and certain land use practices, produce only 7 megatons a year, but we repeatedly do this every year. And of this seven, only half is reabsorbed by the oceans and the forests. The other half accumulates in the atmosphere. As a consequence, there is a continuing growth of this heat-absorbing layer around the earth.

You can imagine that scientists could debate for many decades about the relation or the balance between what is natural variation and what we as humans add, and of course, if this natural system is affected, about what our contribution is.

We now know, through 60 years of measurements, that the concentrations of greenhouse gases are steadily growing. Moreover, through isotope analyses, we know that fossil-fuel use is the main contributor to this growth. A more recent understanding is that our contribution will affect these big flows in a way that reinforces the warming of the planet (so-called positive feedback).

Feedbacks and the natural cycle of ice ages

This can be illustrated by the natural cycle of ice ages every 120,000 years. We had ice on our doorsteps, right here in the Netherlands! It is gone now, but very likely it will return some 60,000 years from now. That is still a long time away. Some geologists will suggest we just wait for the next ice age and compensate for it by global warming and using lots of fossil fuels now. Well, this is an over-optimistic way of looking at the earth, as the timescales do not fit. These ice ages come and go with a timescale of about 120,000 years. The human contribution to the greenhouse effect is a matter of our generation, the previous generation and the next five to ten generations. As a consequence we cannot let the glacial cycle solve the problems of human-induced climate change. But, more interesting, we increasingly understand the glacial cycles. The ice ages are triggered by the Milankovich cycles. Milankovich is the Russian scientist who discovered seventy years ago that the earth shakes a little on its axis, with a variation of solar energy reaching the earth as a consequence. Calculations have been made about how much warming and cooling is brought about by this shifting of the axis. Astrophysics tells us that the first-order temperature variations caused by these Milankovich cycles are considerably less than 0.5°C, while in fact the glacial cycle comes with a variation of global average temperatures of about five degrees. The difference between less than half a degree and five degrees is caused by feedback. Physical feedback can be illustrated by examining the response of the summer ice covering the North Pole. When the ice melts, it reflects less sunlight and it absorbs more energy. As a consequence, the water and the air over it warm up. Biological feedback can be illustrated by tundra response. If the tundras warm up and melt, they are likely to produce more methane. As methane is a greenhouse gas, it adds to the warming of the planet. The scientific community increasingly finds evidence that the ice ages are the result of slight changes in the amount of sunlight received by the earth (Milankovich cycles) reinforced by physical and biological feedbacks as described above. So relatively small changes in the radiative balance of the earth can have large temperature effects.

Another thing we learned from the ice ages is that, 120,000 years ago, in the preceding warm period, the earth was on average about two degrees warmer then it is today. There were very few people living on earth then, and the physical world looked more or less the same, with similar ice caps on Greenland and Antarctica. Paleo-climatologists have now reconstructed the sea-level rise in that period and they come to the conclusion that there have been rates of sea-level rise of one to two metres per century. They tell us this is likely to happen again within the next fifty to a few hundred years, now as a result of the accumulation of greenhouse gases in the atmosphere.

Effects on sea level rise

The IPCC, in its report in 2007, which covered the literature until 2005, was uncertain about the behaviour of the Greenland ice cap and the West Antarctic glaciers and ice caps. Since the year 2000, glaciologists have measured a net production of water from these ice caps. It is still small in terms of sea-level rise: about 0.2 millimetres per year. But this response to the warning planet comes earlier and faster then predicted. Glaciologists suggest that, once this process has begun, it cannot be stopped. They calculate that the sea-level rise from the melting of the edges of the Greenland ice cap could be 20 centimetres in 100 years, and from the edges of the Antarctic ice cap, it could be in the order of another 50 centimetres in 100 years. In 200 years, it could go up to 2 to 4 metres! This is a major threat that we cannot neglect. It is difficult to speak in terms of certainty or uncertainty, but the signals we now see are too clear to ignore.

Another reason why I want to stress the urgency of the matter is that, twenty years ago, scenarios of global warming as a result of

191

human emissions were made. These scenarios are still considered as realistic projections of possible futures. However, from 2000 until 2008, the world was well beyond the highest scenarios in terms of emissions. Of course, you can blame that on the rather rapid economic growth worldwide, including in China and India, but in addition, the industrialised countries have increased their CO_2 emissions. As we are beyond the highest scenario of the IPCC, the Delta Commission, in its advice to the Netherlands government, decided to explore not only the middle of the road scenarios but also the highest scenarios, in particular with regard to their implications for global sea-level rise.

The increased understanding of positive feedback triggers a growing support in the scientific community for the idea that we should deal with this issue urgently. As I said, the issue of climate change can always be disputed, but I know the field and I know my colleagues quite well, including those in the UK, Germany and the US. In the US, for example, Jim Hanssen is called an alarmist. But he has at his disposal all the data on the North Pole and Antarctica ice coming from NASA. Hanssen has come up with the statement that, indeed, the physical and biological feedback of the earth is likely to be stronger than considered in the most recent IPCC report. He makes a plea for reducing the concentration of greenhouse gases in the atmosphere from the present 450 ppm down to 350 ppm, while earlier suggestions from the scientific community usually mentioned 550 or 650 ppm as an unavoidable and possibly acceptable upper level. From geological records, Hanssen concludes that 350 ppm is the critical level, above which the ice caps start melting. His recommendation – returning to a level of 350 ppm within a few decades – is mind-boggling if we consider the present volume of investments in the exploration and production of fossil fuels such as oil, gas and coal. Looking at the past: in 1970 we had 30 megatons of CO_2 emissions in the world; in 2004 we had 50 megatons. Considering the recent analysis of Hanssen and a number of collegues, the world community should reduce emissions in a most radical way. Some suggest it requires a 'war economy' to reach responsible levels of greenhouse concentrations within the next few decades. Realising this, Hanssen suggested that we may for a few decades go beyond the present level but that we should then use this time to take action 'to win from the tipping points'. A responsible goal for the world would then be to transit into a climate-neutral economy by about 2050.

Response strategies for Europe and The Netherlands

Let us now turn to the IPCC and what they say about the response strategies. Bert Metz, our Dutch colleague who was the leader of working group III of the (UN)-intergovernmental Panel on Climate Change, brought the key messages forward rather strongly. He said that the good news is that, according to IPCC, it is technically and economically feasible to avoid most of the projected climate change. The bad news is: there is very little time to do this and we probably need to pay a price in the order of 50 or maybe a 100 or more euros per ton of CO_2 for climate change to be avoided. To achieve this, it will be necessary for the governments to allocate and then take out of the market, step by step, the permits to emit greenhouse gases. The good news is that the ways to do it are well known; the bad news that the measures required will have an effect on the distribution of wealth and income and therefore demand strong leadership to be introduced. Moreover, there is very little time to implement such measures.

At national level we had the former Minister of Agriculture, Mr Veerman, showing leadership on the issue of sea-level rise and coastal protection, which is of course very dear to the Dutch public. Similarly, we need leadership in the field of energy and greenhouse-gas emissions at national and global levels. Not only is the technology there, it is also economically do-able. The companies who have invested in energy efficiency and renewable energies have performed better in the market than their traditional competitors. The technologies available are first of all those dealing with energy efficiency and renewable energies. In the Netherlands that would, for example, mean an extension of the use of heat pumps and more wind, solar and biomass energy. Within a decade, or even less, we can make all our new homes energy-neutral and climate-neutral.

We know there is a debate going on about the use of biomass and that debate will continue. But if you travel in Europe, you see so much land that is available for the production of biomass for energy. There is no reason why we shouldn't use it. The debate focuses on importing biomass from abroad, which occurs potentially at the cost of the production of food and the conservation of tropical forests. That is a valid debate, but there is sufficient land available in Europe and worldwide to produce a significant amount of biomass energy, i.e. 20 to 30 percent of present energy needs, without endangering world food production.

Then there is solar energy: much progress is being made here and more is to come, but it takes time. In the meantime, Carbon Capture and Storage (CCS) may fill the (time) gap. Nuclear energy is an alternative. Both technologies are second-best and it may well be that a full focus on renewable energies and efficiency increases is more economic.

The issue of nuclear energy

In the Netherlands we are at a crossroads. I am sure that we need more electric energy as our society is likely go 'entirely electric', even our cars. In a few years we will have a wide variety of electric vehicles on the market. Within a year the 'plug-ins' will be there, even if that creates problems for some oil companies. Indeed, for reasons of continuity these companies should start to invest in facilitating electric vehicles on a large scale, starting today.

When we go entirely electric, we will need more electric power stations. Simultaneously, we have ambitious national targets for the introduction of renewable energy. This reveals a potential contradiction, as certain types of electric power-plants, such as nuclear and traditional coal power-plants, prohibit the economic introduction of renewable energies. Economics dictates that a traditional coal power-plant or a nuclear power-plant should run on a permanent basis, continuously. Once it has been started, it should not be stopped, as that would be too costly. So nuclear power-plants must run day and night, like traditional coal-fired power-plants. If we invest in that kind of power station, it will be very difficult to introduce wind and solar energy on a competitive basis. Once you have these nuclear and coal-fired power-plants, they will out-compete renewable energies like solar and wind energy.

There is a way out, however: building (modern) coal gasification plants. They produce gas from coal. In turn the gas can either be burned for electricity or stored, the latter in particular in periods when wind and solar energy is produced. So if additional coal power-plants are to be built, and simultaneously renewable energy targets are to be met, priority should be given to coal-gasification plants to allow for renewable energies to enter the system. Moreover, the CO_2 of such plants could be stored underground, thus creating a climate-neutral electricity system.

Presently there is a big debate going on about the technical aspects of this possibility, which is promoted strongly by the group on energy transition specialists in the field. Our government so far is not paying enough attention to these technical connections and interdependencies. But be sure that once you choose nuclear and/or traditional coal-fired power-plants, you may as well forget about economic introduction of solar and wind energy.

Global management of climate change

Let me go back to the global level. Climate change is indeed the ultimate test of international cooperation. Two steps should now be taken. One is that the US, Europe and Russia show leadership in reducing emissions. If they don't, we will never succeed. Secondly, if China and India do not step in within ten years, we will never succeed in meeting the targets proposed by the scientific community. We need the US on board within half a year from now and I expect that it will come. We also need Russia on board and then, within ten years, China will have to accept legal obligations as well, and so will India. As China and India together host about one third of the world population while Europe, the US and Russia together host less than half the population of India and China, it becomes clear that the ultimate key for success in controlling the human effect on the global climate is in the hands of China and India. Looking at the technological side: China and India had economic growth rates of between 8 and 10 percent over the last decade, while the growth of energy use was only half of that: between 4 and 5 percent. Compare that with the situation in the West in the 1960s: our economic growth then equalled the growth in energy use. So China and India are developing in a much more energy-efficient way than we did in our industrialisation age.

To bring these countries on board in the Copenhagen process, direct confrontation with emission targets is not likely to work when our level of per-capita emissions is three to five times as high as theirs. Instead, we could ask them to come up with energy-intensity goals in the order of 50 percent. This implies that for every percent of economic growth the emission should not grow more than 0.5 percent. This is an achievable goal and a positive incentive at the same time. As was indicated by Minister Heemskerk, the Chinese exporters are the best in class. If you want to invest in renewable energy, you should be aware of what is going on in China.

Allocating of CO_2 emission rights

The mechanism with regard to sharing the cost of reducing CO_2 emissions (and other greenhouse gases) will of course be crucial. Will we have a sharing mechanism on a per-capita basis? That would mean: as soon as you are born, no matter where in the world, you would have an equal right to carbon emissions. Ideologically, and in order to achieve long-term stability in the world, this would be the course to take. But of course a transition is required, as there are major differences now.

It is internationally agreed that countries have common but differentiated responsibilities with regard to the control of greenhouse gases. Industrialized countries have started to accept a cap on their national emissions. The next step is to agree on a long-term target of emissions per capita. The transition from present emissions per capita to the long-term per-capita targets is called convergence. The developing countries converge upward while the developed countries converge downward. This approach is generally called a cap-and-convergence model.

Now, should all this be negotiated at UN level? Of course countries are actively participating in the UN negotiations, but let me remind you of the statement of a high-level representative of the US, at the time of the first negotiations on climate change. He said: as soon as the US becomes serious about this issue we probably prefer to deal with only five or six countries and fix a deal within a year. For them, the United Nations system is too complicated. If the problem needs a rapid solution, then the UN may not be the most effective organisation. Of course, the UN will remain the organisation to consolidate the agreements and organise compliance and monitoring.

To conclude: some dilemmas

Let me finish by summarising some dilemmas. The ultimate goal of the UN treaty on climate change is to avoid dangerous anthropogenic interference. But what does this exactly mean? Personally I consider the present level as already dangerous for continuous economic prosperity and social stability on this planet, but who am I? Well, together with James Hanssen and Joachim Schellnhuber, I am among the researchers who have studied this issue for the last thirty years and whose concern about the issue has grown with the growing understanding of climate changes in the past.

Then there is the issue of compensation for the cost of damage and adaptation. The-polluter-pays principle is accepted by the OECD countries as a way to deal with domestic environmental issues. The 'no harm' principle is accepted internationally and ratified by nearly all countries in international environmental agreements. However, the reality is that most developed nations are in a no-response mode when developing countries raise the issue in the UN negotiation context, the major reason being the potentially enormous cost, a minor reason being the practical difficulty in defining damage and adaptation cost. Scientifically speaking, it is still, and will be for a while, very difficult to distinguish between the effects of climate variability and climate change. As a consequence, it will remain difficult to deal with the compensation issue in practical terms. A major effort will be required by the political and scientific community to find a way forward.

Then there is the dilemma of what the phrase 'common but differentiated responsibilities' means. We all know what it means at a meta-level, but what does it mean at operational level? There is legitimacy in the call on richer countries to help the poorer countries to control emissions and to adapt to climate change. Indeed, much can be achieved with money and dedicated funds. However, in the end it is the planning capacity and governance that determine the success of international financial assistance. How will funding for emission control or for compensation of adaptation costs take account of or deal with limited capabilities of governments of countries?

In the end, the biggest dilemma of all is, if you have one euro to reduce poverty now, why spend it on reducing climate change and resulting poverty in the future? My final statement therefore is that we cannot afford to postpone reducing greenhouse emissions until all national and international social distribution issues have been resolved. Climate change is the result of currently using the 'wrong' types of energy and applying the 'wrong' types of land use. We can and should do better, apart from other pressing issues.

PART III

Power Shifts

Energy Issues Redefining Latin American Policies

Reinaldo Figueredo

A s the overall heading of this set of lectures is 'Emerging global scarcities and power shifts' and I was asked to talk on 'Energy issues redefining Latin American policies', I will attempt to provide my views not only as a Venezuelan, whose life has been devoted to the search for a more harmonious attitude on democracy and sustainable development for his country and his region, but also as someone who has searched for a better understanding of the development strategies being pursued for and by developing countries. From the start I would like to underline that the academics in my part of the world have paid relatively little attention to the specific development aspects of this particular set of issues you are dealing with in your lectures. As you have indicated in the background paper to the series, environment, water and energy are inextricably intertwined. Without careful consideration of their respective management, sustainable human development, and, for that matter, the handling of public goods, will likely have major setbacks, not only in the region but worldwide. Today's geostrategic, overall sustainable development agenda forcefully reveals some facts concerning our region, such as the significance of the Amazon forest, a basic world lung and the fact that South America holds 28 percent of the world's fresh water, and that its hydrocarbon reserves are the largest outside the Middle East. The Andean countries, Venezuela, Colombia, Ecuador, Peru and Bolivia – which, until recently, were part of a Community of Nations formally linked in an integration scheme – hold 85 percent of the reserves in oil and gas of South America and more than 20 percent of fresh water. This in itself was, and still is, an essential component of harmonious sustainable human development sought in this part of the world, which is being abruptly challenged by equivocal perceptions on structures to be established within worldwide power shifts.

I will deal with a number of topics highlighting the power shifts and world dynamics on energy issues: the role played in establishing common strategies to ensure a fair return on exhaustible mineral resources of the developing countries; the perceptions behind the global scarcities issues and the economic and financial challenges being faced by all of us; the environmental concern and the unilateral approach being considered by industrialised countries, or, for that matter, the 'beggar thy neighbour' policy likely to provoke additional tensions among producers and consumers. Last but not least, I will discuss types of development cooperation assistance that might pave the way to harmonious energy transition, avoid regional conflicts and enhance the region's potential to achieve greater volumes and diversity of energy supply, thereby contributing to energy security worldwide.

World dynamics on energy issues

Energy issues have persisted as one of the major concerns in the discussions on development and related strategic considerations by the OECD countries since 1973/74. At that time, the consequence of an Arab oil-producers' embargo based upon fundamental political considerations prompted a major international economic crisis, risking destabilization of both the financial and the industrial sector of the industrialised economies. A sudden shift of US$120 billion[1] as 'windfall profits' from these countries to the oil-producing developing countries, in conjunction with the impact and sudden awareness of the vulnerability of their transportation and industrial sectors, highly dependent on imported oil, was seen, specifically by the US, as tantamount to an act of war. The US government even envisaged military occupation of the Arab Gulf countries[2].

President Giscard d'Estaing, concerned that this might ignite a third world war, talked President Ford into jointly proposing an 'Energy Conference' to the OPEC sovereigns and heads of state. Acceptance of the Paris CIEC Conference on Commodities and the ensuing Producer Consumer Ministerial dialogue did not unfortunately lead to a joint convergent strategy on trade and development. OECD countries agreed instead to create the IEA, with the prime responsibility of devising collective emergency response mechanisms to offset impacts of short-term supply disruptions. Also, the method chosen of recycling the 'windfall' gains of developing oil-producing countries and a reactive negative attitude towards OPEC as a whole, perceived as a cartel that should be erased, was not conducive to dispel deeper misunderstandings on what should have been a positive collective approach yet to be fully attained[3]. The Oil Facility set up within the International Financial Institutions also took part in the 'beggar thy neighbour' policies. The Oil Supply Emergency Response of IEA Countries, 2007 depicts the refinement of the joint endeavour and the strengthened coordinated responses to all such eventualities that, since its inception, it has acted upon:

Major Oil Supply Disruptions[4]

Sept. 2005	I Hurricane Katrina / Rita	1.5
March–Dec. 2003	I War in Iraq	2.3
Dec. 2002–March 2003	I Venezuelan strike	2.6
June–July 2003	I Iraqi oil export suspension	2.1
Aug. 1990–Jan. 1991	I Iraqi invasion of Kuwait	4.3
Oct. 1980–Jan. 1981	I Outbreak of Iran–Iraq	4.1
Nov. 1978 – April 1979	I Iranian revolution	5.6
Oct. 1973–March 1974	I Arab–Israeli War and Arab oil embargo	4.3
June–August 1967	I Six-day war	2.0
Nov. 1956–March 1957	I Suez crisis	2.0
	I	

Gross peak supply loss (mbd)

IEA Oil Supply Security Report 2007

Today's energy scenario is far more complex and blurred, with a forced energy transition taking place in the context of the globalisation process and other new issues that were hardly significant in the 1970s. Nowadays, the level of interactivity among countries on the critical issues requiring collective understanding and convergence does not lend itself to the former types of analysis and coalitions. Securing a harmonious energy transition, and tackling the serious lack of clean water and energy likely to generate major conflicts, requires different analyses and tools compared to those established in the context of what was then the East/West confrontation and the North/South divide. Yet we are all aware of the very significant power shifts taking place in the world. These require new visions, some of which timidly seem to surface though still on a piecemeal and self-contained basis, lacking an all-inclusive and comprehensive approach.

Oil demand in developing countries and increased dependency on a number of producing countries generates tightness as well as tensions that might slide into major confrontations. The IEA 2007 World Energy Outlook foresees an increase in oil demand[5] from 84.5 mbd in 2006 to 98.5 mbd in 2015 and 116.3 mbd in 2030. The developing countries will represent a major part of the increased demand.

The IEA warns in its 2007 Oil Supply Security Report that: the risk of oil supply disruptions has grown in recent years and will grow in the near future for a number of reasons. Among them, the IEA underlines that the share of its own production that OECD countries consume will fall from 26 percent of global oil supply to 16 percent in 2030. We will see a continued growth in demand, of 31.8 mbd, predicted between 2006 and 2030. (China and India alone will be responsible for approximately 13.9 mbd of which the former, in 2006 amounting to 7.5mbd, will reach the level of 16.5 mbd.) There will be increased concentration of oil use in the transport sector and insufficient increase in capacity (both upstream and downstream) to keep pace with demand growth. An additional factor is the concentration of oil supply in countries with large reserves – notably Middle East OPEC-member countries and Russia. This will increase global vulnerability, particularly because of the geo-strategic context, given that this source of energy is channelled and delivered to importing consumer countries. The devastating hurricanes of 2005 also demonstrated that in today's market, the severity of an oil-supply disruption is not only a function of the oil lost.

Establishing common strategies

The 1950 dictatorial Venezuelan regime lasted until 1958 with full connivance of the US government and the international oil companies. As soon as the process of democracy was initiated, one of the nation's main priorities was the setting up of a national oil policy and international diplomatic activity to ensure that oil-developing and exporting countries might establish an international institutionalised mechanism to defend their non-renewable energy resources from being exploited in an unfair and inappropriate manner. The main energy policy measures to ensure an adequate exploitation policy to service the requirements of the country's development needs were the enforcement of a physical and economic conservation policy regarding non-renewable resources: the 50/50 share of the benefit derived from hydrocarbon exploitation; no more concessions; and the setting up of a national oil company. As regards the international actions, two Venezuelans, Manuel Pérez Guerrero and Juan Pablo Pérez Alfonso (then Minister of Oil), together with Abdallah Tariki (Minister of Oil in Saudi Arabia), promoted the creation of OPEC at a conference held in Baghdad on 14 September 1960. The founding members of OPEC were Iran, Iraq, Saudi Arabia, Venezuela and Kuwait, responsible for 80 percent of the world trade in oil at the time.

The basic objective of building a common stance was to jointly counter a unilateral announcement of some of the seven sisters of a further reduction in prices, and their determination to have a say in the exploitation of their non-renewable resource. At the time the establishment of OPEC passed almost as a non-event in the international press, but the seven sisters actually took it upon themselves to discredit the main goal of Venezuela, arguing that the country was on the verge of exhausting its reserves, and did not want the Gulf countries to exploit their reserves freely.

If reference is made to this historical event, it is done to underline in the consciousness of Venezuelans that energy resource development is closely related to the type of society and institutional structure required to secure asocial human development. In an article published some days ago in the Dutch press, I made reference to Michael Tanzer's 1974 'Energy crisis and the power wealth struggle' which provided a realistic view of connivances among international oil companies, governments and multilateral financial institutions such as the World Bank and the IMF, which still persist to a certain extent, in forcing biased approaches to far more complicated issues requiring common understanding among producers and consumers on such a vital resource.

The problem in Latin America today is that high energy export revenues in two of the most important countries of the region with very significant reserves in oil and natural gas – Venezuela and Bolivia – and, to a lesser degree, Ecuador, provide scope to their present administrations to carry forward policies that have as an objective the establishment of authoritarian governments, in order to create what is called 'The New Socialism of the 21st Century'. Venezuela's president, in particular, perceives both the neo-liberal globalisation process, as well as the way in which the global warming and overall environmental approach is handled by most OECD countries, as a new phase of capitalist exploitation requiring an appropriate collective response. Closely associated with Fidel Castro and Evo Morales, they are determined that, if necessary, the end-use of energy resources should serve as leverage to create a counterbalancing political power of the so-called progressive forces in Latin America[6].

This particular approach, which Venezuela is forcefully trying to implement, has shifted the lawful economically driven defensive approach with regard to our strategic non-renewable resources in the direction of more prioritising and securing of a 'revolutionary' state of affairs. This is, for tactical reasons, by no way limited to the country of Venezuela itself; the nation is essentially driven to implanting it more broadly in the region of Latin America as a whole, and it includes the induction of those elements that are capable of reinforcing unstable and inflammable societies. The logic behind this is in line with the way in which, in the early days of Fidel Castro's revolution, Cuba conceived to export its revolution to some key Latin American countries such as Venezuela, Bolivia and Nicaragua.

Perceptions on global scarcities and economic and financial challenges

Higher oil prices have led to a significant redistribution of global income from oil importers to oil exporters. In 1974, we were talking of US$120 billion; by 2006, according to the Federal Reserve Bank of New York, oil revenues for oil-exporting countries had risen by about US$970 billion – an increase of almost US$670 billion since 2002 – the bulk of which goes to a handful of countries. In so far as oil prices and oil revenues are concerned, the world has had to adjust to harmful large swings in oil prices. In 1974, as a consequence of the Arab oil embargo and the Israel War, prices hiked from an average of slightly less than US$4.00 a barrel to US$11.40 (the equivalent in 2005 of from US$16.75 to US$45.40 if adjusted to the US consumer price index.) In 1970/80 the 'oil shock' as a consequence of a decrease in Middle East production pushed prices from US$14.00 a barrel in 1978 to $US37.20 a barrel in 1980 (equivalent to US$41.95 to US$88.25 a barrel in 2005).

From 2002, when prices averaged just under US$25.00 a barrel, owing to surging demand by China, prices began a strong upward trend, from an average of US$37.75 a barrel in 2004 to US$53.35 in 2005, US$65.35 in 2006 and almost US$100 at the beginning of the fourth quarter of this year.

Once again, the issue of recycling petrodollars comes to the forefront of financial circuits, although not with the same kind of concern, since the options for oil exporters are basically twofold:

1. increasing imports of goods and services. This, in a certain sense, is a revisiting dynamic of earlier shocks, but this time, as the days of cheap energy are forgone and the world oil peak is somewhere within the timeframe presently evolving, this requires a different attitude.

2. the purchasing of foreign assets in the international capital market stimulated by the dynamics of globalisation. The Federal Reserve Bank of NY in a December 2006 analysis identified revenues for this category of countries exceeding US$1,500 billion, a jump of about US$980 billion since 2002. Half of it, or almost $475 billion, went to acquire goods and services from abroad, and $485 billion went to increased net purchases of foreign financial assets.

Venezuela's oil revenues from between 2002 and 2007 amounted to US$261 billion, in spite of a persistent fall in production as well as in its oil export volume. Exports have fallen by 40 percent in the last seven years, from 2.5 mbd at the beginning of 2000 to approximately 1.5 mbd these days. The downfall in volume terms has been more than compensated by the export price increase, which on average over the period has increased by 150 percent. The net outcome has been an increase of 50 percent of export revenues in the seven-year period. President Chávez has used a considerable amount of this income in providing assistance to several Caribbean, Central American and South American countries contingent upon adopting alignments with his ALBA integration initiatives and proposals to set up development financial as well as regional petroleum companies and a vast energy supply network essentially conceived to counter the US/AFTA and its military presence in the region. A very large amount of foreign exchange has been used in acquiring both from the Russian Federation and Byelorussia sophisticated armaments, as though Venezuela is getting ready to enter into an armed conflict with some of its neighbours!

The environmental concern and actions devised unilaterally by OECD countries.

Venezuela has a prolonged and resentful experience from unilateral actions adopted initially by the US that had negative financial implications in a difficult phase of its development. In the mid 60s the US adopted a 'Clean Air Act' to ensure that fuel oil consumed in the major Eastern cities would meet very stringent, reduced levels of sulphur content as well as of lead in petrol. At that time Venezuela was by far the main fuel oil supplier of the Eastern coast, and the sulphur content of its product was well above what was to be enforced. Given the low market price at the time, Venezuela was getting approximately 0.80 cents per barrel of fuel oil sold to the US, although we explained that our net income would fall to less than 0.60 cents per barrel unless an investment of approximately US$1billion in our refineries was made. We argued that this should be shared by both countries. However, these pleas fell on deaf ears. Global warming, we agree, needs to be tackled at the global level. During the Kyoto process, Venezuela, together with other OPEC countries, made its case that proportionality should be introduced in the corrective measures to be adopted. This means first of all a clear link regarding the level of development, while countries mainly responsible because of their high level of industrial and transportation activities should bear the main burden of the adjustment costs to be made. The carbon tax being considered by OECD members, and particularly in Europe, as referred to by President Sarkozy in his recent visit to China, needs to be pondered against a broader and more constructive approach dealing with the overall issue of 'security of energy supply'.

We believe, as mentioned earlier, that convergence among producers and consumers in constructive dialogues like those that have been patiently established in the International Energy Forum (IEF) would certainly yield a more positive outcome. The new Dutch General Noé van Hulst will soon assume the place of Secretary General, currently held by the Norwegian Ambassador Arne Walther, who has very efficiently laid the ground to ensure that this Forum sets the necessary conditions for essential understandings among producers and consumers. Noé van Hulst will, I am confident, pursue some practical actions, leading the way to conducting a smooth and harmonious energy transition and ensuring avoidance of probable dangerous confrontations. Carbon sequestration is, I am sure, one of the actions that should tackle some of the basic problems.

An important initiative was taken by UN Secretary General Kofi Annan in the setting up of a high-level interagency group on energy presided by a vice-president of the World Bank, Mats Karlsson, and the Under Secretary General José Antonio Ocampo, responsible for the Secretariat. The first report of this group was linked to the attainment of the Millennium Development Goals and the role that 'energy' had to play in this regard. Even if the effort is laudable, the biased approach of emphasising renewables and avoiding the complex 'energy transition' is likely to induce serious shortcomings in attaining sustainable human development, which is precisely what it attempts to achieve.

Considerations regarding development cooperation

We have seen with interest the announcements made by Bert Koenders, the Netherlands Minister for Development Cooperation, regarding the challenges and engagements his government is determined to undertake with respect to fragile states. He himself recognises the difficulties in defining a 'fragile state'. I am sure, for instance, he would certainly not even consider including Venezuela in the list of thirty-five or so countries that fall into that category. In fact, I would argue that a state which does not uphold the rule of law, that systematically violates human rights, that has stimulated social confrontation and disregards the essential formal institutions of a democratic state might well be setting the course of a 'inflammable society'. One week ago, a referendum propelled by the administration that would have, through what many constitutional experts had defined as a statutory Coup d'État was defeated by what Chávez himself qualified as a 'pyrrhic' victory of the opposition – although the margin between the NO vote and the YES approval is far more significant than what was formally announced by the biased Electoral Council. The outcome of this popular consultation has certainly generated shivers among the hard-core followers of the President who until late in the evening of Sunday the 2nd were asking him not to recognise that the Venezuelans had rejected his reforms.

I am certainly not making a case for Venezuela to be included in the category of fragile countries likely to be the subject of Dutch development cooperation. But I do so regarding 'inflammable societies' in our region, such as Bolivia, Ecuador, El Salvador, Nicaragua and Guatemala, whose social cohesiveness hinges on fragile ground and which are therefore likely to enter directly into a geo-strategic dynamic and become 'inflammable societies'.

I could not agree more with your minister regarding the rigidity of 'good governance' conditionality as well as other stiff procedures that have for too long prevented provision of important inputs into these fragile states. I would also concur with him in respect of the Dutch and European Extractive Industries Transparency Initiative, launched for the private sector. That initiative is very much in line with what Ambassador Walther has so ably engaged the UN, the IEA, OECD and many other very significant partners to adopt. This is one of the issues that I would like mind to exchange views on with Noé van Hulst, once he assumes responsibility of the IEF Secretariat.

I would like to conclude with what I had raised earlier regarding the implications of revisiting the inflexibility of conditions, as well as the conceptual identification of the category of fragile countries that should be the subject of specific programmes in development cooperation. In my view, what is still missing is a comprehensive regional or sub-regional approach, preferably complementing whatever specific national or bilateral action is decided upon. That is, an integrated approach to prevent any kind of possibility of 'fragile states' or 'inflammable societies' lapsing into 'inflamed societies', or even worse, a 'vortex' of major dislocations within their own region. This is, in my view, what might happen in Bolivia, where some prospective analysis could perhaps help to promote a more positive role in the Andean Community of Nations. Such an approach might be an important initiative which The Netherlands might wish to ponder together with such countries as Sweden and Norway. I have reasons to believe that such a possibility might become one of the most significant cooperation strategies in the 'energy transition' period, encompassing peaceful resolution of conflicts in a region clouded by potentially extremely stormy weather.

Notes

1 An equivalent to 235 billion in 1997 US$.

2 Schlesinger foreshadowed the possible use of force in September 2004 and Kissinger followed suit in an interview with Business Week in December : "I am not saying that there is no circumstance where we would not use force. But it is one thing to use in the case of a dispute over price; it is another where there is some actual strangulation of the industrialised world."

3 This is in the present deep structural and turbulent world crisis more necessary than ever. It seems that we do not understand or learn from past experience and we find ourselves in the Energy environment reediting what professor Cobby Van der Linde describes as the critical "roller coast" energy price dwindling.

4 IEA Oil Supply Security Report 2007.

5 This has been slightly revised downward in the 2008 IEA World Energy Outlook but does not alter significantly the analysis overview presented at 2007 lectures.

6 Heinz Dietrich a senior counsellor of president Chávez wrote "The strategic defeat in Venezuela; a mortal danger for Bolivia and Cuba" referring to the recently held referendum on Venezuela's defeat of Chávez constitutional 'reform'.

The end of globalization
Europe looking for a workable world order in partnership with Latin America

Cor van Beuningen

G lobalization refers to the process of worldwide economic integration – or, to be more precise, to the sudden acceleration, broadening and deepening of this age-old process of the interweaving of economic (f)actors, in the period after the Second World War. In this accelerated process, technological innovation plays an important role, in particular and most spectacularly in two areas: information and communication and transport. The transport revolution – also fuelled by cheap oil – made possible the relocation of productive capacity to low-wage countries as an integrated part of global value chains; *distance no longer matters*. The ICT revolution further *flattened the world* by providing companies and entrepreneurs from all over the world with the opportunity and the tools to connect to and compete on a levelling global playing field.

At the same time, this acceleration is the outcome of a process of consultation, planning and decision-making, which started with the Bretton Woods Conference of July 1944. Among other things, the World Bank, IMF and the Uruguay Round WTO constitute the institutional fallout of this conference. Bretton Woods was about economic recovery after the Second World War, and about the way towards global growth and prosperity. To that end, barriers had to be removed, such as restrictions on free trade. New arrangements and institutions had to be established to ensure recovery and to facilitate growth. The type of policy that was developed here, and that was later identified by concepts such as neo-liberalism and the Washington Consensus, revolves largely around reducing the role of government in economic life and enhancing the role of the market.

This market is increasingly a global market, and economic inter-weaving largely blurs national borders. Globalization is thus associated with a (relative) *de-nationalization* of the economy. The space for a national government to steer the economic process is dwindling. The discipline of the world market dictates the actions of companies but also of governments, or at least binds them to clear frameworks and instructions. In this sense one can speak also of the *de-politicization* of economic life. National governments have no choice but to adjust, as disengagement is not a real option anymore.

National boundaries no longer matter

Although the margins for national governments to steer the economic process are reduced, many countries in recent years stepped up their efforts to use those margins as effectively as possible. It is all about the ability to constantly accommodate and reposition oneself, to create and exploit opportunities, and to reduce risks and avoid adverse developments (resilience). General keywords are: investment climate, export orientation, niche specialization. Typical for such national policy efforts is that they combine two tracks. On the one hand, they are geared towards maintaining strict monetary, budgetary and fiscal discipline, and towards improving the country's competitiveness through tax incentives, more flexible labour and reform of the social security system. On the other hand, efforts are deployed towards increasing the value of collective assets, in physical infrastructure, education and care, in innovation, research and development, knowledge and social capital . . . On the first track national governments compete with each other in *a race to the bottom*: who is the cheapest? On the second track they are involved in *a race to the top*: who is the best, who is in front with regard to the quality of its assets? The problem is, of course, that these two policy tracks do not easily match: there are trade-offs between them.

The reversal of the globalization process

At a time when most people were still busy adjusting their mindset to a globalized world, the largely unexpected problem of the so called *new scarcities* - of energy, minerals, food and water - signalled a first turning point with respect to the nature and the direction of the globalization process. The sudden imbalance between a sharply rising demand and a slowly reacting supply of these essential but special goods (special, because they are relatively irreplaceable, and because output increase here meets with natural constraints) has led to dramatic price increases in the last couple of years. Between 2002 and mid 2008 oil prices tripled and the prices of basic cereals increased by 140 percent; and with the rise of bio-fuels, the energy and food markets were more directly linked to each other. While the global recession, linked to the financial crisis that marks the second half of 2008, softens the impact of the combined energy and food crises at least with regard to price increases, the problem of the new scarcities, or more generally, the extreme volatility of the prices for those commodities, is bound to continue to have a profound impact on the global structure of production, trade and consumption in the decades to come. One salient aspect of the changed international competitive framework is that oil-price volatility has led to a re-localization of the production of transport-intensive goods (i.e. goods which are relatively heavy and/or bulky). Where previously the transportation revolution was at the root of globalization - *distance no longer matters* - we now experience the reverse movement, at least for transport-intensive goods: re-localization, or reversed globalization.

The new scarcities have also led to a political redefinition of - particularly - energy and food. In the eyes of present-day politicians and states, these are much more than just economic goods. They are redefined as strategic goods, i.e. goods that are directly relevant to national security and sovereignty. National governments thus feel obliged - or legitimized - to meddle with affairs that until very recently were left to the market. National energy supply and food security have suddenly become *Chefsache*, deserving leaders' direct political control and intervention. Old-fashioned control delusion and planning and control reflexes, state interventionism and protectionism can now be seen mushrooming all over the place. Thus, we experience the *re-politicization* of important sectors of the economy.

Of course, the awareness of the strategic and military qualities of energy, food and water is probably as old as politics itself, and as far as the EU is concerned, this awareness was still very much alive well into the twentieth century. Proof are the Treaty of Rome, the European Community for Coal and Steel and the Common Agricultural Policy (which originally focussed on food security). The neo-liberal de-politicisation process only started in the 1980s, with the privatization of utilities and the liberalization of the markets for energy and water. The political definition of food was questioned for the first time during the Uruguay Round of GATT (later WTO) in 1986. And in the 1990s, energy, food and water were subsequently stripped of their political definition and transformed into economic goods like any other. In this way, the last remnants of direct government interference in the economy were eliminated, as remnants from a previous period of short-sighted nationalism and costly protectionism. From now on, the globalized market would ensure efficiency, innovation, optimal allocation of resources and lower prices for consumers.

At least, this was what was thought at that time. Actually, in most EU countries, liberalization and privatization policies are now being questioned and the policy processes that were set in motion along those lines are being revised, postponed or reversed, notably in the field of energy (re. unbundling). And some politicians effectively plead for a return to the original wisdom and the founding principles of the EU – back to the old days.

At the *international* level, energy and food are redefined as strategic goods in the geopolitical sense, i.e. as important assets in international power relations. The possession of, control over and access to these goods affects the behaviour of politicians and states to an almost unprecedented degree. Leaders of energy-rich countries display a new, imperial self-confidence, and energy and food suddenly turn out to have military qualities; re. the energy weapon, and the food weapon. Countries that depend on energy from elsewhere now go as far as it takes to get hold on them; witness therefore the scramble for resources, and blood for oil. In this newly defined context, the fact that national state-owned enterprises possess the lion's share of world energy reserves suddenly acquires a new significance: Gasprom, Pemex, Petro China, Petrobras, Pdvsa, the Arabian monarchs . . . These combined and interlinked processes of re-nationalization and re-politicization of economic affairs, as well as the scarcities-related geopoliticization of international relations, are greatly intensified, accelerated and deepened by the financial crisis that is actually striking global capitalism and is threatening to plunge the world economy into a prolonged recession. The images of desperate bankers turning to their respective national governments for help in order to save the remnants of the global financial system; and of presidents of serious countries redefining neo-liberalism as casino capitalism, nationalizing banks and pleading for the establishment of state funds to secure national ownership of key companies, etc. – few things might better illustrate the ongoing process of reversed globalization. The pace of this process is breathtaking by any standard. This world is anything but flat, national boundaries do matter as much as ever before, national governments again play centre stage in the economic realm, and international relations are redefined as geopolitical power relations.

The promise of globalization was that everybody would be a winner, through the twin process of niche specialization and increasing interdependence. And when all stakeholders shared an interest in economic integration on the globalized market, international power politics and rivalry would lose their meaning and gradually come to an end. Actually, however, the reverse is happening. Geopoliticization is the antithesis of globalization. Geo-economics is subordinate to geopolitics. The global marketplace for entrepreneurs has been integrated in and superseded by the geopolitical arena where, again, national governments play the main characters.

The transition to new world order

This geopoliticization of international relations, driven by the combined effect of the new scarcities and the financial crisis and (the prospect of a deep) economic recession, is taking place in a very particular period of world history, i.e. one that is characterized by the transition in the world order of a unipolar system as we have known since 1989, to a multipolar system. The unipolar world was ideologically dominated by Western liberalism, and it was geopolitically dominated by the US as the sole superpower. This period is now coming to an end, but the outlines of the new world system are not yet clear. There is, however, some consensus among researchers about its economic characteristics. In about ten years' time the world economy will be dominated by three large blocks, each of which accounts for 15 to 20 percent of the Gross World Product: China, the US and the EU. They will be followed by India with about 10 percent and Japan, Brazil and Russia, each with 5 percent or less. The main question then will be how this new economic configuration is processed in the ideological-political domain, i.e. how the current and future political actors will deal with and respond to the complex process of change and re-accommodation on a global level. Are they willing and able to ensure a peaceful transition to a sustainable new world system, or are we in for a long period of rivalry and conflict?

To illustrate this point we may refer to the thesis of Mark Leonard in his *Divided World: The Struggle for Primacy in 2020*. According to Leonard, there are currently four political blocks that are emerging and already equally embroiled in a battle for hegemony. The first two of these blocks are the US and the EU. The difference between the two concerns their vision of the world order; while the US favour a 'realistic' approach to security and use a concept of a world order that is based on power, the EU is in favour of a rules-based international order and an effective multilateral system with well-functioning international institutions. The third block is formed by the autocratic axis Russia–China, countries which attach much importance to national identity and sovereignty, but which share with the EU the option for a rules-based international order – in their case seen as a protection mechanism against Western domination. The fourth block is the Islamic zone, extending from Morocco to Indonesia, not bound by democratic processes nor – in the last instance – by international institutions. This scenario of rivalling geopolitical power blocks – whatever their composition might be - is full of risks. The process will be characterized by instability, polarization, the strengthening of nationalist and militaristic tendencies, and perhaps even include the use of energy, food and water as weapons; thus producing if not open military conflict, the risk of a global recession, shortages of energy, food and water, and the spread of poverty and hunger. In such an atmosphere of generalized and spiralling distrust, the resolution of the current global problems, climate change, loss of biodiversity, security and poverty, issues that precisely require collective action if they are to be addressed with any chance of success, will be fully illusive.

Interacting and spiralling conflictivity

Though the two processes – the transition to a multipolar world order and the scarcity- and recession-driven geopoliticization of international relations – have completely different timeframes, it is becoming perfectly clear that the two processes will greatly influence each other in the years to come, with regard to both pace and direction. The way in which the transition process to a multipolar world order is being dealt with will be influenced by the way in which the scarcities- and recession-driven geopoliticization of international relations is being processed – and vice versa. In fact, interacting polarizations and mutually reinforcing conflictivity, entangled in a very explosive spiralling process, might well constitute the single most important threat to global stability in the years to come.

The EU and short-sighted realism

The EU is heavily dependent on external energy supply: 76 percent of its oil and 49 percent of its gas is imported, and these figures are expected to rise to 94 and 81 percent respectively in 2030. Energy security is a top priority in the foreign policy of the EU. The core of its external energy policy is the promotion of rules-based behaviour on open markets: *Market plus Governance*. This involves the removal of obstacles to the smooth functioning of the market, such as lack of transparency, corruption and cartels, as well as physical and infrastructural barriers to an integrated market; while other measures refer to legal frameworks to promote foreign investment in the energy sector, to human rights, democracy and good governance, security and environment. In conceptual terms, the EU external energy policy is a continuation of its constitutive internal policy paradigm, that is, rules-based market liberalization (*freedom plus responsibility*).

But it is precisely in the energy sector policy that the EU faces the biggest opposition, both from within and from outside. The internal energy market is still not fully open, physical or commercial, and several member states de facto impede the opening of energy markets, especially when it comes to the decoupling of production and distribution, and to the free access of foreign investment (energy nationalism). A coherent EU policy is also effectively undermined by the fact that many member states prefer to secure their energy supply by means of bilateral agreements with third countries, even if these same third countries refuse to incorporate the EU policy principles in their agreements: see Russia, Algeria, the countries of the Middle East . . .

Faced with these obstacles, the EU policy paradigm itself has become the subject of doubt and outright criticism, both from policymakers of member states and from inside the EU bureaucracy. Some criticize the policy paradigm for being politically idealistic, and, for that reason, unworkable and ineffective. They propose to de-politicize the EU external energy policy, in the sense of disconnecting commercial transactions (the buying and selling of goods) from difficult talk about democracy, good governance and human rights. That is, they enter a plea for *economic realism*. On the other hand, there are critics who argue that the EU policy is geopolitically naïve, and they see the need to effectively geopoliticize the external EU energy policy, in the sense of approaching the issue of energy security as set within the wider context of international and global power relations. They argue, in other words, for *geopolitical realism* and for an EU that self-consciously participates in the geopolitical power game of the major producing and consuming countries in the world arena. Both these alternative policy proposals must be strongly rejected. They are dangerously short-sighted. They would only reinforce the very tendencies that generate instability and disruption of energy supply as well as of the world economy and society as such. Given the complexity of the energy transition, given the scarcity- and recession-related geopolitical vulnerabilities in a period of fundamental transition in the world order, the energy issue can no longer be left to the market. And against the geopolitical realists: how would playing the geopolitical power game ever produce a peaceful, viable and rules-based world order, including a functioning global market, a functioning financial system and a functioning energy system?

It is of course an undeniable fact that the EU policy paradigm – i.e. rules-based market liberalization – is inherently vulnerable and weak. It is based on trust and, in order to function, a certain degree of mutual trust is needed between all parties involved. If this trust is not there, the EU policy concept will be seen and understood as naïve and therefore unworkable. But this is just another illustration of the problem associated with all collective action: trust is necessary in order to have the parties refrain from making use of individual degrees of freedom now, in favour of a better outcome for all in the future (*freedom plus responsibility*). Surely, on this fragile basis, the EU is an extremely vulnerable undertaking, and the same is true for its constitutive policy paradigm. But the EU has no other choice but to stick to what it is, and to do what it should do, precisely because this fragility and vulnerability are at the core of its constitutive force.

In the EU policy, all efforts should be aimed at reversing the process of geopolitical block formation and polarization, and to facilitate a peaceful transition to an effective and sustainable new world system. This new world system will necessarily be multipolar in nature, but it should be one in which the various actors feel recognized in their legitimate interests, one which generates a broad willingness to settle and compromise, to continue the dialogue and to commit oneself to a rules-based international order and institutions. To facilitate this, the EU has to behave itself consistently as the champion of multilateralism, of international rules, order and cooperation. The EU is to behave as the soft power for the good, and it must be willing to go as far as it takes in *not* accepting the power and polarization game, but in giving and fostering trust, even if that means increasing its own vulnerability; as far as it takes, in exercising soft power. The Union cannot be nor do otherwise, if only because the fate of Europe, its security and prosperity, including its energy and food security, depends on a workable world order.

The EU: Latin American partnership and alliance

In this perspective, the first partner for Europe in this enterprise – and one that could prove to be of invaluable importance – should be Latin America. For too long now, Latin America has been the big absentee in the EU foreign policy. The continent possesses almost one third of the world's fresh water, favourable physical conditions for the production of food and bio-fuels, the most important oil reserves outside the Middle East, gas, copper, iron – you name it. These assets will not only be important for the economic development of the LA countries but also – eventually – for the EU. They will also be crucial in addressing and solving some of the global problems of our times: energy and food security, climate change and biodiversity, and poverty reduction. But most importantly, LA shares with the EU its preference for multilateralism, for a rule-based international order and institutions. On a more profound level, Europeans and Latin Americans share a common set of beliefs and convictions regarding how we should live together and what kind of society we really should strive for, both at the national and at the global level. It is easy to recognize the real existence of such a shared value base by comparing it with Chinese, Slavic or even Anglo-Saxon basic beliefs. Surprisingly, however, Latin Americans seem to be much more aware of this fact than Europeans. Also, to Latin Americans, the strong historical and cultural ties that connect the two are much more alive. From their side, there is still a very real interest to develop a partnership and alliance that goes much deeper than the rather sterile negotiation ritual of the EU-LA summits. What is required is dialogue, mutual trust and the will to invest in a durable partnership and in an alliance for the good on the world scene. The issues that used to frustrate the Latin Americans – the agricultural protection and the fact that the Europeans are partners with the US on this crucial issue in the WTO; the migration issue; the way Spain is enabled to use the EU to further its own interests in Latin America – should be dealt with immediately, as a sign announcing a new era in the relationship. Both sides should be working within an integrated framework that gives due weight to the interests of each partner as well as to the pursuit of common purposes. Thus, energy policy should be made part of a framework that incorporates security and defence, food production and poverty reduction, economic and commercial relations, and political and institutional cooperation.

Latin America: energy and distrust

This new partnership or alliance between LA and Europe might also be instrumental in addressing a number of problems that LA societies are currently facing. These problems have been given different names: bad governance, young democracies, fragile states, or better fragile *societies*. The bottom line is that LA societies suffer from a growing lack of public trust; and that *dis*trust is gaining the upper hand in the relationships between groups, between citizens and their government, as well as between the nations on the continent. Of course, this problem is not new, and it is not exclusive to LA; but it is becoming more serious. Where distrust is spreading, social unrest will block economic growth. Nationalism and militarism will frustrate development and fruitful regional cooperation, and protectionism will come in the place of profitable exchange on open markets. And where distrust is spreading, the common effort to address the shared challenges of our times – energy and food security, climate change and biodiversity, and poverty reduction – will turn into a hopeless enterprise. The logic of distrust and confrontation is a spiralling process, one that is self-feeding and self-propelling.

Problems related to spreading distrust and inflammable societies threaten to interfere with a rational and fruitful use of the rich natural resources of the continent – for growth and development, and for the fruitful integration of LA economies and societies in the world community. Instead, energy resources are used as an asset in a spiralling process of distrust, of hegemonic power and conflict. And when distrust comes to dominate the relationships, the vicious circle of distrust – when left to its own devices – will end up producing widespread energy scarcity on the one hand, and conflict and war on the other hand. Let us illustrate the point with a few concrete cases, taken from LA reality in the last couple of months (second semester of 2007).

Last June and July, in the southern winter, Santiago was confronted with power-cuts and with heavy air pollution. Its power-plants received only a small fraction of the gas that it had contracted with Argentina, so they had to return to expensive imported diesel and coal. Argentina itself had a shortage of gas, receiving only a fraction of the gas that it had contracted with Bolivia. So it had to buy expensive electricity in Brazil, and it had to subsidize the owners of gas-driven cars to compensate for the price differential with gasoline, in order to save gas needed for residential heating. The gas shortages also seriously affected Brazil, especially its industrial zone and power-plants in Sao Paulo and Rio. Chile, Argentina and Brazil are currently building gasification plants, to import and process LNG that is much more expensive than the gas from Bolivia.

All these problems are being caused by the fact that Bolivia is not able to fulfil its contractual obligations for the delivery of gas to Argentina and Brazil. The reason behind this is, that for three years now, no investments have been made in exploration and exploitation. Foreign investors and companies are very cautious to invest because of the political situation in the country. In October, the Bolivian Minister of Energy made a trip to Miami, Washington and Brasilia, trying to attract new investments, but he met with a lot of distrust. Now, finally, it seems that Brazilian Petrobras will come to the rescue and invest in a mixed enterprise for the exploration and exploitation of gas. Petrobras felt that it was the principal victim of Evo Morales' so-called nationalisation, so they were reluctant to deal with Bolivia; but Petrobras itself is under heavy pressure to deliver gas to Rio and Sao Paolo. But also, there was political pressure, through the intervention of Marco Aurelio Garcia, Lula's principal political advisor on external relations. His motive is a geopolitical one: to not leave Bolivian gas to the PDVSA, that is, to Chávez's mercy.

The second example relates to gas in Bolivian society. Gas has been a hot issue in Bolivia for some years already. Former president Sánchez de Lozada's plan to sell gas to Mexico and the US (involving eventually Chile) produced a popular uprising that led to his retreat and flight from the country. The present crisis in the country is, again, related to the control and distribution of gas revenues between central government and the opposition concentrated in the regions where the gas is produced. In Bolivia, gas has become the fuel for a spiralling process of distrust and conflict. Gas, which should be an essential asset for the development of the poorest country of the continent, is setting the country on fire.

The third situation relates to energy nationalism and regional confrontation. In November, Lula proudly let the world know that Brazil had found huge reserves of oil and gas, in the deep sea in front of Rio. It should be clear by now, he said, that God is Brazilian, referring to the Brazilian wealth of natural resources. Just a few days later, Lula announced a 50 percent increase in the defence budget for the acquisition of new weaponry in 2008 and in subsequent years. Already in 2008, US$5 billion will be spent on weapons. Brazil, Lula said, is the happy owner of fresh water, of energy, minerals and food, and those are exactly the things that the world now is in great need of; so we have to be able to protect ourselves and these valuable assets. In that same week, the magazine *Veja* published the results of a survey conducted among high army officials: it turns out that almost two thirds of them consider that an armed conflict with neighbouring Venezuela and Bolivia is very well possible. In the past two years, as a matter of fact, Venezuela has bought Russian armaments for more than US$4.5 billion. The point here is not, of course, to picture Brazil as a warlike country, as it would probably be the last one on the continent interested in promoting instability; but Brazil's behaviour might be seen as an expression of the sense of alertness that is spreading all over the continent.

The fourth example draws more on regional hegemony. In the first week of August, Lula and Chávez both made a trip to a number of LA countries. Lula visited Mexico, Honduras, Nicaragua, Panama and Jamaica. In Mexico he promoted an agreement between Pemex and Petrobras for the deep-sea oil exploration and exploitation in the Gulf of Mexico; an idea, by the way, that was heavily criticised by opposition leader Lopez Obrador who warned against the sell-out of national interests. Lula's other mission in Central America was to promote partnerships for the production of ethanol and biodiesel, or, in his own words, 'to promote a world market of clean, cheap and renewable fuels, and to diversify the energy mix, generate new jobs, democratize the access to energy sources'. Of course, Brazil is in need of CA partners because these countries have free access to the US market, whereas the Brazilians pay a tariff of 54 cents per gallon of ethanol. Chávez for his part visited Argentina (where he signed a contract to build a LNG plant), Uruguay (where he signed a treaty on energy security), Ecuador (where he committed to invest US$5 billion in a new refinery in Manabí) and Bolivia (establishing a new mixed enterprise, starting with an investment of US$600 million in new explorations).

Quite a spectacle: two leaders simultaneously on an energy tour through the continent! While the Brazilians are very careful not to address any matter of competition for regional leadership, let alone confrontation with Chávez, Chávez himself is not so shy. According to Chávez this is, however, not a dispute on continental leadership but a confrontation of different energetic models. Venezuela promotes regional integration on the basis of sharing petroleum and gas, while Brazil is fighting for a model based on agrofuels, similar to the model that is promoted by the US. Indeed, Bush made a bio-fuel trip in LA in March, after signing a cooperation agreement with Brazil on the production and commercialisation of bio-fuels in January 2007. The Brazilians of course hope that this cooperation eventually might lead to the lifting of the US import tariff on ethanol; which would involve a significant geopolitical re-alignment in the Western hemisphere.

Conclusions

Latin America is to occupy a prominent place on the new world map. Energy and politics are intricately intertwined, both in the EU and in LA and elsewhere. The energy issue threatens to disrupt integration and development processes both in the EU and in LA. A solid EU–LA partnership, covering topics such as energy, bio-fuels and food; institutional development and regional integration; and technology and scientific research, will be of great benefit to both continents. At the same time, there is an urgent need for a EU–LA alliance on the global scene, marked by the geopoliticization of the new scarcities (the redefinition of energy and food commodities in terms of national security and strategic power) and the transition from a unipolar to a multipolar world order.

Together, the EU and LA should act as the force for the good. They may divert the ongoing process of geopolitical block formation and polarization, and act and behave consistently as the champions of multilateralism, of a world order governed by international rules and institutions.

Notes and references

1 See the European Commission, 2006, Green Paper on Energy; 2007, Strategic
Energy Review, and 1994, Energy Charter Treaty.
Leonard, Mark, 2007, *Divided World: The Struggle for Primacy in 2020*,
London, CER

China and India: Angels or Devils for Latin America?

Javier Santiso

T he Development Centre of the OECD works a lot on the issue of China. China is very important for us. We just released the second edition of a book on *One Thousand Years of Economic History of China* by a very well-known economist, Angus Maddison, who is a very close collaborator of ours. So, with the help of others, we take, from time to time, a long-term view, as we have been doing on this issue. We were presenting this study in Beijing last month.

Why am I saying all this about the importance of China? Well, because, obviously, China is changing the world economic balance nowadays. This rebalancing is probably the most important event we are witnessing today. Most crucially, what we are witnessing today and what we will be dealing with for the next years - that is this massive plug of the Chinese economy in the world - will lead to a major rebalancing of the world's nations.

As a former banker working on emerging and developing markets, I know the buzz-word is 'decoupling'. Well, this may be the wrong expression for what is going on, but maybe we should talk more about rebalancing in terms of the wealth of nations and the distribution of wealth within nations, and also about the tensions that may result from this. This rebalancing is very important because we tend to think, when we look at world economic issues, and above all if we look at them from an OECD perspective, that somewhere there is a centre and somewhere there is a periphery.

When we use the word 'decoupling' we are still thinking that somehow the periphery is decoupling from the centre. Figure 1 demonstrates why people are afraid that the centre is less and less the centre and the periphery less and less the periphery. Fifty years ago, the OECD countries represented 60 to 70 percent of world GDP, and now they are reaching levels that are below 50 percent.

Figure 1   Share of world GDP in 1952, 1978 and 2003

0%	10%	20%	30%	40%	50%	60%	70%	80%

1952

1978

2003

- USA
- Europe
- Japan
- USSR
- China
- India

Source: OECD Development Centre, 2008; based on OECD Statistics.

So even in terms of share of GDP the balance is changing. If we look at what is going on in terms of foreign direct investments (FDI), in 1970, 100 percent of outgoing FDI was coming from OECD countries. At present they are reaching levels that are below 85 percent for 2006, and they are already below 80 percent in 2007. We are witnessing a major change here and obviously we could multiply the examples as we see in Figures 2 and 3.

Figure 2   Share of Outward FDI, 1970–2006

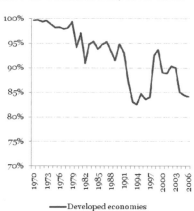

———Developed economies

Source: UNCTAD, World Investment Report 2007

Figure 3   World Investment Shares, 1970–2006

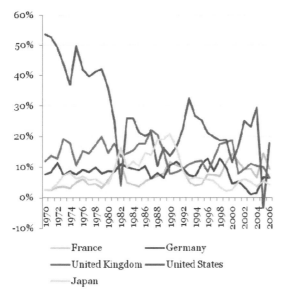

Source: UNCTAD, World Investment Report, 2007

Part of this is related to the Chinese story. China is investing abroad - but not only China, also India, Brazil, Mexico, South Africa, Egypt, Turkey and so on. We can show the official figures of the Chinese Ministry of Commerce in Figure 4.

Figure 4   China's Outward Foreign Direct Investment (1979–2006)

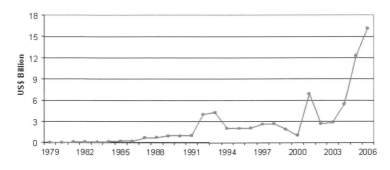

Data sources: Ministry of Commerce and China Statistics Bureau

231

The numbers are still not very large but they are approaching US$20 billion of outgoing FDI, and obviously this trend will continue over the next year. There are also more and more relations between China and Africa. The Development Centre published a study in 2006 on the Chinese presence in Africa and in 2007 another study on the Chinese presence in, and relations - above all trade and investment relations - with Latin America.

I want to make three points here. The first one is about the helping hand that is coming from what is called the Asian drivers, not only China, but beyond China - in particular, India. The second point is about specialization, and, in particular, trade specialization. The third point is about infrastructure as a key for competitiveness. The rise of China can also be seen as a wake-up call for Latin America.

Trade competition: an echo of the Asian boom

I am coming back to this long-term series, starting back in the sixteenth century, from the Angus Maddison study. In Figure 5 the dark and light lines represent the evolution of shares in world GDP of India (dark) and China (light). Until the middle of the nineteenth century, China represented more then 30 percent of world GDP, and if you add this to India's share, the total was roughly 50 percent of world GDP. This was already the case in the middle of the nineteenth century, in what we call today the emerging market or developing countries.

So maybe what we have been witnessing over the last 100 years of world economic history is just a 'parenthesis'. There is another way of showing this by expressing China's GDP as a percentage of world GDP in bars (see Figure 6.)

Figure 5　Evolution of share in world GDP, 1500-2001

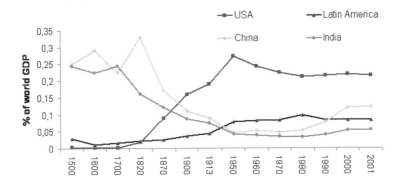

Source: OECD Development Centre, 2008; based on Maddison (2003)

'The World Economy Historical Statistics'

Figure 6　China's GDP (percentage of world total), 1500-2045

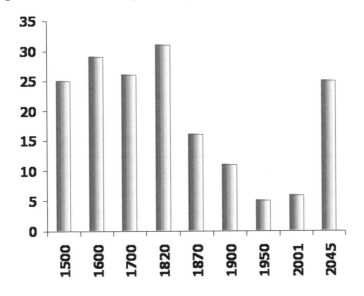

Source: OECD Development Centre, 2008; Based on:

International Financial Statistics and Angus Maddison, 2007

You see China already reaching nearly 35 percent of world GDP in the mid nineteenth century and projected to reach similar levels in the middle of the twenty-first century. According to projections by Angus Maddison, in seven or eight years' time China will already be overtaking the US in terms of nominal GDP (see Figure 7).

Figure 7   Comparative levels of GDP, China, United States and Latin America, 1900-2020

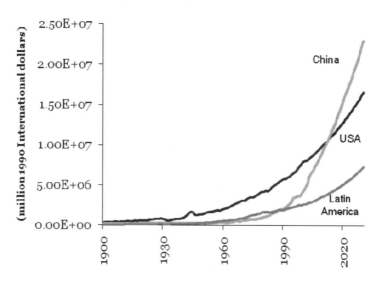

All this is an illustration of what I have been saying, which is that perhaps the last 100 years of world economic history from that point of view has been a parenthesis. There are big differences between now and yesterday. The biggest difference with the past is that the Chinese economy acts as a plug in the world economic system. The impact in the past has not been the same because, in the middle of the nineteenth century, this one country, this empire which was China, was a closed economy.

Incidentally, the title of a book we have published recently on China and Latin America is called *The Visible Hand of China and Latin America*. This is a reference to Adam Smith and his book *The Wealth of Nations*. When Smith was writing his book, he was thinking about how Scotland could grow – this was his obsession – and the country which he had in mind, which was his benchmark already at that time, was China! So not everything is new. What is new is the Chinese or Asian plug in the world economy. The speed of the process is also new. We have done a comparison showing the Chinese take-off since the end of the 1980s and compared it with the take-offs at the end of the 1950s. We took exactly the same years with other countries like Mexico, Brazil, South Korea and Japan, thereby including both Asian and Latin American countries (see Figure 8).

Figure 8 **Take-off of China compared to other countries, GDP in constant prices, 1987-2007**

GDP in constant prices

Source: OECD Development Centre, 2008; based on Datastream

(Economist Intelligence Unit)

What you see is that, yes, there were other take-offs that were impressive. Perhaps the Japanese one was most impressive of all, compared to Brazil, Mexico and the others, but the speed, the nearly vertical line representing the take-off of China has not been seen in the past in any other country.

The Asian boom and its impact on Latin America

When we look at this phenomenon from the Latin American point of view it is important to note that China alone already represents a larger share of world output than the whole continent of Latin America (see Figure 9).

Figure 9   GDP share of world output (WEO, 2005)

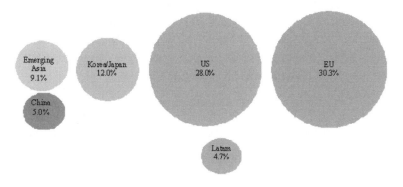

Source: OECD Development Centre, 2008

It is also important to note that Latin America is witnessing a boom in its trade relations with China. This can be very easily explained when you look at the endowment of Latin American countries, mainly in natural resources, including soft and hard commodities. So not only oil, gas, iron ore and copper – and we will be talking about those later – but also food and agro-industrial products, soybeans, for example, are exported from Argentina or Brazil to China. But you also have countries like Venezuela, which is basically an oil-exporting country; Chile and Peru, which are exporting copper; and Argentina, Colombia and Brazil, which are exporting agricultural commodities in addition to, in the case of Brazil, iron ore (see Figure 10).

Figure 10 Natural resources as a percentage of Latin American exports to China

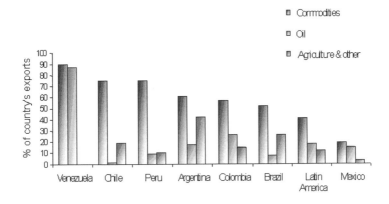

Source: OECD Development Centre, 2008; Based on: National Balance of Payment.

So Latin America is gifted with a lot of natural resources, both soft and hard commodities, that are exactly fitting to the demand of China's very quickly growing economy in need of raw materials that are produced and exported by Latin America.

China as a trade angel or trade devil?

So in the short term this looks like good news to Latin America. It looks like China might be more of a trade angel than a trade devil for Latin America, depending on the time horizon.

I will come back to this point because there are a lot of questions and issues to discuss in relation to it. The positive side can be illustrated by looking at the classical concentration index, which shows how Chinese products are competing with other products of developing countries in third markets.

Figure 11 Export competition with China for selected countries, 2000-2005

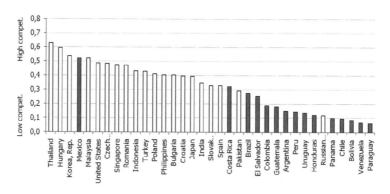

Note: CS and CC coefficients calculated with exports of country i and exports of country j (China, India)

Source: OECD Development Centre, 2008; based on WITS Database, 2007.

If the index approaches 1 this means that nearly 100 percent of the products are directly competing in third markets with Chinese products. So you see that Thailand, Malaysia and some Eastern European countries, but also the US and other OECD countries, are in direct competition with China. This is less so the case with Latin American countries. The exception in Latin America is Mexico and some Central American countries.

Obviously this is the other side of the same story, because Latin American exports, with Mexico as an exception, consist to a large extent of commodities, and are therefore not in competition with China, which does not export commodities, but above all manufactures.

This also raises challenges for Latin American countries. For Mexico it means that it has to catch up in terms of competitiveness with China and, beyond China, also with India. For the other countries this means another challenge, which is how they can diversify their trade beyond commodities, to add value and employment in the industrial sector. When you have such big players as China already increasingly occupying the space — and not only China but also India and Vietnam and Indonesia – obviously for these developing countries the trade diversification issue nowadays is very much different to the way it was twenty or thirty years ago. We carried out the same exercise for Indian exports, showing the same picture, only with lower levels, which means that there is less direct export competition in third markets with India and that there is less competition from the side of most Latin American countries compared to other Asian and Eastern European countries. If you look more carefully at this trade specialisation issue, again not everything is good news for Latin America (see Figure 12).

Figure 12 Vollrath's Relative Comparative Advantage Index for selected Latin American countries, 2005

Good	Product Name	Argentina	Brazil	Chile	Colombia	Mexico	Peru	Venezuela	Average LAC
0	Food & live animals	3.12	1.80	1.24	0.92	-0.16	0.61	-3.32	0.98
1	Beverages and tobacco	1.93	1.73	2.40	0.03	1.69	-1.48	-2.03	1.16
2	Crude mater.ex food/fuel	0.96	1.92	2.53	0.85	-0.63	2.65	-1.01	1.40
3	Mineral fuel/lubricants	1.57	-1.02	-2.30	3.43	1.36	-0.63	7.15	1.21
4	Animal/veg oil/fat/wax	4.28	1.40	-1.08	-0.34	-2.32	-0.51	-5.40	0.90
5	Chemicals/products n.e.s	-0.98	-1.33	-0.81	-1.04	-1.19	-2.04	-2.14	-1.17
6	Manufactured goods	-0.41	0.61	1.38	-0.40	-0.81	0.27	-0.90	-0.22
7	Machinery/transp equipmt	-2.06	-0.64	-1.57	-2.44	0.13	-3.93	-4.34	-0.71
8	Miscellaneous manuf arts	-1.27	-0.40	-2.52	0.07	0.27	0.21	-4.00	-0.21
9	Commodities nes	0.63	8.91	1.74	1.26	-1.21	9.78	2.04	0.81

n.e.s. = not elsewhere specified

Note: Positive values of the index reveals a comparative advantage, whereas a negative indicates a comparative disadvantage.

Source: OECD Development Centre, based on WITS Database, SITC Revision 3 (three-digit classification), 2007

In light figures you see the relative comparative advantage indices, which are negative, meaning that the Latin American countries in the table do not have a comparative advantage for those commodities, while the black figures, on the other hand, indicate in which commodities countries do have a comparative advantage. So you see, for example, that Latin American countries with a few exceptions do not have a comparative advantage in manufactured goods and machinery and transport equipment. The exceptions are Brazil for manufactured goods, and above all Chile. For most of the Latin American countries trade specialization and comparative advantage are in food and live animal products, beverages and tobacco, crude oil, minerals, iron ore, and so on – mostly commodities again. As I was saying, in the short run this is good news because there is a lot of demand coming from China and beyond in Asia. This explains also, by the way, why for the first time in the history of Latin America this continent looks like it is shifting more and more towards Asia.

Until the 1980s the bulk of the trade relations for Latin America were with the US. In the 1990s there was a shift in the direction of Europe with more and more investments coming from Europe. So you had two pillars acting as exogenous engines of growth for Latin America: one was the United States, and after that came Europe. Now you have Asia as a third pillar and exogenous engine of growth. A country like Chile, for example, is exporting more than 36 percent of its total exports to Asia, 15 percent to China alone, which means that it is trading more with Asia than with any other continent in the world, including North America and Europe.

Now this is the reality that we are witnessing for a lot of countries in the region like Peru and Argentina. The good news is that this implies trade diversifications in terms of destination. Latin American countries are trading more and more with partners in Asia and no longer only with Europe and North America. They are now trading also with Middle Eastern countries and so on, but the bulk is with Asia.

The flip side of this is the export concentration in terms of products. The OECD will be monitoring the export concentration for Latin America on an annual basis looking at the Herfindahl Hirschman Index (see Figure 13).

Figure 13 Export concentration in products for Latin American countries, 2001-2006

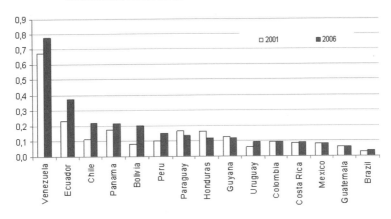

Source: OECD Development Centre, 2008; Based on ECLAC and World Trade
            Integrated Statistics

This is the same type of index as we have seen before, so if you go up to 1, this means that you have exports that are more and more concentrated in a single commodity. What does that means for Venezuela, for example? In 2001 Venezuela was already exporting oil to the amount of nearly 70 percent of its exports. In 2006 this had increased to nearly 80 percent. While the export concentration index is moving up, trade diversification in terms of the composition of export is worsening. You see the same movement in Ecuador, but even in Chile export concentration is increasing, albeit at a lower level than in the other two countries.

It is a very different story if you look at nations like Mexico, Brazil and some Central American countries that have a more diversified basket of export products. In the case of Central America, the basket consists more of agricultural products; in the case of Brazil and Mexico it is more related to manufactured products. But you see that the trend for some other countries is worsening, which means that export concentration is increasing and diversification decreasing.

241

Figure 14 shows how Latin America is increasingly looking towards Asia for its exports.

Figure 14 Latin America: exports to China as percentage of total exports

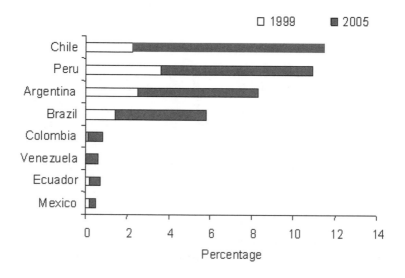

Source: OECD Development Centre, 2008 and UNCTAD, 2007

I mentioned Chile earlier, but it not only Chile, this is also the case with Peru, Argentina, Brazil, Colombia and others. It is also part of the rebalancing that we are witnessing, the explosion of South-South relations that go beyond the pure OECD-non OECD or North-South relation. This is what you could call a South-South rebalance.

Latin America's performance on trade infrastructure

Although China is also a trade opportunity, it raises challenges in the medium term for Latin American countries, as I have been mentioning. Compare, for example, the trade performance of some countries in Latin America with China in terms of shipping time needed for exports – factors such as this can be considered as a wake-up call for Latin America. According to the World Bank the shipping time needed for exports in terms of days on average by Latin American countries is much larger than in China. This is, in particular, the case for Colombia, Venezuela and Peru. (Figure 15).

Figure 15 Time for exports

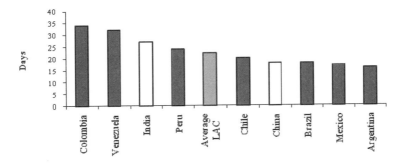

Source: Based on Doing Business Report, World Bank, 2007

This is also the case for the costs of exports, which incorporates not only shipping costs but also trade union transaction costs and so on, which for Latin American countries are on average much higher than for China.

Figure 16 Costs of exports

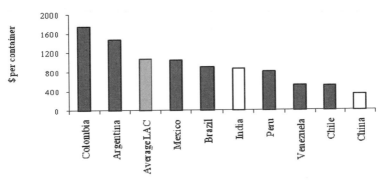

Source: Based on Doing Business Report. World Bank, 2007

Finally, just remember that China is investing nearly 10 percent of its GDP in infrastructure, while Latin America is investing only 2 percent of its GDP. There is a huge room for manoeuvre, for jumping in between the two numbers of 8 or 9 percent, for filling the gap. Some countries are already trying to catch up with big investment projects. These projects are now being developed for Brazil, Mexico, Chile and Panama, but it was about time.

Because, obviously, you are losing competition if you look at the number of days that you need to travel from Mexico along the Pacific Coast to Los Angeles, which is four days of shipping, and twenty days from there to China.

Figure 17 A wake-up call for reforms: The proximity to export markets

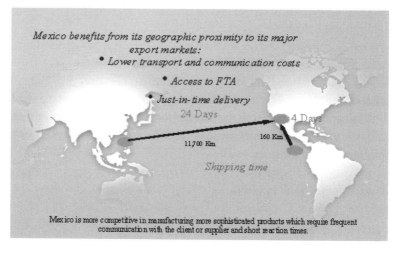

But for the moment this comparative advantage is lost in transaction costs and so on because the infrastructure in Latin American countries is in such bad shape. A possible catch-up can only be achieved through improving the infrastructure, including ports, airports, railways, roads and so on. Massive investments are required because competitiveness will not come from lower wages. On the contrary, wages are on average four times higher in Latin America than in China. Catching up with China can therefore only

244

be achieved through lowering these trade-related costs by investing in better infrastructure.

If you also take the countries of the Pacific Rim into the equation, including Australia and Canada, and you look at the literature on the governance curse, the oil and raw material curse and so on, it is interesting to see what is happening. This comparison is even more telling if you not only include the Pacific Rim countries but also Norway.

Norway as a country is endowed with raw materials and has still been able to diversify. I think we have to rethink what we say about the commodities malediction. It depends what governments do with that. When Norway discovered its oil, it did not have an explosives industry, tanker industries or seismic industries. Norway managed to develop those very value-added intensive industries by making them more competitive and going for international competitive bidding.

The same goes for Canada and Australia. They have huge clusters related to those commodity industries but with very high value added. So now they have seismic industries that are high-performing world leaders. It all depends on how the country, not only the governments but the society and the corporations, react to the situation. It is sad to say that we do not have many countries like Australia, Canada or Norway in Latin America.

Let me add that to have growth is not the same thing as having development. Peru is growing at an 'Asian' rate of growth of 8 percent. But what is the quality of this growth in terms of distribution of wealth within the country? In 2006, Peruvians went to vote, but in spite of its annual growth rate of 8 percent, its huge exports, low inflation and smooth running in terms of the macro economy, people did not feel that, in their day-to-day lives, infrastructure was improving or that their access to education was improving. So obviously, for the lowest quintile, growth is not the same as development.

With the commodity boom that we have today, much depends on whether Latin American countries surf actively or passively on this wave. If they do not prepare in a much more sustainable way for what comes after it, life will become much more complicated for them. I mentioned infrastructure as an issue, but obviously investments are need for a longer-term perspective. which does not mean that more has to be spent.

Take education or innovation, which are also important in relation to the competitiveness of Latin America. You may know that the OECD published the Pisa report on education. It shows that Mexico, Brazil and other Latin American countries are spending nearly the same amount on education as, for example, Poland. But the return on investment in education in terms of efficiency, looking at the scores in mathematics and so on, are much lower in Latin America then in Poland. So it is not so much the amount of money you invest but also the efficiency of your investment in education that counts.

The amazing thing is that for the first time ever in the history of Latin America the question in terms of forecasts of economic

Figure 18 Real GDP growth outlook: investment banks' forecast changes

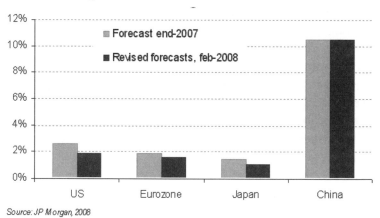

Source: JP Morgan, 2008

growth, behaviour and development for 2008 and 2009 is no longer about what will happen with the US economy, the sub-prime crisis, the real crisis in the US. The big question now is: what will happen with China? If China is more resilient, this means that commodity markets will be more resilient, and if commodity markets are more resilient that will mean that Latin American countries, from a macro-economic point of view, will be more resilient.

Figure 19 Commodity prices (100 Basis Index = 1975)

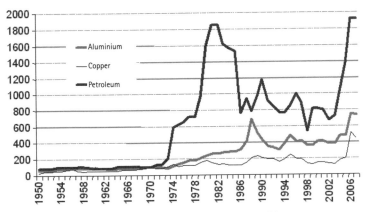

Source: OECD Development Centre, Latin American Economic Outlook, 2008

Here we see the massive shock that we are facing in terms of commodity prices. We show here aluminium, copper and petroleum. My colleagues are doing the same exercise for food prices. When you compare long series even of the last 100 years for these metals and others, you are facing a terms of trade shock that is pretty impressive. So that means that in the face of these developments China is becoming more important for Latin American countries then it has ever been before.

China–Africa Energy Relations

Yang Guang

I will deal with the subject of China-Africa energy relations and their impact in three sections.

Firstly, very briefly, I will give some background on China-Africa relations in general; secondly I will be more specific about China-Africa energy relations; and finally I will try to evaluate the impact of China-Africa energy relations in different areas.

China–Africa relations in general

When we talk about China-Africa energy relations we have to bear in mind that China-Africa relations have a very long history, going back to the eighth century. For instance, the very famous navigator Jen Hue made three visits to the East Coast of Africa in the early fifteenth century.

This relation was interrupted later on by the colonization of the African continent and it was not resumed in a massive way until the 1950s and '60s of the twentieth century, when Africa was decolonized. Since then, China-Africa relations have become a kind of strategic cooperation. Between 1960 and 1980 this strategic cooperation was based mostly on political considerations and came in the form of a kind of politically neutral support.

Since 1980, China-Africa relations have seen some change. Economic cooperation has become a new and very important dimension. Since the year 2000, when the China-Africa Cooperation Forum was formed, the relation has become much stronger. This Forum as a new mechanism has provided a very strong impetus to the bilateral relations. The value of trade and investment has increased since then and the Chinese government has also increased its assistance to African countries.

The forms of assistance have also diversified. Apart from the grants and loans provided to Africa, the Chinese government has exempted foreign aid loans that African governments owed to the Chinese government at the end of 2005. China has also removed the import duty on a large number of African products to favour their entrance into the Chinese market.

As China considers its relation to Africa as a kind of strategic cooperation, it has observed some principles which have not changed for many years. For instance, China cherishes equality and mutual respect in its relations with Africa and is reluctant to impose any political conditions on African countries. At the economic level, for instance, China looks for win-win situations and adheres to the principle of shared development.

China-Africa energy relations

With rapid economic growth over the past thirty years China's demand of energy has significantly increased. So far China has managed to achieve self-sufficiency of energy supply to a large extent: 95 percent of energy consumption is supported by domestic production simply because coal is the leading energy carrier in China's primary energy structure and it accounts for around 60 percent of China's total energy consumption. This was the case in 2002 and will still be the case in the year 2020 (see Figure 1).

Figure 1 China's primary energy demand, 2002 and 2020

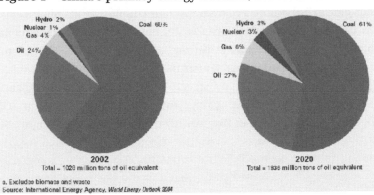

a. Excludes biomass and waste
Source: International Energy Agency, *World Energy Outlook 2004*

But there are some problems with the oil supply in China. China used to be a net exporter of oil in the past but with the increased demand and consumption of oil China became net importer of oil in 1993. With the growth of demand of oil and the weakening of the supply of oil domestically you can see that the gap between demand and domestic production has been widening to such an extent that by the year 2006 China had already become the third largest importer in the world, next to the United States and Japan. (see Figure 2).

Figure 2   China's oil-demand and domestic supply, 1990-2005

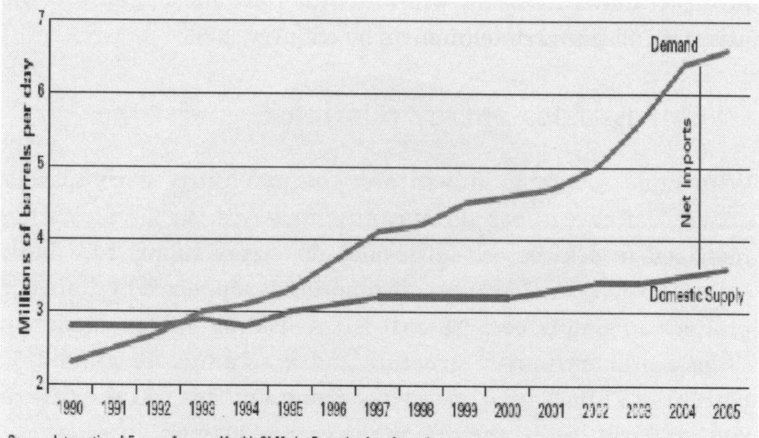

Source: International Energy Agency, *Monthly Oil Market Report* (various issues)

With China's requirements to import more oil from abroad, Africa has gradually become a more important supplier for its oil imports. In 1995 the share of Africa in China's import of oil was 11 percent, but by 2005 it was already 31 percent, and Africa became the second largest source of oil imports, after the Gulf. (see Figure 3).

By 2005 Angola provided 14 percent of China's oil imports and became supplier number two, just after Saudi Arabia. (see Figure 4).

Figure 3   China's crude imports by region, 1995 and 2005

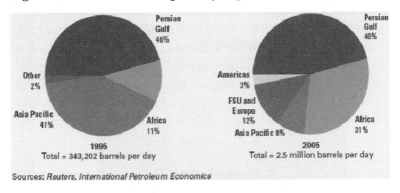

1995
Total = 343,202 barrels per day

2005
Total = 2.5 million barrels per day

Sources: *Reuters, International Petroleum Economics*

Figure 4   China's crude imports by country, 2005

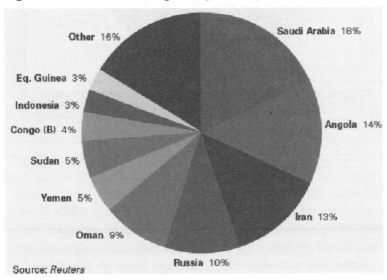

Source: *Reuters*

Apart from buying oil from international markets, Chinese companies, like many others, have also invested abroad to produce oil. This is just what many companies in oil-importing countries are doing. Some people argue that this kind of overseas investment in oil industries is organized government behaviour. Actually, I think that that is wrong.

Figure 5   Chinese NOC's production in Africa, 2006

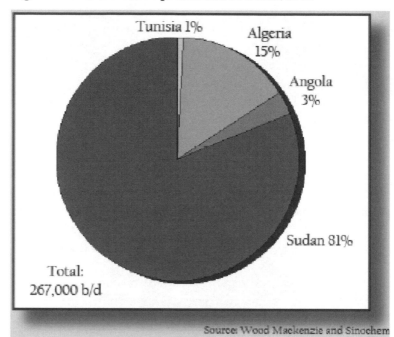

Tunisia 1%

Algeria 15%

Angola 3%

Sudan 81%

Total: 267,000 b/d

Source: Wood Mackenzie and Sinochem

If Chinese companies invest abroad they are basically driven by economic motivations. Firstly, because, as the domestic resources are scarce, the oil companies in China need to make use of resources abroad to continue their production, and, secondly, because since the year 2000 constantly high oil prices have given a very strong incentive for Chinese oil companies to make profits abroad. And thirdly, many African countries have improved their investment environment, making it very attractive for Chinese oil companies.

The fourth reason is that Chinese companies find that they also enjoy some comparative advantage compared to the Western-established major oil companies, especially because their cost of labour and equipment made in China are much lower. When I talk about the cost of labour I am not only talking about the cost of operators but also of the salaries of the managers, the physicists and the geologists.

The fifth reason is a rather technical one. This is because African crude oil in many of the cases has a low sulphur content and this fits nicely with the requirements of Chinese refineries. As a lot of Chinese companies that are active in Africa also own refineries in China, they can put the crude oil they get from Africa directly into their refineries in China without having to make additional investments to upgrade their refineries.

Finally, as the Chinese government also sees the importance of diversification of the sources of imported oil, it provides some incentives to Chinese companies, for example by providing subsidized interest loans by the Exim Bank and also by providing insurance by the National Export Credit Insurance Campany. The Chinese companies benefit from these incentives.

The impact of China-Africa energy relations

Here I would like to discuss three kinds of impact; firstly, the impact on the international oil price. As is shown in Figure 6, since the beginning of the new century the crude oil price has increased significantly, both in real and in nominal terms.

Figure 6   Crude oil prices, real and nominal

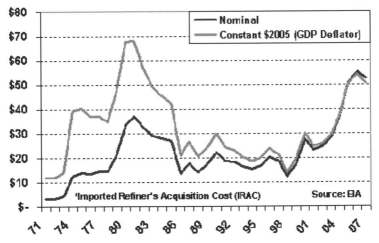

253

There are many reasons for this. Some people argue that this is because of the devaluation of the US dollar. This may be true, but this can only explain why the nominal oil price has increased. But the question is why even the real oil price in constant US dollars has increased significantly. Other people argue that this is because of speculations in the financial market. This may also be true, but this does not explain why the international market and the forward market did not play a similar role in the 1980s and 1990s, despite the fact that the oil forward market has been in existence since the early 1980s.

So in my personal opinion, when we talk about the increase of oil price we should not neglect two very important factors. They are the fundamental factors behind the high international oil price. First is the tight spare capacity of supply (see Figure 7). Spare capacity of supply is defined as the kind of existing capacity that is not yet put into use and can be mobilized and put into use immediately if some shortage or some disruption of supply occurs in another part of the market. For a very long time, this kind of spare capacity was very large and it played a role as guarantee for the security of the international oil supply.

Figure 7   Erosion in OPEC spare capacity

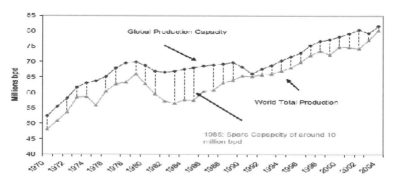

Source IMF:NP

* Spare capacity around 2% of global oil demand in 2004 despite increase in OPEC production capacity

254

But with the constant increase of demand and the shortage of investment in the oil industry since 1992, basically because of the low oil price, the spare capacity of production has been eroded: it became smaller and smaller. In Figure 7 you can see that in 1983 the world spare capacity was 1,300 barrels per day. On the other hand if, by the year 2006, smaller and medium-sized oil-exporting countries stopped producing and exporting, then we will not be able to find alternative sources of supply. What the market will face is an absolute shortage of oil supply.

What makes things worse is that not only the spare capacity of oil production has declined, but also the spare capacity of refineries and of tankers for oil transportation has declined. If you look at Figure 8, you can see that by the year 2004 no spare refinery capacity existed anymore.

Figure 8   Cushion of spare capacity declined in all parts of the oil supply chain

So the shortage of capacity of supply is a very important reason behind the high oil price, as it makes the international oil market very vulnerable and very sensitive. In this regard China has contributed to some extent to this kind of decline of supply capacity. But China is not the only one, because countries like the

US and India have also increased their imports significantly over the past six or seven years.

The other very important reason behind the high oil price is the very tight geopolitical situation in the oil-producing areas, especially in the Middle East. If you look at the history of international markets you can see that since the 1950s the market has experienced many disruptions (see Figure 9), but most of them were not caused by economic factors. Most of them were caused by geopolitical tensions, especially in the oil-producing areas in the Middle East.

Figure 9   Major world oil-supply disruptions

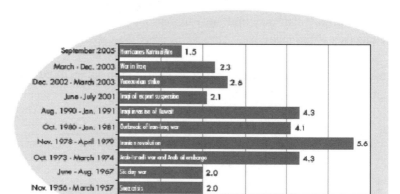

Unfortunately, since the beginning of the new century, the situation in the Middle East has become much worse compared to the situation in the 1990s. The war in Iraq, the Iranian nuclear issue and others have contributed to the aggravation of the situation in the Middle East. All these changes have made the international oil market even more vulnerable and may lead to further disruption of oil supply.

The second impact I want to discuss here is whether China's relations with Africa have threatened Western interests. I would say not. Or, I could say that this kind of argument is a bit exaggerated.

Let me just give you a couple of figures to demonstrate this. First, the volume of all trade of oil: by the year 2006 only 10 percent of the oil produced in Africa flowed to the Chinese market. At the same time 32 percent flowed to the US and 36 percent to Europe. So by 2006, China was not taking the bulk of African oil.

Secondly, according to an evaluation done by the consultant firm Wood Mackenzie in March 2007, the values of assets owned by different kinds of oil companies in Africa are also very telling. Nowadays most of the oil resources or asset values are still owned by African countries themselves. African countries own around 55 percent of all asset values, Western oil companies or so-called International Oil Companies own 33 percent, while Chinese companies owned only 22.6 percent of the total asset value of investments in Africa.

Figure 10 Commercial value of oil investments in Africa

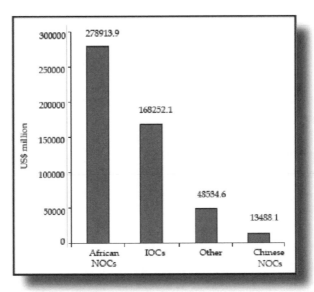

Source: Wood Mackenzie, March 2007

Thirdly, although China can produce some oil in Africa, its production is still limited compared to the major Western oil companies. In Figure 11, you can see that the production of Chinese companies represents approximately one third of the production of Exxon-Mobil or Total from France.

Figure 11 2006 Production in Africa by selected companies

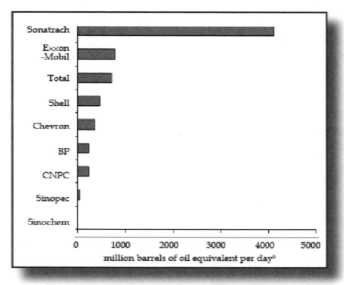

Source: International Oil Daily, Wall Street Journal, Wood Mackenzie & Sinochem

Finally, I want to discuss what kind of impact China-Africa oil relations have had on African countries. Firstly, I think that China, by developing energy ties with African countries, has contributed to their development, even if Chinese companies, like I said before, have benefitted as well. If you look at the macro-economic indicators, all those countries having energy relations with China, such as Sudan and Angola, have achieved very rapid growth rates in the year 2007. Sudanese growth rate, for example, has been 12.8 percent, and the Angolan growth rate has been 15.9 percent.

Secondly, Chinese investments have helped African countries to improve their production structure and promote their industrialization process. Chinese companies also paid attention to possibilities of forward linkages, for example in the Sudan. When the CNPC went to the Sudan for the first time, the first thing they did was to explore and develop oil resources. Then they moved to build their first refinery and now they are building their second refinery. The first refinery already made the Sudan self-sufficient in oil products of different kinds. This was done in just over ten years. Compare this with, for example, the Anglo Persian Oil Company established in Iran in 1906. Over a hundred years have passed and still Iran has still not been able to achieve self-sufficiency in oil products. It still has to import 60 percent of its gasoline from abroad while for Sudan this has been achieved in just over ten years. This is a very big achievement.

In addition, some of the secondary products of the refinery nowadays are used to produce chemicals and fertilizers in factories. This is what I saw when I visited Sudan last January: with the growth of this kind of industry, a small town emerged next to the refinery. There used to be the desert, but now there is a small town. Urbanization is making progress.

Thirdly, Chinese oil companies are increasingly aware of the importance of fulfilling their corporate social responsibility. This has resulted in more contributions by Chinese companies to social development in African countries. For instance, I have made calculations showing that when Chinese companies invest in Sudan 71 percent of the labour-force is Sudanese.

Over the past ten years, CNPC, China's leading company, also spent a lot of money on social expenditures, including building 22 schools, 101 health clinics, a bridge and a road, and also supported African students to carry out their studies in China.

Finally, the Chinese CNPC has also paid a lot of attention to environmental protection, for example by constructing an artificial lake near its refinery in Sudan. The lake is very beautiful and its water is processed from the waste water of the refinery: it is very clean and attracts many birds and fish.

China is also paying attention to the political situation in the African region, and contributes, along with the other permanent members of the Security Council and Germany, substantially to UN Peacekeeping Operations. So far it has dispersed approximately 1,700 peacekeepers around Africa. Many of those are not stationed in oil-producing nations. Some of those are also based in oil-producing countries. In Darfur, for example, there are more then 200 Chinese peacekeepers, so I would not say that the presence of peacekeepers is directly linked to whether there are oil resources or not. On the other hand, there is a kind of general approach in Africa. Because of the tribal linkages and Africa's very complicated international relations, conflicts in Africa may very easily spread to other countries. So if you want to contribute to stability and peace in Africa, you need to do it wherever you have conflicts and not just focus on oil-producing countries.

As China has an interest in stable international relations contributing to uninterrupted supplies of oil and raw materials, it has made some diplomatic efforts to reduced tensions, not only in Africa but also in other parts of the world, and especially the Middle East. Let me give you a few examples. In the Middle East one of the breakthroughs in Chinese diplomatic history has been that it has, since the late 1990s, sent a special envoy to discuss the Palestinian issue. His mandate was to mediate between Israel and the Palestinians so that they could sit together and talk.

China has also cooperated with the international community, and especially the other permanent members of the Security Council, in peacefully resolving the Iranian nuclear issue. I think this is also related to the energy security concern. In Africa, one of the typical examples is Chinese efforts to persuade the Sudanese government to show more flexibility with regard to the concerns of the international community on the Darfur issue.

A final word on democracy. To my perception, the Chinese government has no specific idea on or preference for any political regime, because its policy has always been not to interfere in domestic issues in other countries. This makes sense because, if you look at the diversity of cultures and histories of different kinds of countries, you cannot impose one model on them.

Moreover, these countries are also in different stages of development and for each stage of development there might be a specific solution. So if you talk about democratic and authoritarian regimes you need to be very careful with your prescriptions. Personally, I think democracy is very good. It reflects one of the highest values of humankind, but you need to accept different kinds of form or realization : you cannot just impose one model on all kinds of countries.

New Scarcities, International Trade and Climate Change

Frank Heemskerk

I would like to take this opportunity to consider some of the trade aspects of scarcity. First, I will discuss open markets and competition, and the crucial elements of trust and confidence they need in order to work. Secondly, I will address the issue of carbon leakage and the role trade can play in climate-change-related policies.

I will not consider water, even though shortages can have profound consequences for communities, particularly the very poor.

Social justice should not to be left to markets

I believe open markets are the most efficient way to organise economic activity and allocate scarce resources, globally and at home. No other form of organisation can provide a real alternative. But 'believing in a market economy does not mean embracing a market society', as Lionel Jospin famously said.

Governments and regulators have a very important role to play in providing and safeguarding social assets, and in providing social justice, i.e. basic services like education, health care, pension systems and social security. That is not something to be left to markets.

Consent and confidence

However, market performance and trust in open markets are not determined by regulation or regulators alone. Market participants themselves play a key role in fostering the consent and confidence necessary for trade. Anyone who takes part in an internet auction on a website like eBay will look closely at the feedback available on the buyers and sellers. Are they dependable? Do they keep their word? There are encouraging signs that the same mechanism is at work in the globalisation of economic activity. 'World connectors' and networks like it play that important role.

What can a Minister for Foreign Trade do? My mission is to implement trade policies that open up opportunities to people who are currently excluded.

Opening up markets in a globalising environment

Building on the development assistance we provide, we must help the poor overcome the entry barriers to the global market. That 'development dimension' will remain important well beyond the current Doha Round. At the same time, we must care for groups in our own countries that are in danger of exclusion. Social justice means preparing people for tomorrow, through education and training and by meeting basic needs. It is not about protecting yesterday's profits and vested interests. Protectionism does not protect people.

There are fears that globalisation will lead to a race to the bottom, to a general lowering of standards, especially social and environmental standards. But many data show that foreign buyers and investors bring high standards with them, which then spread. And conversely, that companies trading or investing in more demanding markets take home the higher standards they encounter. International trade and FDI bring international standards to developing countries.

The example of food scarcity

In decades past, food scarcity was overcome by protectionism, by export restrictions and by consumer subsidies. This resulted in the exclusion of the poorest countries, denying them access to the big agricultural markets of the US and Europe.

A better response, which these days is at the fore of European policymakers' thinking, is innovation and improvements in technology. We already have a raft of technological measures that can increase food production relatively quickly. Higher productivity per hectare is possible if we invest in better production and irrigation methods and, above all, in the prudent liberalisation of specific sectors in developing countries.

Competition policy

Let me take competition policy as another example where we should move from protection to open markets. Powerful cartels and the abuse of dominant positions cannot be tolerated in a free market. The trading community agreed, in 1996, at the WTO Summit in Singapore, that competition had to be addressed. But the matter was effectively scrapped from the Doha Round in 2003. Some countries thought competition was one item too many on an already full and challenging agenda. Others were reluctant to address the issue of market regulation and anti-cartel measures because they thought it might jeopardise their own autonomy. Clearly, the public good lost out. Powerful cartels extract tens of billions of dollars from developing countries. And yet, to my disappointment, the international community is unable to organise a collective response.

Global markets need global governance

As I pointed out earlier, markets can only work if people believe in them; if there is trust. People consent to business transactions because they trust other parties and have confidence in the outcome. The authorities have always played a part. In simpler times they enforced the accuracy of weights and measures. In today's more complex world, states intervene in many more ways to ensure that markets work efficiently. Rules are necessary to sustain consent and confidence in the markets. But it is precisely in the area of rule-making that states have been unable to keep pace with global economic integration. Global markets need global governance.

There is a compelling case for greater global and corporate governance. Regulatory cooperation has received a boost from the recent credit crisis. A connected global economy, facing global challenges, can only be addressed by global, multilateral responses.

Climate change

Turning to climate change, it is amazing how dramatically the political debate has moved over the past few years. The Al Gore film, *An Inconvenient Truth*, and the Stern report have been influential. What can trade policy contribute? Is trade part of the problem or part of the solution?

At the moment, unfortunately, trade is part of the problem. Transport using carbon-based fuels is an inherent part of modern trade. But to suggest that we should stop trading with faraway places would be going too far. For where are these faraway places? They are mostly developing countries. Trade has driven development and poverty reduction in Asia and we cannot deprive other regions of the same opportunities just because transport is involved.

Sustainable globalization means spreading access to the benefits of an open world, not excluding whole groups of countries on the basis of geography, particularly as developing countries face the greatest challenges when dealing with the consequences of climate change.

Let's look at the positive side. How can trade help us meet the challenge of climate change? Achieving emissions targets – Kyoto and its successors – will depend on the technologies available to industry. Maximising trade in green technology will drive down emissions.

So we need an open global market in environmental technologies, one that allows green technology to be traded freely, with the least cost and impediment, from North to South and also between the economies of the developing world. The Doha Round negotiations to liberalize trade in environmental goods and services – a market worth some US$550 billion – must be revived!

Open trade is essential to ensure sustainable globalisation in the face of climate change. Without the stimulus of open markets, the growth and innovation we need to meet the challenge of climate change will not be forthcoming.

I will use carbon leakage to illustrate the various aspects that need to be addressed by trade and environmental measures.

Carbon leakage

Carbon leakage is the risk that strict standards on CO_2 emissions here will lead to production 'leaking' away to poorer countries with lower standards. It is frequently used as an argument against higher environmental standards.

The Dutch government broadly and warmly supports the European Commission's proposals on the Emissions Trading System. But, equally, I understand that anxieties and uncertainties must be addressed. We need objective criteria this year to identify sectors at risk of carbon leakage, and a clearer view of the overall implications. We will then be in a better position to identify specific measures in the light of the results of the climate negotiations.

That said, some governments, politicians and companies are calling for trade measures to solve carbon leakage. They generally advance three reasons for trade measures:

1. They protect competitiveness here in the Netherlands or in the EU;
2. They combat environmental degradation abroad (outside the EU); and
3. They put pressure on otherwise unwilling negotiating partners.

To stimulate the debate, let me illustrate what these measures might mean in the real world. This example will make clear that using trade measures to put pressure on such negotiating partners is not a very effective approach.

China produces a third of the world's steel, but exports only 8 percent of that amount. The remaining 92 percent of its steel production is for the domestic Chinese market and is not for export. Given these figures, will trade measures have a big impact? What is more, Chinese exporters are best in class, also from a climate point of view. The problem lies chiefly with the other 92 percent of Chinese production, which is purely domestic. Will trade measures affect the firms responsible?

As Trade Minister, I do not make climate-change policy. But I do know something about the effects of trade measures and about the WTO. Experience shows that there are usually more efficient instruments to solve a given problem than trade measures.

Another argument often used for trade measures against carbon leakage is that our competitiveness is at stake. We're imposing compliance costs that companies in other parts of the world do not have to pay. However, the first, best and most efficient solution probably lies in mechanisms to control the cost of doing business, notably by cutting taxes, cutting red tape and reducing the administrative burden for companies on the one hand; and in stimulating innovation and allocating emission rights freely on the other.

Finally, if we want to take carbon-leakage measures elsewhere because our main concern is the environment, it is probably more efficient to focus on polluters *there* rather than on imports *here*, which may be produced in modern factories that are more carbon friendly than some of our own.

So trade measures are very likely to be the 'second-best' option.

Nevertheless, when might their use be justified? Turning to WTO conformity, Director-General Pascal Lamy has explained that the only answer to whether the WTO allows carbon leakage measures is: 'It depends.' This does not mean that anything goes, but that any measure will have to be carefully tailored.

Last March, the European Council highlighted the importance of international negotiation as the best way to counter carbon leakage. Broad international support would also enhance the legitimacy and effectiveness of trade measures in the handful of countries that are unwilling to cooperate.

The European Council was wise to put the climate-change negotiations before trade measures; the outcome can now inform our evaluation of any trade measures that are proposed.

Climate change is precisely the kind of global common ground that requires global governance. Trade threats and beggar-thy-neighbour policies have no place here. Instead we have a framework of rules, dialogue and conflict resolution. Current trade and financial institutions were established in response to the errors of the 1930s. Climate change must not lead to a repetition of those errors. An expression of collective responsibility is required after the crises of 2008.

To conclude

I trust you agree that social justice, open markets and sustainability are important issues, and that trade policy has a contribution to make in all these areas. There is no better mechanism than the market for distributing scarce resources, whether they be energy, food or greenhouse gases. We need to work harder on regulatory cooperation, governance and rule-making to foster the confidence and consent that are crucial to the effectiveness of the markets. For that to happen in a global world – in a connected world – we need trust and confidence and therefore networks like World Connectors.

Summary of Lectures and Conclusion

Bernard Berendsen

The 2007-2008 SID lecture series on Emerging Global Scarcities and Power Shifts started from the assumption that energy, food and water are becoming more scarce, which will result in steady price increases that may well continue for some time to come. The economic downturn that started in the middle of 2008 might very well put this assumption to the test, but the lectures clearly demonstrated that these scarcities are interrelated. One example is energy prices and environmental concerns affecting the production and utilization of bio-fuels that compete with food for land and water. Price changes of raw materials, energy and food also have direct consequences for the relative position of countries on the economic world map as well as for the development perspectives of developing countries. Power shifts between and within regions are the consequence of shifting money and of trade flows increasing relative wealth in some countries and continents and decreasing relative wealth in others.

In this summary as in the book the lectures have been arranged in the following way. The scene is set by the lectures on *emerging global scarcities* in food, energy and water. They not only demonstrate how they are interrelated but also what considerations played a role in policy setting and formulating policy responses.

In the area of *food*, Gerda Verburg, the Netherlands Minister of Agriculture, Nature and Food Quality, spoke about the challenge to find a new balance between social, economic and ecological interests with regard to food, bio-fuels and bio-diversity. Rudy Rabbinge focussed on the issue of bio-fuels versus food production, followed by Kornelis Blok who considered the role of bio-energy under the limitations of climate change. Andre Faaij put the production of bio-fuels into perspective by pointing out that only 20 million hectares of land worldwide is used for the production of crops for bio-fuels, whereas 5,000 million hectares is used for food production. In the end, he concluded, there are no simple choices and resources need to be diversified from food crops to perennial crops and from cultivated to marginal and degraded lands.

In the area of *energy* Michael Klare gave an overview of global energy competition, qualifying energy as the most pressing, the most difficult and the most dangerous issue facing the world community today. Jonathan Stern spoke about the European response to the Russian challenge, starting from the assumption that Europe will have to import some of its oil and increasingly also gas from Russia. Catrinus Jepma was less optimistic about Russia being prepared and able to invest more in enhancing its capacity to produce oil and gas in response to increasing demand abroad. All three gave attention to the geopolitical consequences of the growing scarcity in energy, notwithstanding the recent downfall in energy prices. Coby van der Linde, coming at the end of the series in September 2008, felt compelled to answer for the sudden downswing in oil price after reaching its climax in July 2008. She insisted that due to lagging new investments, increasing demand worldwide and rising marginal cost of supply, energy prices are bound to go up again in the end.

Finally in the area of *water*, Jan Lundqvist related growing water scarcity to the food crisis, climate change and the growing demand for bio-fuels. He concluded that we should have a closer look at what is happening in the food chain and see how we can reduce losses there and wastage in the household sector. Michel Camdessus focussed on water as a basic human right and linked it to sanitation. With regard to the water-related Millennium Development Goals, he noted Africa is lagging far behind. He therefore highly recommended the Rural Water Supply and Sanitation Initiative, which has the ambitious aim to tackle the main obstacles toward the MDGs and the implementation in 2025 of the African vision, namely water and sanitation for all.

Secondly, *climate change* was given attention in three lectures. First, Gurmit Singh dealt with the phenomenon of climate change itself, the international negotiations over the last two decades and the position of the different countries and country groupings in the negotiations. Jan Pronk gave special attention to the position of developing countries in the debate on climate change and its effect on their development perspectives. Finally, Pier Vellinga insisted that the risk of irreversible climate change is too great to be allowed to happen but that it is technically and economically feasible to do something about it. It will be a race against time and global cooperation will be the bottleneck: climate change is the ultimate test for international relations.

The last lectures dealt with the subject of *power shifts*. Reinaldo Figueredo raised the subject of energy issues redefining Latin American politics. Cor van Beuningen made a plea for a new partnership between Europe and Latin America that may also contribute to Latin America making rational and fruitful use of its natural resources. Javier Santiso focussed on China and India and how economic growth in these emerging economies is affecting trade relations with Latin America. Yang Guang paid special attention to the increasing role of China in Africa. Frank Heemskerk finally asked how trade can help us to meet the challenge of climate change and argued that maximising trade in green technology will drive down emissions.

Emerging Global Scarcities

Food

Gerda Verburg began by making a distinction between public goods (biodiversity and climate), semi-public goods (land and water) and private resources (food and fuels). This illustrated the complexity of issues the lecture series was dealing with and marked the responsibility of governments with respect to claims which different, competing uses make on both private and public resources.

She wanted to respond to the challenge of finding a new balance between social, economic and ecological interests with regard to *food, bio-fuels and biodiversity*. Starting with food and food production, she noted great improvements in Asia and Latin America, while Africa is lagging behind. World food production has outstripped the enormous growth in population; the average yield has doubled; new crop varieties, fertilizers and other quality inputs have boosted productivity. However, the costs of inputs are rising and there is little scope to increase the area of land or the amount of fresh water available for agriculture: another manifestation of a new emerging scarcity.

New investments and more innovative solutions in relation to production are required, she concluded. It is a matter of improving productivity, facilitating chain development, stimulating local and regional markets and improving access to the international markets. But the intention to increase food production is competing with the growing demand for biomass to generate energy, so sustainable development could be threatened.

Climate change to a large extent is caused by CO_2 emissions that result from the use of fossil fuels for energy production. Global warming as one manifestation of climate change results in rising sea levels. Climate change and global warming affect the prospects for food production, biodiversity and the development potential of developing countries in many ways. The increasing scarcity of fossil fuels, as well as the damaging effects of climate change and global warming make the development of alternative and more sustainable energy resources, including renewables and biomass, even more urgent.

This process is further stimulated by the recent spurt in economic development in other regions. This presents opportunities for developing countries and a chance to reduce their dependence on imported oil and develop the rural economy, but Verburg warned that 'we have to make sure that bio-fuels come from sustainable sources'.

She finally raised the issue of biodiversity. Biodiversity is required to maintain our ecosystem, which should be able to address the needs of future generations. The challenge is to find a way to counter-balance human activities and to cancel out the negative effects of that behaviour on biodiversity, for example by creating ways of paying for biodiversity and reducing the impact of our country on biodiversity in other countries.

Rudy Rabbinge focussed on *food and bio-fuels*. First of all, he noted the importance of agriculture in economic development, which is again recognised and demonstrated in one of the latest World Development Reports and also in present Dutch development cooperation policies. He sketched three ways of responding to external challenges in a historical context at the time of the industrial revolution: forcing structural change by way of liberalisation, the British way; preserving the existing structure by protectionist policies, the French and German response; and raising productivity and enhancing competitiveness through innovation, the Dutch way.

Rising productivity has now become the characteristic of modern agriculture, exemplified by the green revolution, not only in Asia in the 1970s, but also before that in Britain and the US in the late 1950s and the Netherlands in the early 1950s. As a consequence, agricultural growth has been substantially larger than world population growth.

Rabbinge distinguished seven mega-trends in relation to agricultural productivity growth: (1) increase in productivity increased per hectare, per man hour and per kilogram of external input, (2) change in the character of agriculture from skilfulness in the utilization of input to industrialisation, (3) improvement in chain management, (4) better management of the environment, landscape and nature, (5) movement from a linear to an interactive knowledge model, (6) more attention to matters of food quality and diet composition and (7) introduction of agricultural production for bio-energy.

Rabbinge doubted the wisdom to go along with the seventh mega-trend. In order to come to grips with the food versus bio-fuel issue he considered it necessary to better understand the basics of the primary production process and understand that only a very small part of the energy that comes from the sun is used by plants to produce proteins, fats, starch and so on; there is an annual energy efficiency of between 0.5 and 2.3 percent only. This alone should bring us to the conclusion that second-generation bio-fuels are to be preferred over first-generation fuels.

But there are other considerations. Firstly, the emission of greenhouse gases is different for the different types of agricultural products. Secondly, there is depletion of the soil: inputs are required in the form of fertilizer, but also reserves of phosphorus are limited. Thirdly, large areas of agricultural land would be needed to produce bio-fuels, and, finally, the energy efficiency of bio-fuel production is limited.

Rabbinge is sceptical about using marginal land for energy production to avoid competition with food. If land is marginal, it requires more inputs to yield the same productivity as on richer soils. And if the economic value of energy crops is lower than that of food crops, economic production of energy crops will not be feasible on marginal land.

Instead of presenting bio-diesel as the solution, Rabbinge pleads that we move away from a bio-fuel to a bio-based economy, where new products with high added value in new markets are predominant. We should also move away from the petro-chemical route towards the bio-chemical route, which is much more useful for making highly sophisticated products.

He concluded that food security can be obtained, but that it requires a diet change that does not jeopardise food security. Diet change is already taking place in the developing world, for which high-productivity agriculture and productivity increase per hectare are required. Moving in the direction of bio-fuel may have detrimental effects because of growing competition from different claims. Solar energy might bring the ultimate solution while bio-mass will only play a minor role.

Kornelis Blok, in his comments on Rabbinge's lecture, made reference to a number of scenario analyses to demonstrate what the role of bio-energy might be under the limitations that climate change is posing us. Those limitations force us to reduce the use of fossil fuels drastically and to opt for a combination of reducing energy use and making use of a range of different sources. In the scenarios presented by IPCC, conventional fossil fuels will gradually be phased out and there will eventually be a huge contribution from biomass. He admitted that there is a lot of debate surrounding all these energy sources and strategies, which include nuclear energy, bio-energy, carbon storage and even energy conservation. He concluded that we will probably need all those options and probably cannot do without any of them.

He then focussed on the role of biomass for energy purposes and noted that in the agricultural and food production cycle there are all kinds of residues resulting in waste flows that seem to be a good and ample source of energy, even if part of that may be required to maintain soil fertility.

There is also the question of whether in the future there will be enough land available for direct energy crops. Here he again referred to scenario analyses with varying levels of population growth, varying diets and so on, and also with different technology development and GDP growth rates. Especially with high technology development and low population growth, there is the likelihood of increasing areas of abandoned land, especially in Russia, but also in China, Latin America and Africa, indicating that land available for the production of bio-energy might be increasing. The most optimistic scenario ends with bio-energy production of more then 1000 exajoules, while in the lowest scenario it is more or less equal to the current production level of between 200 and 400 exajoules.

According to Blok there are ample opportunities for the development of local bio-energy systems. Experiments with plants like jatropha have demonstrated that the development of local bio-energy can also contribute to local prosperity. Locally produced bio-energy can be used to feed diesel engines and supply electricity to local grids. Charcoal is another interesting example with all kinds of applications, including the production of iron and steel. Other local energy sources include the production of bio-diesel from fat of pigs and the production of ethanols from waste streams.

Blok concluded that it is extremely important to introduce a system of checks and balances, such as certification systems, for bio-energy. This is all the more important if you want to develop bio-energy systems worldwide where much larger economic interests are at stake. There are sustainability issues related to soil, water and air pollution; biodiversity and the conservation and preservation of forests; and the effects on the climate. Certification systems should result in the production and processing of biomass in a sustainable way. Monitoring systems are required to ensure that results are achieved as intended.

Andre Faaij refuted the negative picture of bio-energy that has developed in the media and insisted that it is a very important option, on the one hand to mitigate climate change and on the other hand to provide a large part of our future energy supplies. The main controversy that has developed in the public debate is focussed on bio-fuels, which still make up a minority of bio-energy.

To put the figures in perspective, Faaij pointed out that at this moment we use a little more than 20 million hectares of land worldwide for producing bio-energy, compared to 5,000 million hectares to secure our food supplies. Nonetheless, we are confronted with a number of issues that are interconnected and need urgent attention: climate change, biodiversity losses, crises in agriculture and sustainable food production as well as the necessity to abate poverty and secure development.

With bio-energy as a complex issue, we may still be able to draw lessons from scenario analyses as was done by the IPCC, with variations in food trade, technology development, population and GDP growth. The result of the low trade and technology development and high population scenario is that the category of abandoned cropland expands at the expense of forest land, and probably becomes depleted and destroyed. On the other hand, with rapid technological progress the result would be that agricultural land-use could be cut in half. There would be much more land that would no longer be needed for crop production.

So in terms of suitability for energy production there will be different pathways and crops to choose between, including perennial crops. Even taking into account the limitations of, for example, water and biodiversity, Faaij dared to say that biomass could be developed to the extent that it contributes about one third of the future world's energy supply.

Major preconditions are: investments in agriculture and livestock development and increased water efficiency. These do not come about without controls. In this regard he referred to the Cramer sustainability criteria.

So bio-energy is definitively not a given. To make this happen, resources need to meet the criteria, and the resource base needs to be diversified and shifted from food crops to perennial crops, and from cultivated to marginal and degraded lands. We will have to push hard for technologies that can be used for second-generation bio-fuels and, in combination with coal gasifiers, introduce biomass into the energy system. So, he concluded, bio-energy is really at the crossroads, at the nexus of land-use, development, energy and climate. We have to aim for more benefits in more areas at the same time. Governance is key to achieving those benefits.

Energy

Michael Klare in his lecture on *global energy competition* argued that energy is by far the most pressing, the most difficult and the most dangerous issue facing the world community today and for the rest of the twenty-first century. It touches on virtually every issue of international affairs, from war and peace to the global economy, and especially the global environment and global warming. Solving the energy problem is the overriding issue, and at the same time it is clear that at this moment there is not any government, any international organisation or any will-power to solve this problem in an effective manner.

Up until the beginning of 2008 the demand for energy has been growing in an unprecedented manner. The industrialised world will, in the coming years, continue to use high levels of energy, while newly industrialising societies, especially China and India, are expected to use vastly more energy than in the past. So the question is: can we expect the world energy industry to be able to supply this additional energy to satisfy both the old industrial societies and the new? While answering this question we should take into account the limited lifecycle of conventional fuels – natural gas, oil and coal – and that at a certain point in time all of the rich sources of these fuels will have been exhausted, and production, after having reached its peak, will go into decline.

With oil, we are currently already very close to peak production worldwide. The rate of new discovery has been falling since 1970. With natural gas we are less far along the curve, and we probably have a decade before we reach the peak moment of natural gas production, around 2020, but then it too will begin a decline. Coal is different because it is relatively abundant, but the environmental costs of getting at it will be increasingly prohibitive.

There are economic and geopolitical consequences and Michael Klare focussed on the latter.

For example, China is taking steps to gain control over foreign sources of supply in competition with Japan, the US and Europe in places where it has historically never gone before for supplies of foreign energy – in the Middle East, the Caspian Sea area and in Africa – and is beginning to collide with these foreign powers.

While global demand is increasing, there are very few countries left in the world that actually still have the capacity to increase production. There are the Persian Gulf countries: Iran, Iraq, Kuwait, Saudi Arabia and the United Arab Emirates. There are four African countries: Angola, Nigeria, Sudan and Libya. There are the Central Asia countries: Kazakhstan and Azerbaijan. Then there are Russia and Venezuela.

So what we see is increasing competition taking on two different forms, diplomatic and military. On the diplomatic front we have the state visits. On the military front we see arms transfers, military aid and other military services and military alliances with these countries. This is happening in Africa, the Caspian Sea area and the Persian Gulf. In 2008, for example, the US announced a

US\$20 billion arms package to Saudi Arabia and the other members of the Gulf Cooperation Council. China is becoming one of the leading suppliers of military technology to Iran and of arms to Sudan. This is true not only of arms, but also of military support, military training, military advisory services and military intelligence.

We see Africa gaining a strategic position, gaining the attention of the US, which established a new military command for Africa, AFRICOM, which became operational in 2008. The only reason one can imagine for this is that the US expects Africa to be its leading supplier of oil, the only one that is left to surplant the Middle East as its major supplier by 2015. We also see a rising interest of China in Africa.

In the Caspian Sea area it is not only China and the US but also Russia competing for geopolitical influence. Russia does not need energy, but it wants to control the transportation of energy from the Caspian Sea to Europe and see to it that the future gas production from those countries travels by Gasprom. As a consequence there is both a Russian military base and an American military base in Kyrgyzstan, only 40 miles or so apart.

Apart from the increasing risk of the military presence of superpowers in those areas there is also the increasing likelihood of violence in the countries themselves because of what is sometimes called the resource curse. This occurs in countries that have no other sources of income and where the state collects the revenues or the rents from the production of energy. This leads to authoritarian regimes to keep rivals at bay and rivals have no other choice but to rely on force of arms to change the government. So there is a natural inclination towards internal violence in all of these so-called petro-states dominated by the production of oil.

Klare mentioned two examples: Nigeria and Iraq. In both countries the US has chosen to ally with the central government against the interests of the local population in the oil-producing areas in those countries.

He concluded that we see increased competition for energy from the outside intertwined with the tendency of oil to exacerbate and heighten the internal divisions, a situation he finds comparable to the situation in the Balkans in 1914 at the start of the First World War. So he asks, 'Are we running the risk of ending up in another World War?'

Jonathan Stern, speaking about *the European response to the Russian challenge*, focussed on fossil fuels, in particular oil and gas. He started from the assumption that much of the oil and gas that Europe will have to import will come from the Middle East, largely in the form of oil. Some of it has already come, and will probably continue to come in the future from Russia.

There are two problems related to this situation. First is the problem of overdependence and the risk that this situation will lead to commercial and political blackmail. The second problem is that these are politically unstable regions and conflicts between countries could lead to supply disruptions.

Stern agreed that these are not new arguments, but what *is* new is that prices until the summer of 2008 had been much higher than in the past, that, for various reasons, supplies are not expected to increase substantially, and that new emerging economies like China and India are intent on attracting new oil and gas supplies towards their economies.

So the real question is: can Europe obtain adequate oil and gas supplies in the 2010s, and, if so, how much is it going to pay to obtain those supplies? This question has, however, been obfuscated by the preoccupation of scientists with the question of the carbon-emission problem: if you are convinced that the burning of fuels creates an unsustainable climatic situation, then the question about where the oil and gas supplies are going to come from pales into insignificance.

Turning to the question of Russian oil and gas supply in the future: it is clear that this is of more concern to Europe than to Russia. Russian oil exports have been levelling off recently and there has been criticism about the lack of investments and the wrong tax regime. Gas exports, on the other hand, have increased significantly in the post-Soviet period, but they are unevenly distributed over

Europe: while the UK is one of the biggest gas markets in Europe, the Netherlands only imports small amounts of gas from Russia. For the future it is important to note that virtually all the important contracts between Russia and the European countries have been extended recently and they are long-term contracts.

The problem with Russian gas in terms of European security has been that with the break-up of the Soviet Union the countries through which the gas flowed became independent, in particular Ukraine, Belarus and Poland. Two problems ensued: firstly, Russia and Gazprom are now trying to move all CIS countries to a market price for energy, and particularly gas. Secondly, Russia and Gazprom will try to solve the transit dependence by building two new corridors: the North Stream Pipeline through the Baltic Sea and the South Stream Pipeline, which is intended to go straight across the Black Sea. If all this goes ahead Russian gas will have three routes: the central route through Ukraine and Belarus, and the northern and southern routes, and Gazprom will be able to arbitrage between these three routes. At the same time it does not look like Russia has an alternative for exporting gas to Europe and the Atlantic basin, for example by exporting gas to China.

The question remains as to whether there will be sufficient supplies. Because of the commitments already made we can expect the peaking of Russian gas supplies to Europe around the early 2010s, but no further increase is to be expected until the late 2010s, if not until 2020.

Looking to other potential suppliers, Africa is a very important place but there are many uncertainties. There are big hopes for Azerbaijan, but not quickly, even if European politicians have vested an enormous amount of hope in the Nabucco pipeline. As Stern puts it, the geopolitics of Central Asia is not yet a European game, as the Chinese already have agreements to import significant amounts of gas from Central Asia.

The conclusion is that if Europe is not going to have incremental gas supplies in 2015/2020, most countries are going to have to obtain and develop their coal, with all the negative consequences for reaching carbon targets. The alternative is to go for a combination of renewables and gas. This means that Europe will have to change its attitude and improve its relationship with Russia and its other gas suppliers.

In his comments, *Catrinus Jepma* was less optimistic about Russia being prepared and able to invest more in enhancing its capacity to produce oil and gas. He pointed to another problem, which is that domestic demand in Russia and the CIS countries will increase, while the convergence of the export price level on the one hand and the domestic price level on the other, is going to be very slow. As demand elasticity is low, price increases will not lead to a slow-down in the demand. Jepma expects that in the end the Netherlands may very well have to decide to reintroduce coal as a relatively abundant and classic fossil fuel.

With regard to the question of domestic demand in Russia and the CIS countries, Stern considered it much more important to see old energy-inefficient and very energy-intensive industries replacing their plants. They could cut their energy usage by 40 percent and produce the same goods. As a matter of fact, Russia faces a tremendous challenge to replace its complete capital stock. So for Russia it is not an energy question, it is a question of how you can have a modern economy if you do not replace your capital stock.

Coby van der Linde admitted that, with the recent changes in oil prices, she had a lot to explain. Still, with all the links between energy, climate change, terrorism, nuclear proliferation, democracy and nation building, security is becoming increasingly more a question of energy security.

Already since the 1970s we have seen a change in ownership, and consequently quite a lot of energy, in particular oil, is now under the save guardianship of states. But while everybody is thinking about 2030 as though a lot of our current problems will already have been resolved, van der Linde was afraid that we are not paying enough attention to the transition problems. Those problems are related to the fact that the demand for energy, despite the current turmoil in international economics, is still increasing, particularly in China and India and other developing countries. Also, reserves are concentrated in only a few countries that are hesitant to invest in new capacities, and other solutions that we had in the past, such as reserves in the North Sea and in Alaska, are no longer available.

With the upcoming crisis we see an increase in bilateralism as an alternative to globalization and multilateralism. We also see governments playing an increasingly important role, not only in the energy sector but in the financial sector as well. So our geopolitical relations and the world system and its underpinnings in economic terms are changing rapidly. Southern wealth funds are main actors now, particularly when it comes to investments needed to make the transition into sustainable energy happen.

Those investments are, nevertheless, lagging behind for a number of reasons. While nation states are increasingly important in the oil market, their motive to invest differs in comparison to international oil companies: because of the turbulence in the financial markets the state has to manage the underground wealth at least as much as the above-ground wealth. And if the dollar depreciates, oil exporters will have a negative return performance on their capital. Also, the oil-producing countries have to make a bigger effort to get the oil out of the ground, so the marginal cost of supply is rising. When market prices have been going down the international oil companies have been thinking again about delaying certain investments.

So van der Linde expected that in the coming years there will be increased discussions among nations and companies about how we are going to structure the future energy market. Europe should realize that its position in the area of energy, oil and gas is different to that of the United States, with Russia as its neighbour on the continent. Energy will stay on the agenda for quite a while and we will have to live with higher prices, if only because we have created a mismatch by being too optimistic of what we can do and not paying enough attention to what we are unable to do in managing this transition into more sustainable energy.

Water

Jan Lundqvist drew attention to problems related to the food crisis, like rising food prices, new demands on water and land, climate change, strong economic growth, especially in emerging economies like China and India, and finally changing patterns of consumption and consumer behaviour. He came up with the conclusion that we should look more closely to what is happening in the food chain: *from field to fork.*

While there is a need to increase food production worldwide, at the same time people are throwing away substantial amounts of food. Is it reasonable to talk about such an increase in food production when we have such huge losses and wastage of food?

As regards water, with a population increase worldwide from 1.65 billion in 1900 to around 6 billion now, expected to rise to 9.5 billion by 2050, the water withdrawal index is rising quickly. The agricultural sector makes up the largest part of it, then we have industry and, thirdly, the municipal or household sector which is much smaller, a fraction of the total.

While the increase in water-withdrawal rate is roughly two and a half times as rapid as the demographic change, the question is whether the water supply can continue to grow fast enough to meet rising demand.

With population increase we see also rising incomes, in particular in China and India. While in the year 2000 there were about 0.8 billion people living in countries with per-capita GDP above US$10,000, in 2050 around 7 billion people, or 80 percent of the world population will be expected to live in countries with annual GDP above US$10,000 per capita. This raises tremendous historic opportunities, but rising income will not only lead to more investment but also to more consumption, and a large proportion of that will be in food. This again translates to an increase in pressure on water resources to produce that food.

With rising income levels there is a clear trend toward water-intensive diets, but at the same time there is quite a variation in water intensity between countries with comparable income levels because of different diets. For example, India is mainly a vegetarian society while China has a high meat consumption. There is also a difference in the usage of water in the production of food, depending on the use of irrigation or rain-fed systems.

Climate change and climate variability also affect water availability and water usage. Around 1.4 billion people are living in 'closed basins', where all the water that is available has already been committed to users. So there is no free water. At the same time, there is a tremendous variation in water quantity from one year to another. This creates problems for both farmers and planners.

Water is also becoming scarcer as a consequence of additional water being required to produce biomass for the production of bio-energy and feed stocks. The additional bio-energy is still expected to be only a small proportion, of around 10 percent, of total energy demand in 2050. Likewise, the amount of land that is allocated to grow feed stock for energy production is a fairly small part of total available land. At the same time, it is likely that the total amount of water that is required to produce the additional crops or the feed stock could be quite substantial in relation to what is needed for food production.

All in all, we could expect an increase in additional water requirement to produce additional food, from about 7,000 to 11,000 cubic kilometres. There are similar estimates of additional water requirements for the production of bio-fuels, and increased demand comes also from other agricultural products, from urbanization and industrialization as well as from the 'environmental flow' to sustain the existing aquatic systems. Finally, climate change and global warming also result in increasing demand of water.

One way of dealing with the food and water problem is to reduce losses in the food chain from production to consumption, dealing with post-harvest losses, reducing the amount of feed for meat production by diet change, and reducing the amount of losses in distribution, retail and so, and the wastage in the household sector. What we see, in fact, is a big difference between the amount of food that is available at field level and the amount available for human consumption. We also see that the situation is different in the developing countries, where the main problems occur in the first part of the chain, and in the rich countries, where there is a much bigger challenge in the latter part, on the consumption side.

One of the difficulties to deal with this is the problem of the right incentives. If we could reduce the losses and wastage in the food chain, this would reduce the pressure on resources; it would be a potential gain to farmers as well as the consumers, and it would be an opportunity to make it possible for farmers to cultivate other crops - food crops as well as bio-energy and other crops.

So we need incentives for farmers, the food-processing industries and the supermarkets, and we need policies to change the behaviour of consumers, which is much more difficult than changing the behaviour of producers. Consumption is part of our private life and part of our democratic system. Sensitizing consumers is also more difficult because they are farther removed from the countryside, the place where food is produced. So policies in this area have to be very strategically designed and should not be of a general nature only. Consumers, moreover, are often not aware that they throw away so much food and are also not aware of the damaging effect this has on the environment. So information campaigns about these issues might be important.

Industry is now becoming more aware of and concerned about the water situation in the world. Benchmarking has been introduced in the food industry, but it would be sensible also to introduce benchmarking in other parts of the food chain. Finally, support for farmers, especially small farmers, could be important, to help them solve transport and storage problems and to reduce post-harvest losses.

Michel Camdessus referred to water as a vital human need, the satisfaction of which can only be made more difficult by the consequences of climate change. He also considered it a human right and more than a Millennium Development Goal: it is a requisite for the achievement of the other MDGs, such as ending poverty, improving education and ensuring gender equality. Moreover, effective water-resource development and management are funda-mental to sustainable growth and poverty reduction.

While the world is on track for access to water, on a regional basis there is a widening gap between sub-Saharan Africa and the rest of the world. This has justified a particular concentration on the case of Africa. Progress remains dramatically insufficient for sanitation, although water and sanitation should always be linked.

As part of the Hashimoto Action Plan, Camdessus particularly recommended the establishment of a water-operator partnership to help international organisations improve their mutual coopera-tion and to ensure that water is no longer an orphan of interna-tional organisations and that proper governance and sources of financing are guaranteed.

In view of the special difficulty of the water and sanitation problem in rural areas of Africa, and of the certainty that they will be among the parts of the world most severely affected by climate change, Camdessus drew attention to a special initiative that has been launched recently, the Rural Water Supply and Sanitation Initiative (RWSSI), a well-designed instrument for achieving the water-related MDGs and for working towards the implementation in 2025 of the African vision, namely water and sanitation for all.

Climate Change

Gurmit Singh began by describing the phenomenon of global warming, the factors contributing to it and how it affects us all, pointing out that 'some are more culpable than others'.

This, he stressed, is the basis for the UN Framework Convention on Climate Change (UNFCCC), agreed upon in 1992. The Convention has as its objective the stabilization of greenhouse gas concentration in the atmosphere at a level that would prevent dan-gerous anthropogenic interference with the climate system. This implies that the eco-system adapts naturally to ensure that food production is not threatened and to allow sustainable develop-ment to occur. There is the underlying precautionary principle that in the absence of scientific consensus we take action where there is a general agreement and that we should respond on the basis of common but differentiated responsibilities as defined in the Convention. This implies that those that have emitted most must take action first and then the others will follow.

This is the whole basis of the Kyoto Protocol of 1997 and the reason for having Annex I and non-Annex I country groupings. As a matter of fact, in each group, you have all sorts of countries with different vested interests: rich countries, countries with high per-capita consumption, those who are wasteful of energy, those whose very existence is at stake if the sea level rises, and so on.

Looking to the future, Gurmit Singh noted that developing countries are increasing their CO_2 emissions and that, in terms of cumulative CO_2 emissions, developing countries will be overtaking developed countries in 2045. 'So', he noted, 'the South are the culprits themselves.'

According to the International Panel on Climate Change (IPCC), the consequences of these developments will be drastic, especially if temperature increases exceed 2° C. For Singh, the only way to look at global warming is to see it as an emergency and treat it as a war, mobilizing resources and shortening the time-frame to achieve the 80 percent greenhouse gas reduction that is essential to avoid the 2° C temperature rise.

At the same time, he insisted this war must be fought in a sustainable development context, 'because we also have to eliminate absolute poverty' and make sure that sufficient means are made available for technology transfer as foreseen already in the UNFCCC as well as in the Kyoto Protocol.

Singh singled out the EU as a global player and asked to what extent the EU is a political driver. The European Commission and the European Parliament seem to be drivers but then the question arises as to how much weight they have in decisions that are taken by the EU political leaders. Individual member nations show uneven commitment. The EU style of compromising within and internationally weakens strong leadership. 'The EU should not compromise itself into uselessness but strike out for something that is really strong and take risks,' Singh argued.

287

He also considered the Alliance of Small Island States as interested in the climate change debate, but remarked that Singapore has been the quietest and least active member, despite being its richest. He put his hopes on the renewable energy industry, as well as the developers of mitigation and adaptation technology in the North. Business, he noted, is not totally opposed to action to tackle climate change anymore and he hopes this action will become stronger and stronger.

Reducing energy consumption, on the other hand, boils down to two things: the affluent in all countries have to make sacrifices in many wasteful areas, but at the same time should they be assured that they can still have a good quality of life. The corollary to that is that those who are developing economically, especially in the vast nations of China and India, must tone down their aspirations for ever higher energy and resource usages, and still recognize the possibility of having a better quality of life.

Regarding the Bali meeting in December 2007, he concluded that there was not very much of a breakthrough. Beyond Bali, the roadmap is just weak and vague. He did not expect the US to take drastic action, under whatever president. He remarked that we have never seen a president or Congress interested in jointly taking action.

Pier Vellinga stated firstly that the risk of irreversible climate change is too great to be allowed to happen, and, secondly, that it is technically and economically possible to avoid the major part of the projections of climate change. 'But it will be a race against time and it is an ultimate test for international cooperation.'

In the climate debate, there is, even with the IPCC report on the table, still a hard core of scepticism, in our own country and in the world. He concludes: the earth is warming up and the pattern we measure clearly reflects the greenhouse theory. Through sixty years of measurements we know the concentrations of greenhouse gases are steadily growing. Moreover, we know that fossil fuel use is the main contributor to this growth, and that this is reinforced by so-called feedback mechanisms. This also means that we should deal with this issue urgently.

For example, with regard to the sea-level rise, glaciologists suggest that this response to the warming planet is coming earlier and faster than predicted and that, once this process has begun, we cannot stop it. So we should reduce, according to one leading expert, the concentration of greenhouse gases in the atmosphere from the present 450 parts per million (ppm) down to 350 ppm, instead of the earlier-mentioned level of between 550 and 650 ppm as an unavoidable and possibly acceptable upper level.

Now, according to the IPCC, it is technically and economically feasible to avoid most of the projected climate change. On the other hand, there is very little time in which to do this, and we probably need to pay a price in the order of 50 or even 100 euros per ton of CO_2 in order to avoid it. But to reduce CO_2 emissions leadership is required at the national and the global level. In the Netherlands one should focus on techniques dealing with energy efficiency and renewable energies. For example, within a decade or even less we can make all our new homes energy- and climate-neutral. More use could also be made of biomass, to the extent that 30 percent of present energy needs should be covered.

Talking about nuclear and coal-fired power-plants, Vellinga warned that 'once you have them, they will outcompete renewable energies like solar and wind energy'. He argued that modern coal gasification plants are a way out as they produce gas that can be stored, in particular in periods when wind and solar energy is produced. So this is a way for renewables to enter into the energy system. Moreover, the CO_2 produced by such power-plants could be stored underground, thus creating a climate-neutral electricity system.

Vellinga ended by summarising four dilemmas. The first is the one related to the question of what is dangerous anthropogenic interference. He, with other scientists, considered the present level to be already endangering continuous economic prosperity and social stability on this planet. But not everybody agrees.

The second is the question of how to deal with the costs involved in the compensation for damage and adaptation to climate change. One of the problems here is that it is still difficult to make a distinction between the effect of climate variability and climate change. The third is the question of what the concept of common but differentiated responsibilities means at an operational level. Much can be achieved with money and dedicated funds, but in the end it is the planning capacity and governance that determine the success of international financial assistance. The final and biggest dilemma is what to prioritise, poverty reduction now or reduction of climate change and resulting poverty in the future. His answer is: 'We cannot afford to postpone reducing greenhouse emissions until all national and international social distribution issues have been resolved.'

Jan Pronk dealt with *climate change and development,* and more specifically with the negotiation process on climate change and the position of developing countries in it. He began by referring to conflicts in the African belt in which he had recently been involved as an illustration of disasters and conflicts that are related to the problem of climate change and are a reason to deal with it urgently. He explained that politicians have to start from the assumption that the annual capacity of the earth to absorb greenhouse gases is limited and that, with the present high levels of emissions in the US and elsewhere, and the big increases in Asia and other regions speeding up their economic development, the carrying capacity of the earth will be surpassed very soon. The consequences will in particular be borne by people living in developing countries.

While there are uncertainties with regard to the effects of climate change, it was decided already in 1992 at the Rio Summit that our policies should be based on *the precautionary principle.* In order to address the problem of climate change it was decided to come to a worldwide agreement to stabilize the concentration of greenhouse gases in the atmosphere. In order to achieve that, the reduction of emissions of greenhouse gases had to be drastic. The targeted reduction agreed upon required a major transformation of the world economy and technology, and that process should start in particular in those countries that have had the highest emissions in the past.

Jan Pronk stressed that climate change is a global problem, that it is urgent, that it is the result of past activities as well as of present activities, that it is to be considered as, in economic terms, an external effect of economic behaviour, that it is massive in its effect and is also long-term. This means that it is an external effect, not of a flow variable, but of a stock. The past flow and the present stock are to a very large extent the result of activities of countries in the North, so it is necessary that in particular those countries should start to act on the basis of the *principle of preferential treatment*: those who were in advance have to step back in order to give room to others who are not yet at the same level. This is also referred to as the *principle of common and differentiated responsibilities*.

Agreements would have to be based on these principles, including concrete targets in relation to these. Because of the uncertainties, people would have to be creative in terms of instruments, and be flexible and innovative, and this had to be dealt with on the basis of binding law. This resulted in the Kyoto Protocol in 1997, and, beyond that, in the process of the subsequent Conferences of the Parties who participated in the Protocol.

The process was successful because at the time there was a worldwide awareness of a global threat, because there was a conducive political climate and psychological atmosphere and there was full agreement on the process with, on the International Panel on Climate Change, an independent secretariat.

Since then there have been a lot of changes. Firstly, there is now much higher economic growth. We also have higher emissions then we expected ten years ago, and we know now that the whole mechanism of climate change is more complex and that the natural and physical consequences are greater then outlined ten years ago: there are more disasters and climate change is an additional factor contributing to greater conflict potential. There is also a much greater than expected shortage of fossil fuels for energy utilization and a greater perceived energy insecurity within nations.

There have also been some positive changes: we know more in terms of scientific research; there is greater awareness amongst the people of the problems; there is more technological research in private industry; and, finally, Europe is playing a more positive role in the international field.

Two question marks still hover: (1) the outcome of the Bali meeting is vague: it is not a roadmap and there is no direction, and (2) bio-fuels do not appear to be a sustainable energy alternative.

Countries are still blaming each other and countries are still not implementing, there is a lot of shifting things forward, and there is a lot of focus on procedures, institutions and the financial question: who is going to pay for what? The power question still plays a role, and there is an inclination to focus on secondary approaches in order to avoid mitigation.

Too much emphasis on adaptation means that attention is lead away from necessary mitigation. There is a built-in inclination amongst all policy makers not to mitigate but to compensate: *the fake approach.* Instead, it is still necessary to think about long-term targets of equal emissions per capita of all inhabitants of all countries.

For the Netherlands, this may mean returning to very simple sustainable alternative sources of energy: solar power and wind. It is a matter of spatial planning, and, as a former minister responsible for spatial planning, he knows how difficult this is.

It may also be acceptable to go for carbon absorption underground, but we should avoid deforestation. Going back to basics is the only way that developing countries can see that we are serious; and then they also may be ready to be serious.

Power Shifts

Ronald Figueredo dealt with the subject of *energy relations redefining Latin American politics.* At the beginning of the 1970s an Arab oil-producers embargo prompted a major international crisis. An Energy Conference was proposed to the OPEC countries, but this unfortunately did not lead to a joint convergent strategy on trade and development. The OECD countries agreed instead to create the International Energy Agency, with the prime responsibility of devising collective emergency response mechanisms to offset impacts of short-term supply responses. The way chosen was not conducive to dispel deeper misunderstandings on what should have been a positive collective approach.

Today's 'energy scenario' is far more complex and blurred within an enforced energy transition in the context of globalization and other new issues that were hardly significant in the 1970s. Securing a harmonious energy transition and tackling the serious lack of clean water and energy, likely to generate major conflicts, requires different analyses and tools to those established in the context of what were then the East/West confrontation and the North/South divide. We are now all aware of the power shifts taking place in the world; this requires new visions.

Recently oil demands and dependency on a limited number of oil producing countries increased, adding to the tightness as well as tensions which could slide into major confrontations. The risks of oil-supply disruptions has grown. The OPEC, set up in the 1960s, had as its objective building a common stance, jointly countering a further reduction of the oil price and having a say in the exploitation of their non-renewable resources.

The problem with Latin America today is that high export revenues in two of the most important countries of the region with very significant reserves in oil and gas, Venezuela and Bolivia, and to a lesser degree Ecuador, provide their administrations the opportunity to carry forward policies with an objective to establish authoritarian governments in order to create what is called 'The New Socialism of the 21st Century'. This approach has resulted in prioritizing and securing a 'revolutionary' state of affairs, essentially driven to implant it in Latin America's region and induct those elements that are capable of reinforcing unstable and inflammable societies.

Against this background we have seen a significant redistribution of global income from oil-importing countries to exporting countries. From 2002, when prices averaged just under US$25.00 a barrel, owing to surging demand by China, prices began a strong upward trend, from an average of US$37.75 a barrel in 2004 to US$53.35 in 2005, US$65.35 in 2006 and almost US$100 at the beginning of the fourth quarter of 2007. The issue of the recycling of petrodollars has come to the forefront again, but not with the same kind of concern as before, since the options for oil exporters are basically twofold: (1) increasing imports of goods and services, and (2) purchasing foreign assets in the international capital market stimulated by the dynamics of globalisation.

In December 2006 revenues for this category of countries exceeded US$1,500 billion, a jump of about US$980 billion since 2002. Half of it went to acquire goods and services from abroad and half of it went to increased net purchases of foreign financial assets. For example, Venezuela recently used a very large amount of foreign exchange in acquiring both from the Russian Federation and Belarus sophisticated armament, as though Venezuela is getting ready to enter into an armed conflict with some if its neighbours!

Figueredo believes that in the area of global warming and other environmental concerns convergence among producers and consumers in constructive dialogues would certainly yield more positive outcomes than in the past, would lead the way to conducting a smooth and harmonious energy transition and ensuring avoidance of probable dangerous confrontations.

What is needed is a comprehensive regional or sub-regional approach complementing whatever specific national or bilateral action is decided upon. An integrated approach is crucial to averting the possibility of 'fragile states' lapsing into the category of 'inflamed societies', as some people believe might occur in the case of Bolivia.

Cor van Beuningen responded by looking at the broader picture of *geopoliticization of the energy issue and its implication of EU policy making* in the present context of a worldwide economic downturn, asking whether this might imply *an end of globalisation*, and then moved on to the prospects of a EU-Latin America partnership and alliance. The geopoliticization of the energy issue is to be understood as the product of two coinciding developments. On the one hand there is the rather sudden imbalance between the sharply increasing demand for, and the only slowly responding supply of, energy. On the other hand, these scarcities are produced at a moment in world history that is marked by the transition of the world order, from a unipolar system as we have known since 1989, to a multipolar system at present. In his view, in about ten years the world economy will be dominated by three major blocks: China, the US and the EU, each one accounting for 15 to 20 percent of world GDP, followed by India with about ten percent, and Japan, Brazil and Russia each with 5 percent. The big question is how this new economic configuration will come about. Will the old powers be willing and able to facilitate a peaceful transition, or will they be in for a prolonged period of rivalry and conflict?

Such is the context and the challenge for the design of an EU policy for energy and food security. All efforts should be directed now to divert the ongoing process of combined geopolitical block formation and polarization, and instead to facilitate a peaceful transition to a viable and sustainable new world system, necessarily multipolar by nature, and one in which the different actors feel recognized in their existence and their legitimate interests. This new system should generate and foster a broad willingness to accommodate, negotiate and participate, and should eventually be committed to a rule-based order and to effectively functioning international institutions.

Van Beuningen believes that the first partner for Europe in this enterprise should be Latin America. The continent possesses almost one third of the world's fresh water, as well as favourable physical conditions for the production of food and bio-fuels. It also has the most important oil reserves outside the Middle East, as well as gas, copper and iron. But most importantly, Latin America shares with the EU its preference for multilateralism, for a rule-based international order and institutions and a common set of beliefs and convictions regarding how we should live together and what kind of society we really should strive for, both at the national and the global level.

This new partnership between Latin America and Europe might also be instrumental in addressing a number of problems the Latin American societies are currently facing: bad governance, young democracies, fragile states, or, better put, fragile societies. Latin American societies suffer from a growing lack of public trust and that *dis*trust is gaining the upper hand in the relationship between citizens and their government, as well as between the nations on the continent.

Problems related to spreading distrust and inflammable societies threaten to interfere with a rational and fruitful use of the rich natural resources of the continent, for growth and development. Instead energy resources are used as an instrument in a spiralling process of distrust, of hegemonic power and conflict.

Together, the EU and Latin America should act as a force for the good. They should divert the ongoing process of geopolitical block formation and polarisation and act and behave consistently as the champions of multilateralisation, of international rules and institutions.

Javier Santiso focussed on *China and India* and the changing *trade relations of Latin America* with these two emerging economies. The Development Centre of the OECD did some work on China to demonstrate how China is changing the world economic balance. What we are witnessing is this massive plug of the Chinese economy in the world implying a major rebalancing of the world of nations. Until recently we used to think that somewhere there was a centre and somewhere there was a periphery. Now we are finding that the centre is less and less the centre and the periphery less and less the periphery. This applies to the share of GDP: OECD countries in the past represented between 60 and 70 percent of world GDP; now they are reaching levels below 50 percent. In terms of foreign direct investment, OECD used to represent nearly 100 percent of FDI; at the moment they are already below 80 percent. At the same time Chinese FDI is increasing, approaching US$20 billion in 2006.

Taking a long-term view, China and India had been occupying a much more important position in the world economy in the middle of the nineteenth century, with China representing more than 30 percent of world GDP – and, together with India, about 50 percent. So, Santiso concludes, what we have been witnessing over the last century of world economic history is just a 'parenthesis''. The big difference now is that the impact of the Chinese economy at the moment is much greater than in the nineteenth century because this one country, this empire which was China, was a closed economy at the time. What is also new is the speed of the process: the take-off of China, compared to those of Japan, Brazil, Mexico and others, has been most impressive of all.

What has been the impact on Latin America? It is important to note first of all that China alone represents a larger share of world output then the whole of Latin America. Also, it is significant that Latin America is witnessing a boom in its trade with China. This can be explained by the endowment of Latin American countries, mainly in natural resources that exactly fit the demand of China's very quickly growing economy in need of raw materials.

In the short term, this seems like good news to Latin America. While Chinese exports are competing with other products of developing countries such as Thailand, Malaysia and some Eastern European countries, this is less the case with Latin American nations. This raises challenges for them, however. Those exporting manufactures have to catch up in terms of competitiveness. For the others, this means another challenge, which is how to diversify their trade beyond commodities.

The increasing demand from China and beyond in Asia explains why, for the first time in its history, Latin America is increasingly looking towards Asia. In the 1980s the bulk of trade relations for Latin America were nearly only with the US. In the

1990s there was a shift toward Europe, with more and more invest-ments coming from Europe. Now there is Asia as a third pillar and exogenous engine of growth. The good news is that this implies trade diversification in terms of destination. The flip side of this is the export concentration in terms of products.

Although China is also a trade opportunity, it raises challenges in the medium term for Latin American countries. For example, the time needed for exports in terms of days on average by Latin American countries is much larger than in China. This is also the case for the costs of exports, which incorporates not only shipping costs but also trade union transaction costs, which in Latin America are on average much higher than in China. The difference in competitiveness is exemplified by the share of investments in infrastructure: 10 percent of GDP in China and only 2 percent in Latin America. A possible catch-up can only be achieved through improving the infrastructure. Massive investments are required because competitiveness will not come from lower wages – there are on average four times higher in Latin America than in China.

Taking the countries of the Pacific Rim into the equation, including Canada, Australia and New Zealand, all endowed with raw materials, it is clear that we have to rethink what we say about the 'commodities malediction'. Quite a few of them have been able to diversify and develop huge clusters of industries related to those commodities with very high value added. So it all depends how a country, not only its government also but its society and the cor-porations, reacts to the situation. It is sad to say, Santiso concludes, that we do not have many countries like Australia, Canada and Norway in Latin America.

With the commodity boom that we have today, much depends on whether Latin American countries will surf, actively or pas-sively, on this wave. If they do not prepare in a much more sus-tainable way for what comes after it, life will become much more complicated for them.

Finally, coming back to China and its importance for Latin America, if China is more resilient in the face of the financial cri-sis, this means that the commodity markets will be more resilient and that means that Latin American countries, from a macro-economic point of view, will be more resilient.

Yang Guang focussed on *the energy relations between China and Africa* against the background of their relations in general. China has a long history of relations with Africa, going back to the eighth century. This relationship was interrupted by the colonization of the African continent and resumed only in the 1950s and 1960s of the last century when Africa was decolonized. Between 1960 and 1980 this strategic cooperation was based mostly on political considerations. Since 1980 China-Africa relations have seen some change, and the economy has become a new and very important dimension. Since 2000, when the China Africa Cooperation Forum was formed, the relation became much stronger and it provided a very strong impetus to the bilateral relations. The value of trade and investments has increased and the Chinese government has also increased its assistance to African countries.

In its relations China has observed some principles that have not changed for many years. For instance, China cherishes equality and mutual respect and is reluctant to impose any political conditions. Also China looks for win-win situations and adheres to the principle of shared development.

With rapid economic growth over the past 30 years, China's demand of energy has significantly increased. Ninety-five percent of energy consumption is supported by domestic production, and coal accounts for 60 percent of China's total energy consumption. Since 1993, China has become net importer of oil, and the gap between demand and domestic production has widened to the extent that by the year 2000 China has already become the third largest oil importer, after the US and Japan.

With China's need to import more oil, Africa has gradually become a more important supplier. Africa's share in China's imports of oil was 11 percent in 1995; in 2005 it was already 31 percent. Africa became the second source of imports after the Gulf countries. Angola, by 2005, provided 14 percent of China's oil imports, just after Saudi Arabia.

Chinese companies also invested abroad to produce oil. As private companies, they were driven by economic motivations. They wanted to make use of resources abroad to continue their production, and since 2000 constant high oil prices have given them a strong incentive to make profits abroad. At the same time, African countries have improved their investment environment to make it more attractive for Chinese companies to invest. Finally, Chinese companies find that they also enjoy comparative advantage because of low labour costs and low costs of equipment made in China. African crude oil is also in many cases low in sulphur content and this fits well with the requirements of Chinese refineries.

Finally, as the Chinese government sees the importance of diversification of the sources of imported oil, it provides some incentives to Chinese companies, for example by providing subsidised interest loans by the Exim Bank of China and insurance by the National Export Credit Insurance Company.

Yang Guang believes that China-Africa oil relations have contributed to the development of the countries where it has invested. Chinese investments have helped African countries to improve their production structure and promote the industrialisation process. Moreover, Chinese oil companies are increasingly aware of the importance of fulfilling their corporate social responsibility and they are paying attention to environmental protection.

China also pays attention to the political situation in Africa and contributes substantially to UN peace-keeping operations. Many of these operations are not in oil-producing countries. China is convinced that conflicts in Africa may very easily spread to other countries, so to promote stability and peace in Africa it is necessary to contribute wherever there are conflicts and not just to focus on oil-producing countries.

Frank Heemskerk, speaking at the closing conference of the lecture series, agreed that social justice is not something to be left to markets and that governments and regulators have a very important role to play. But he still insisted that opening up markets in a globalizing environment is the best answer if we want to care for people that are in danger of exclusion: 'protectionism does not protect people'.

Globalization brings many benefits to other markets, such as higher standards and technologies. Taking the example of food scarcity, he pointed out the response of innovation and improvements in technology to increase food production relatively quickly and allow for the introduction of energy crops. With regard to competition, he argued that powerful cartels and the abuse of dominant positions in markets cannot be tolerated, if only 'because they extract tens of billions of dollars from developing countries'. But markets should be made to work efficiently by rules that are necessary to sustain consent and confidence.

With regard to climate change, the question is whether trade is part of the problem or part of the solution. Trade is a problem to the extent that it implies transport using carbon-based fuels. Trade may also be part of the solution, as maximising trade in green technology will drive down emissions.

Heemkerk took carbon leakage as an illustration of the various aspects of trade versus environmental considerations. Carbon leakage is defined as the risk that the introduction of strict CO_2 standards will lead to production leaking away to countries with lower standards. Therefore we need to develop criteria to identify sectors at risk of carbon leakage and to get a clearer view of the overall implications.

The question now is whether trade measures can solve the problem of carbon leakage. Heemskerk argues that trade measures are not very effective, and that the best and most efficient probable solution lies in mechanisms to control the cost of doing business, and in stimulating innovation and allocating emission rights more freely.

Heemskerk concludes that climate change is precisely the kind of global common ground that requires global governance. Trade threats and beggar-thy-neighbour policies have no place here. Instead we should have a framework of rules, dialogue and conflict resolution.

Contributors in order of Appearance

Bernard Berendsen is member of the Advisory Council on Foreign Relations of the Ministry of Foreign Affairs in the Netherlands. He started his international career at the Central Bank in Sudan in 1969. In 1970 he joined the United Nations Economic Commission for Asia and the Far East in Bangkok, Thailand. He completed his PhD thesis at the Erasmus University in Rotterdam in 1978 on the subject of regional models of trade and development dealing with issues of international trade, economic development and integration. He joined the Ministry of Foreign Affairs in the Netherlands in 1975. After various assignments in The Hague he became Director for Africa in 1994, was posted in Jakarta from 1997 until 2000 and became Netherlands ambassador in Tanzania before retiring in 2005.

Gerda Verburg was a member of the House of Representatives of the States General for the Christian Democratic Appeal (CDA) from 1998 to 2007. During this period she was among other things spokesperson for Development Cooperation. Verburg has also been a member of the Social and Economic Council and the Labour Foundation. She has served on the executive committee of the European Trade Union Confederation, and on the boards of the Interchurch Organisation for Development Cooperation, the Royal Dutch Equestrian Sports Federation (KNHS) and Stichting Geuzenverzet. Verburg has been actively involved in the promotion of civil society in Central and Eastern Europe. On 22 February 2007 she was appointed Minister of Agriculture, Nature and Food Quality in the fourth Balkenende government.

Rudy Rabbinge is Professor of Sustainable Development and Food Security at Wageningen University. From 1999 until 2007 he was a member of the Upper Chamber. He is a member of the Scientific Council for Government Policy (WRR). Rabbinge has published more than 200 works in the scientific area.

Kornelis Blok is Professor of Science, Technology and Society at the Copernicus Institute, Utrecht University and is Managing Director of Ecofys. Ecofys is active in research and consultancy in the areas of energy-efficiency improvement, renewable energy and climate change. He is a lead author for the Third and Fourth Assessment Report of the Intergovernmental Panel on Climate Change. He was research director of the inter-university Netherlands' Research School for Environmental Sciences (SENSE).

André P.C. Faaij is Professor of Energy System Analysis at the Copernicus Institute for Sustainable Development (Faculty of Science) at Utrecht University. He has a background in chemistry and environmental sciences and holds a PhD on energy production from biomass and waste. He worked as visiting researcher at the Center for Energy and Environmental Studies at Princeton University and at King's College, London University. He is a member of a variety of expert groups in bio-energy and energy policy, research and strategic planning. He works as an advisor for governments, the EC, IEA, the UN system, GEF, OECD, WEF, the energy sector and industry, strategic consultancy and NGOs.

Michael T. Klare is a Five Colleges professor of Peace and World Security Studies, whose department is located at Hampshire College. He is defence correspondent of *The Nation* magazine, and author of *Resource Wars* and *Blood and Oil: The Dangers and Consequences of America's Growing Petroleum Dependency* (Metropolitan). Klare also teaches at Amherst College, Smith College, Mount Holyoke College, and the University of Massachusetts, Amherst. Klare serves on the boards of directors of Human Rights Watch and the Arms Control Association. He is a regular contributor to many publications including *The Nation*, *TomDispatch* and *Mother Jones*, and is a frequent columnist for *Foreign Policy in Focus*.

Jonathan Stern is Director of Gas Research at the Oxford Institute for Energy Studies where he is creating a research group that will carry out independent research and commentary on international gas issues worldwide. He is also Honorary Professor at the Centre for Energy, Petroleum & Mineral Law & Policy, University of Dundee and holds fellowships at both the Royal Institute of International Affairs' Sustainable Development Programme and the Department of Environmental Science and Technology at Imperial College in London. He is Chairman of the British Institute of Energy Economics and Member of the Board of Advisors, Institute for Energy, Law and Enterprise at the University of Houston.

Catrinus Jepma is currently Professor of International (Environmental) Economics, appointed at the University of Amsterdam, the University of Groningen, and the Open University, the Netherlands. Since 2005, he has held a chair in Energy and Sustainability at the University of Groningen and is scientific director of the Energy Delta Research Centre (EDReC) of the same University. He currently chairs the National Working Group on Clean Fossil Fuel and Carbon Capture and Storage and CNG for mobility, and is actively engaged in the national energy transition management plan towards sustainable energy systems.

Coby van der Linde has been the director of the Clingendael International Energy Programme since September 2001. She was a senior researcher at Clingendael from 1998 onwards, on secondment from Leiden University. Her career before joining CIEP was predominantly an academic one at the Universities of Leiden and Amsterdam, where her research focussed on international energy markets. In the 1990s, she was a visiting scholar at the Oxford Institute for Energy Studies (OIES), at the Energy and Environment Programme of the Royal Institute for International Affairs (Chatham House, London) and the Colorado School of Mines (Golden, Colorado). In 2004 she was appointed to the Chair of Geopolitics and Energy Management (part-time) at the University of Groningen. She is also a member of the Dutch Energy Council (Energieraad).

Jan Olof Lundqvist is Senior Scientific Advisor at the Stockholm International Water Institute (SIWI) and chairs the Scientific Programme Committee for the World Water Week in Stockholm. Through decades of leading research, including 100 publications, Professor Lundqvist has extensive experience and networks within academia, the UN system, bilateral programs, the NGO and private sectors.

Michel Camdessus was Managing Director of the International Monetary Fund (IMF) from 1987 to 2000. He was educated at the University of Paris and earned postgraduate degrees in economics at the Institute of Political Studies of Paris and the National School of Administration. He was Deputy Governor and Governor of the Bank of France from November 1984 until his move to Washington DC. He is currently president of the Semaines Sociales de France and is a member of the Commission for Africa. He is also a member of the pontifical Commission for Justice and Peace and of the Africa Progress Panel (APP).

Gurmith Singh is a well-known environmentalist and social activist. He is the chairman of the Board and founding executive director of the Centre for Environment, Technology and Development in Malaysia. He is the founder-president and an advisor to the Environmental Protection Society. He is also a member of many national and international societies and committees. Singh has organised and managed national and international courses, workshops and studies on environmental issues. In 1993, he received the Malaysian Government's Langkawi Award.

Jan Pronk is Professor of Theory and Practice of International Development at the Institute for Social Studies, The Hague. From 1973 to 1977 and from 1989 to 1998 he was Minister of Development Cooperation and from 1998 to 2002 Minister of Environment. In the last capacity he chaired the international climate negotiations in 2000 and 2001 (COP VI, The Hague and Bonn). Thereafter he was Special Envoy of the Secretary General of the UN, preparing the UN Summit on Sustainable Development in Johannesburg, 2002. Jan Pronk is President of SID-International.

Pier Vellinga is Professor of Environmental Sciences and Climate Change at Wageningen University Research and Vrije Universiteit Amsterdam. Originally he specialized in Coastal Engineering, contributing to the Deltaplan of the Netherlands. In 1987 he became advisor to the Netherlands Environment Minister on Climate Change. In that period he helped to shape international climate policies, and he was one of the initiators and first bureau members of the Intergovernmental Panel on Climate Change. In 1991 he joined the Vrije Universiteit as Professor of Environmental Sciences and as Director of the Institute for Environmental Studies. In 2007 he took up a position at Wageningen University Research as well, to lead the National Climate Change Research programme Knowledge for Climate. Pier Vellinga is a board member of several research institutes and environmental organizations in the Netherlands and abroad.

Reinaldo Figueredo has occupied several senior and high-level executive positions in Venezuela in the Ministry of Energy and the Foreign Trade Institute, and has served as a minister of the Presidency of Venezuela and of Foreign Affairs, a member of parliament, Chairman of the Commission on Privatisation, Vicechairman on the Defence Commission and President of the Venezuela Institute on Foreign Trade. He has now retired and is presently Associate Fellow at the Netherlands Clingendael Institute of International Relations International Energy Programme.

Cor van Beuningen is the Director of SOCIRES, a Dutch-based thinktank specializing in governance, democracy and civil society organizations in the public domain. He holds Masters degrees in regional planning and in public administration. Van Beuningen has twenty years of experience in international cooperation, including ten years of field experience in Latin America, Africa and Asia, being employed by both governmental and non-governmental development agencies. He is advisor to the Netherlands Institute for Multiparty Democracy, and to several other public and private institutions involved in non-commercial public-private partnerships, both in the Netherlands, in Eastern Europe and elsewhere.

Javier Santiso was appointed Director of the OECD Development Centre in 2007. He joined the OECD in December 2005 as Chief Development Economist and Deputy Director of the Development Centre. He has been the Centre's Acting Director since July 2007. He began his career in 1995 at the Latin American Centre, University of Oxford. Member of the editorial committee of *Problèmes d'Amérique Latine*, Santiso is the author of over sixty articles on international economy. His most recent published book is entitled *Latin America's Political Economy of the Possible: Beyond Good Revolutionaries and Free Marketeers* (MIT Press, Cambridge, Mass, 2006) (also published in French). He was a visiting Professor at Johns Hopkins University Paul H. Nitze School of Advanced International Studies. He sits on the advisory council of the Centro de Investigación Latinoamérica Europa (CILAE).

Professor **Yang Guang** is Director-General of West-Asian and African Studies at the Chinese Academy of Social Sciences (IWAAS-CASS), Beijing, China. He received higher education from the Beijing Foreign Language Institute, L'Institut des Études Politiques de Paris and the Graduate School of the Chinese Academy of Social Sciences. Joining the Institute of West-Asian and African Studies in 1978, he is now Director-General of the institute, senior research fellow and professor. He was also elected Executive President of the Chinese Association for Middle East Studies, Executive President of the Chinese Society for Asian and African Studies and Vice-president of the Chinese Association for African Studies. Most of his research is devoted to economic development and energy studies.

Frank Heemskerk is a Dutch politician. He was a member of parliament for the Labour Party between 2003 and 2006 and is currently Minister of Foreign Trade within Economic Affairs.

Heemskerk was educated at the University of Amsterdam. He worked for ABN AMRO and made a career in the banking world. In the 2003 elections Heemskerk was elected into the Tweede Kamer. In parliament he specialized in the relationship between market and government and in the reform of the healthcare system.